THE
EDUCATION
OF A TEACHER

THE
EDUCATION
OF A TEACHER

Essays on American Culture

HOWARD WOLF

Foreword by Edgar Z. Friedenberg

PROMETHEUS BOOKS

Buffalo, New York

90 89 88 87   4 3 2 1

Library of Congress Cataloging-in-Publication Data

Wolf, Howard Robert, 1936-
     The education of a teacher.

     Originally published between 1968 and 1986.
     1. Education, Higher—United States. 2. College teaching—United States. 3. Educational sociology—United States. I. Title.
LB2325.W58 1987   378.73   87-10885
ISBN 0-87975-374-9

To John Lancaster,
Curator of Special Collections, Amherst College Library

The poet, in utter solitude remembering his spontaneous thoughts and recording them, is found to have recorded that which men in crowded cities find true for them also.

Ralph Waldo Emerson,
"The American Scholar"

In most books, the *I,* or first person is omitted; in this it will be retained; that, in respect to egotism, is the main difference. We commonly do not remember that it is, after all, always the first person that is speaking.

Henry David Thoreau,
"Economy," *Walden*

Most Educators of the nineteenth century have declined to show themselves before their scholars as objects more vile or contemptible than necessary, and even the humblest teacher hides, if possible, the faults with which nature has generously embellished us all, as it did Jean Jacques, thinking, as most religious minds are apt to do, that the Eternal Father himself may not feel unmixed pleasure at our thrusting under his eyes chiefly the least agreeable details of his creation.

Henry Adams, "Preface,"
The Education of Henry Adams

Let us guard against stripping our science of its share of poetry. Let us also beware of the inclination, which I have detected in some, to be ashamed of this poetic quality. It would be sheer folly to suppose that history, because it appeals strongly to the emotions, is less capable of satisfying the intellect.

Marc Bloch, "Introduction,"
The Historian's Craft

Contents

Foreword

The Education of a Teacher is a treasure for several reasons. The reason which I think might be most important to its author is the depth, clarity, and imagination with which the book demonstrates, in a variety of contexts, what it takes to make a good teacher. Wolf doesn't tell the reader that, and I'm not sure he thinks he knows. Maybe no one does, and anyway, as his book clearly shows, sometimes nothing works. But he knows what the ingredients are and the limits within which the proportions may be varied and still provide sustenance for mind and character, so that the power—and the need —to love and to understand would grow and go on growing.

That is what the dissenting students of the sixties, who have meant so much to both Wolf and myself, expected it to do. The fact that it didn't go on growing accounts for much of their rage and for their rejection of letters and history, which Wolf so greatly deplores. Some of the more moving passages of this book detail his stratagems to bring these essentials to their attention, so that they would have them when they needed them to make sense of their lives.

The second reason why *The Education of a Teacher* is a treasure —to me, this is actually the first reason—is the respectful and loving, though never sentimental, account of these students that Wolf consistently gives. The documentary value of this account is further enhanced by the fact that the book consists of essays written at various times from 1968 to the present: it gives the reader invaluable evidence of how the ensuing years affected our perception of the conflicts of the sixties, in which both he and I took part, at SUNY-Buffalo; and especially of the radical students we valued and who frightened us so much on their behalf and on our own. It is a great relief to read, after twenty years of ridicule and vilification, a book by someone else who appreciated them and much of what they were trying to do.

In his writings during the seventies, however, Wolf adopts an elegiac tone that is the one thing that troubles me about this book. The essays he wrote then are studded with comments about how long ago the sixties seem; his perceptions of the students of the seventies seem to agree with, say, Christopher Lasch about their narcissism, though Wolf's observations are much richer than Lasch's. The most exciting parts of Wolf's book recount his friendships with particular individuals: those are really beautiful. But he writes about them, sometimes, as if they and their causes—our causes—are as good as dead, especially in the papers written in the seventies. His most recent papers are much feistier.

In 1972, commenting on two *New York Times* articles celebrating the decline of student radicalism, Wolf wrote:

> I did not agree wholly with this unveiling of a generation's tombstone—there were and are still, after all, signs of innovations and redirected energies on campus and in the society—but it was self-evident to close observers of American society, especially those on campus and in the classroom (an accurate theatre of evolving and shifting consciousness), that these elegiac forecasts were essentially correct. This does not mean that there will be no more struggle in America, that the radical impulse is dead. But it does mean that tactics will be scaled down, and mass support diminished. . . . So the question has become for me and some of my students: How can the significant gains of the sixties—personal, social, and political liberation, the careful nurturing of individual and social energy—how can these introspective, ecological, and participatory gains be preserved without giving way to what has come to be felt as an overreaching of boundaries, an excessive and, in many cases, irreparable testing of social and perceptual limits?

This question cannot be answered in general terms. It can only be answered in relation to the issues that must be confronted and the degree of repression prevailing at any given time. These factors determine what responses are excessive and whether damage to social limits is justifiable even though it may be irreparable. I found this passage precise, elegant, and moving. But I'm not sure how students at Fort Hare University or the University of the Western Cape would respond to it. Well . . . I'm pretty sure.

The quietism of the seventies is attributable, surely, to many different factors. Demoralization was certainly one of them, and Wolf reminds us how frightening and crazy those days were. But it wasn't just that the students of the seventies were cowed into submission, although they had reason to be. There was also the fact, avoided in subsequent discourse, that the student radicals had begun with reason to believe that it was *they* who were upholding the principles for which our country was supposed to stand, and that the structures of power, formal and informal, must ultimately support them when push came to shove. What happened, instead, was quite a shock.

Wolf makes less than I would of the *fact* that universities are indeed key synapses of the American power structure, and that their complicity with it in punishing student protest was quite thorough. So among those quiet students of the seventies, there must have been many very like those we had cherished during the sixties, but who seemed careerist by comparison because a career was all they were prepared to buy from *us;* all, perhaps, that a university, despite its ethical pretensions, still seemed qualified to sell.

I share completely Wolf's conviction that history and the liberal arts are indispensable resources in any important struggle, inner or outer, that may engage us. But when dispensed by official agencies, they are properly suspect: not because we may be teaching in bad faith—that seldom happens—but because that knowledge deemed to be of most worth is, in Pierre Bourdieu's phrase, *a form of cultural capital* and does indeed partake of the ideology that declares it to be the mostest and the bestest. The students came to realize that, too.

I have no fear whatever that young men and women in the nineties will be predominantly morally obtuse and insensitive to the needs of other people; preoccupied with technology at the expense of their humanity. What *does* terrify me is the prospect that, as the eagles launched by an unchanging policy come home to roost—not only from Vietnam but from Angola, Chile, Nicaragua, Namibia, El Salvador, Libya, Grenada (who knows how long the list may have grown?)—the young people I love may once again be buried in eagle-shit if they disturb it again, as they will and must. There may not be much a teacher can do about that, but I wish more of us would try. Howard Wolf does, quite often.

Edgar Z. Friedenberg, Professor *emeritus*
Dalhousie University

Preface

A writer is perhaps the last one to know what his work stands for. This is an old, but reliable, saw. He writes from inner promptings, and however public his material may feel even to him, it is only an audience outside of him, other than him, who can decide, after all and finally, if and how his work holds up.

Still, it is difficult, if not impossible, for a writer not to imagine that he indeed knows something special about his own work—something like a parent's feeling that, in the end, only he understands his child, even when that child feels misunderstood by the parent.

So, I will indulge myself a little. These essays turn out to be something like an autobiographical chronicle of American culture in relation to university life during the postwar period. I say "turn out" because I never planned really to teach for such a long time, and I didn't expect, when I thought about writing as a younger man, that I would choose education, in any of its aspects, as a subject. But I took to the subject the moment I began to teach: the classroom seemed to me from the beginning to be a theatre of human possibility.

These essays also chart a course of personal and cultural movement that I could not have predicted at the beginning of my teaching career. The Vietnam war shaped, to a large extent, my sense of what a university might and should be; then, the end of that prolonged war and its aftermath forced a redefinition. It took a while to see these changes; now I may see them too clearly.

Whatever I may claim to see clearly now, I didn't see lucidly at any one point along the way. But it would be foolish, of course, to deny the order I see in them now, and I'd like to believe that a unified imagination was at work even when I was unaware of it.

The essays move through a number of phases discernible to me, phases I've indicated in a table of contents but hesitate to elaborate further here because I don't want to reduce the complexity of the experiences I hope have been captured in the essays.

The reader may be surprised that there is a strong autobiographical element in these essays about education and culture. The field of education—especially "higher" education—has been exempted pretty much from subjective and literary treatment. University professors, to say nothing of administrators, don't like to see the personal side of their objective and rational commitments. There is more to be said about this subject, and I hope I've said some of it in these essays.

I've tried over more than two decades in teaching to oppose this tendency to deny the uses of the imagination in education. I've tried to humanize the place where my colleagues, students, and I have lived our all too human, but usually unexpressed, lives.

I've changed these essays only slightly: in getting rid of gross repetitions, in improving word choice, and in burying properly dead sentences. These essays stand mostly in the order in which they were written, with only a few rearrangements for the sake of coherence. I want to preserve the time of their lives, like snapshots.

Acknowledgments

It is always difficult to put a book together. It is especially demanding, if also rewarding, to bring together materials from most of the stages of one's writing career. You need the help of others to meet the challenge. I am grateful to the staff at Prometheus Books, especially to Doris Doyle, Victor Gulotta, and Donna Sheinberg, for their understanding and support. I am deeply grateful to Linda Bogdan, secretary in the Office of English Undergraduate Studies, for the hard and careful work she did in preparing my manuscript. She is a critic as well as a secretary and deserves recognition beyond my enduring respect. I owe a lasting debt to Ramona Whitaker, a scrupulous and meticulous editor. F. Curtis Miles has been a selfless proofreader. To my close friends—Carl Dennis, George Hochfield, Mac and Katka Hammond, Martin Pops, Mark and Anne Shechner, Alan and Anne Spiegel—I say thanks, as always, for listening and sharing over the years.

THE
EDUCATION
OF A TEACHER

Setting Out

The Education of a Teacher 1

At the end of August 1962, I stood on a dune overlooking the Atlantic Ocean with a girlfriend who was getting ready to spend a few years in Paris on a Fulbright. She was young, creative, and Bohemian. Paris wouldn't disappoint her. I was about to launch a career in teaching as a teaching fellow in Boston. I had to prepare myself to earn a living and, besides, Cambridge was mecca for a would-be writer and Americanist, especially if I could find a spacious room on leafy Harvard Street.

Still, I was edgy. I had tried teaching a few years earlier and had given it up because I'd been assigned to teach grammar to three sections of nursing students at another large university. I hadn't seen the point, then, of helping students master the period. I'd skulked off in the middle of the night and sent a telegram to the chairman, saying I'd been drafted. A number of small wars at the time made my excuse for so rapid an exit seem plausible.

Ready for another go at teaching, I wondered if I'd stick with it. As I looked at the waves surging towards the wide, sea-foamed beach, I saw, coming through the grass, a whitehaired man whom I recog-

This essay is reprinted with permission from *New Directions in Teaching,* vol. 6, no. 4 and vol. 7, no. 1, A Double Issue, 1979-80.

nized as the retired soccer coach of my alma mater, a man respected as much for his wisdom as for his athleticism. I introduced myself. He remembered me slightly, or so he said, and we brought each other up to date on our lives. He'd just retired and was expecting to paint full-time. I told him I was off to Boston to start a teaching career.

"What do you think of that?" I asked.

"A great adventure," he said; "the question is, though: Who will love first?"

I didn't really know what he meant in this context by "loving," but I was pleased that he thought an adventure, not flight, lay ahead for me. Given my uncertainties about teaching and what I might be asked to teach, I wasn't sure I'd even get to unpack. His words stuck with me, and I often went back to his question; but I came to see over the years that the shape and quality of the "teaching love" change *in* time and *with* time in its shifting course.

I returned to New York City for a few days before going to Boston and found myself on the last night sitting on the lip of the fountain in front of the Plaza Hotel. I'd always gone there when I was on the verge of a major decision. Manhattan was a magical place for me, imbued with radiant possibility.

For all my doubts about teaching, the purpose of a literary education seemed unassailable: to teach, in the Arnold mode, the best that had been thought and felt, to present students with the high points of Western civilization, and to ask them to engage themselves with these heightened possibilities.

There could never be enough time, of course, to teach all the important works, and few people ever had been properly educated to teach them all (Eliot was an exception), but there didn't seem any doubt about the importance of certain works, their significance and place in a curriculum, their appropriateness in a common culture. It didn't occur to me that evening, with the fountain suffused in lambent and Steichenesque light, that I would come, for a few years, to see the mission of a literary education in a different set of terms; that I would, for a while, become a radical, a progressive, an innovative teacher; that I would discover several versions of what the old man meant by "Who will love first?" and even come to wonder if the university was the place for love, or if love of learning and true collegiality even were possible in America in the late twentieth century.

How did my affirmation of the Arnoldian ideal get shanghaied by history? What forces compelled me to become interested in new directions of teaching? What other forces, after Vietnam—for that is the crucial element here—moved me in other directions and still keep me in motion?

What kind of love is possible now, and am I willing, after almost two decades of teaching, to inaugurate the teaching passion? Can I find ways to love preliteracy, illiteracy, philistinism, and an artificial cosmology after the generation of student protest? Can I make, have I made, a transition from the age of Frisco to the age of disco and its neoconservative aftermath?

I spent only one year in Boston (1962 to 1963) and didn't have much occasion to think about the old coach I'd met on the dunes. Love didn't seem to be an issue. It wasn't on my mind. I was trying on an elemental level to figure out how to get through six hours of teaching a week without the students mistaking me for a fellow student; I would seek this case of mistaken identity a few years later.

I wasn't satisfied with the regular curriculum (the standard anthology of readings and style/grammar handbook) and tried to slip in some of the techniques and insights of the freshman English sequence I'd taken at college. It had been a famous course, lorded over by a brilliantly difficult professor (his name keeps popping up, I notice, in essays like these); some of the semantic strategies of that English 1-2 got me through some difficult hours when I thought I might have nothing to draw from the well.

I'd bike to school on most fall and spring days, and when I was uncomfortable with the standard lesson for the day, I'd usually be able to think of one of those English 1-2 devices before I got across the Charles River bridge.[1] Maybe I'd tell them to describe the light reflected off the Boston State House at different times of the day (like Monet's Rouen) and then ask, "How has the building changed for you?" I'd hit them, finally, with the big twentieth century relativist question: "Is there really *a* State House?"

These questions and other mind-twisters aroused interest, but I never felt that I could settle their serious philosophic implications, and I'd bike unsteadily back across the Charles. I loved living in Cambridge, but I thought, after a year, that there were too many correct opinions floating around Harvard Square for me to find my own way and voice, so I headed for the Midwest and the University of Michigan.

I packed my few possessions into a tiny Fiat 600 and drove, with two shock absorbers, to Ann Arbor. After the long drive, the bouncing, the jostling, I knew when I got there that I'd have a better chance at becoming an original teacher if I left English 1-2 behind. (It's still lying somewhere near Toledo, and I only reach for it when I'm desperate.)

As it turned out, I didn't have to search out a method for very long. The New Left and the antiwar movement came into view quickly. By the spring of 1964, there was radical activity on the Michigan campus—speeches on the steps of the library, SDS manifestos. I sensed history bearing down on all of us and knew it would make itself felt in the classroom. It did. Students wanted their educations to be "relevant" to the implications of the war: imperialism, capitalism, racism, the accumulative peril of Western technology, the Big Lie of official language, the role of the university as a wing of the Establishment.

Although I wasn't politically engaged, I responded to these issues and pitched discussions of our assigned books in their direction. I put in other readings that were to the point: Orwell, Sartre, Caudwell. I started out at the University of Michigan in a three-piece suit and was "into" faded jeans (dungarees, then) and work-shirts by the end of the third year (shades of James Agee and the populist affectations of the 1930s). I went to rallies and sit-ins, listened to the issues, and brought some of them, like deer on a fender, into the classroom.

But it soon became clear that no discussion in class, however relevant, was going to change the course of history, and I began to wonder: How was history changing the students in the classroom? What could be done about it? If I couldn't make the classroom relevant to history in the largest sense, how could I make history relevant to the classroom? Or how could I discover the relevance of history in the classroom? It might work in that direction.

I might not have gotten anywhere with these questions if I hadn't taught for a year at Eastern Michigan University in Ypsilanti, Michigan. The students of EMU, not as sophisticated as their Ann Arbor contemporaries, forced me to ask basic and primary questions about education. They didn't confront me with relevancy or the failure of the university to deal with the real issues (as they were called). They confronted me instead with the concrete fact of their intimidation, silence, diffidence.

I didn't understand this silence and fear of participation, but I knew something had to be done about it. I began asking them to discuss their readings in small groups. I then asked them to appoint a discussion leader who would represent the group. This technique began to work without my fully understanding its dynamics. It inaugurated the second phase of my brief career as a radical teacher.

I didn't quite understand why this group approach made open discussions possible and even comfortable, but I kept at it and was pleased when a college friend, a young psychoanalyst, John Zinner, wrote that the work I was doing was consistent with the newer trends at the National Institute of Mental Health and at the Tavistock Clinic in London.

I stuck with this group and surrogate-spokesman method for a year and took some of its assumptions with me when I left Ann Arbor in 1967 to begin a job at the State University of New York at Buffalo.

Driving across Southern Ontario in the late August heat, slightly nauseated from smoking, I wondered again if I'd stick with the job. Old fears come back for me at crossings and thresholds. When I got to the university, then a tower of experiment, rising above the Niagara escarpment, I began to write about my experiences at EMU and to put some of my insights at the service of new techniques.

I came to see that silence and fear of participation were standard features of education in America. Most elementary and secondary school teachers had overemphasized the role of their authority. Students were rebelling against this imposed authority by refusing to learn, by refusing to risk rejection. The Vietnam war, as a massive instance of the misuse of authority, found an audience among American students ready to throw off the shackles of authority. But it's never been easy for Americans to rebel: on the one hand, the students wanted to show anger towards authorities, elders, and fathers who had been imposing knowledge of one kind or other from grade school to Vietnam; on the other hand, the prospect of showing these feelings, of giving vent to an accrued history of resentment towards the learned, wasn't acceptable either at an unconscious or at a social level.

Caught between a personal history of defeat from kindergarten to the threat of draft, the American student became silent in the classroom. This silence found its opposite expression in the streets, but even there, passive resistance—despite the hype and paranoia of the Johnson and Nixon administrations—seemed to be the dominant mode of defense.

Other variables contributed as well to this passivity in the face of imposed learning: America's historical anti-intellectualism, the media (television, radio, newsmagazines) with their denial of value, their pitch for commodities, their presentation of people as products, their emphasis on stars and celebrities. All these elements diminished the value of the average viewer, and this diminished sense of self, in turn, was passed on to the student-viewer.

I came to see some of these issues through my writing, and I tried to do something about them. In place of group discussion and the spokesman/instructor-surrogate approach used at EMU, at SUNY-Buffalo, I now tried to make my classes more therapeutic.

Making use of some of the psychiatric and psychoanalytic models fashionable in the mid- and late 1960s, I asked students to come to terms with some of their resentments by making them public, by discussing them in a group, by asking other students to respond and "to share" (a famous verb of the period) the fears and anxieties of their contemporaries. Between 1968 and 1970, I became more of a therapist, I think, than a teacher of literature, though I didn't want to admit this.

Instead of teaching a course in Literature and Madness (typical of those days) in the fall of 1969, I first asked students to write up their "own crises." We would discuss them, I suggested, instead of borrowing life from literature. It occurred to me after awhile that we didn't have to "write up" these crises; we could just present them in class. Students took to this suggestion. I don't doubt that it may have been an easy way for some of them to get through a course. But for others, for me, it was a response to the times.

Where my students were exploring on all fronts, were testing limits all around (through defiance of the draft, through drugs, through communal living, through new approaches to, and the understanding of, art and music), where my students were becoming participants and subjects all around, I pretty much had limited myself, though I didn't think of it in these terms, to experiment in the classroom. I was reaching, I suppose, for a "high" in teaching.

Some of these experiments were risky in their own way. This became quite clear at the end of that semester when a student, who hadn't been attending class (because of a heroin problem, as it turned out), appeared in class one day and tried to become part of the group. The solidarity we had formed was so airtight that he was shunned. When he tried to get into the group, he was told to stay out. He responded by crying out and beating his hands against the wall. It seemed clear then, if it hadn't before, that we had gone too far. I, as a teacher certainly, had gone too far, had sailed too deeply into therapeutic waters.

This student had rights and privileges that we had violated as a group. I never felt quite the same way again being therapeutic in a classroom. It had seemed possible for a while that the classroom—like the tide of revolutionary history we thought we were living through—might move without injury beyond the limits of individual and national history. I sustained this typically American illusion between 1968 and 1970.

My constraints, as much as my lack of constraints, embarrassed me somewhat, but I'm pleased in retrospect that I didn't cross my Rubicon and destroy a life's history of interest in teaching literature and writing. I came back to it in the end. It saved me when history seemed to have fled. If I hadn't been able to write after the spring of 1970, after Kent State and Cambodia, if I had savaged my literary side too much during those years when I was trying to get students to find a way to love, when I was trying, in my way, to fight the war, I don't know what future would have been possible for me as a teacher after the years of protest.

I tried in the years immediately following Kent State and Cambodia to sustain some sense of experiment in education. But my experiments were mild for me, if not to most of my colleagues. I taught a course in Drama of the Family and tried to get students to relate their personal and family histories to the lives of the characters in the plays. Although I emphasized understanding the plays, not the lives of the students, I always hoped that deeper connections would be made between the plays and the students' inner lives. This quest for the inner life will surely go down as one of the great preoccupations of the twentieth century. It may go down, as well, as one of the great myths of our history.

I tried other "soft" experiments in humanistic education between 1970 and 1973, between the end of the Vietnam era and the emergence of what I've come to call the age of disco. I asked students to write poems in a modern poetry course that would be discussed alongside and equally with the "official" poems of the anthology. Without making comparisons of quality, without assuming that the official poems were more important or complex than the student poems, we asked for instance, "How does x's experience of parental loss agree with or differ from Sylvia Plath's?"

It seems a tired question now, but there it was, part of the period's lingering preoccupation with trauma, guilt, the weight of the middle-class family, the need to confess and be forgiven. There was no way for me, or most of my students, to escape the impress of this intellectual and psychological history. We were there and we asked these questions.

I might have gone on with these somewhat fainthearted attempts to sustain the experimental mode of the 1960s, but a sabbatical leave came along, and I took it in California.

Living in California for a while might have made me take hope in the possibility of experiment again. It had started there with the Free Speech Movement at Berkeley in 1964, and the atmosphere of experiment hovered like the smog in L.A. But I became more certain, while living there, that the quest for self-expression (which is what most of us were up to) was very much an American phenomenon that needed to be questioned and, perhaps, checked.

I began to write about my 1960s experiences in order to figure out how I had become the sort of person that I was: What had led me to a particular marriage, to a particular approach to teaching and politics? What, in the history of my family in America, had made me what I was? I was trying to crawl out from under narcissism through self-awareness (perhaps the greatest American Houdini act of them all).

Sitting in my garden in the Berkeley hills, the air scented with plum, magnolia, and fuchsia, I began to grapple with my personal history, a literary and self-searching campaign that was to occupy me for the next five years. The conditions for battle were ideal, if somewhat tilted in my favor. The more deeply I probed the lives of my family—the procession of characters who defined the 1960s for me—and myself, the further I went in locating the fulcrum of each character's "character," the more it seemed that the balancing point of selfhood took its equilibrium and disequilibrium from the weight and moment of history and generational style.

Starting as a preoccupation with self, my memoir moved more and more towards an encounter with history. History itself, its assumptions, its attitudes, and its atmosphere, seemed to be something of an unconscious element in human conduct. I could see my father, myself, and my students—I could see these three generations of Americans—following general patterns of flight. If this discouraged me somewhat because it crimped the wings of individual and narcissistic ascent, it yielded a feeling also of joined destiny and shared migration.

By the time I finished and published my memoir (*Forgive the Father: A Memoir of Changing Generations,* New Republic Books, 1978), I had already begun to ask students in a Literary Journalism course (a new direction for me) to look for the personal element in history, for the historical element in the self. Orwell was important again, but for a different reason: for his autobiographical imprint in "Such, Such Were the Joys . . ." and "Why I Write."

"Who will love first?" took on a new twist. Now it occurred to me that the answer wasn't one-sided. It was more a question of loving the students so that they could come to love themselves a bit more, so that their writing would seem more an act of self-affirmation, even if that affirmation brought them, ironically, to the limits of the self: to an encounter with history.

I didn't have a technique of instruction so much as an attitude, a disposition, a willingness to believe that there were depths and complexities, fears and passions (I had seen these in the 1960s; I had risked facing them in class) that students could write about. I no longer believed in enacting these passions as living drama, but I wanted to act as something of a midwife, a Leboyer of prose instruction.

The last two or three years have been ones of pedagogic encouragement and enticement. Drawing up whatever I possess of humor, charm, evocation, and poetic language itself; drawing upon as many human resources as I can, I have asked students to discover their selves in relation to the real and symbolic history of our times.

So I've gone back to the beginning, in a way, to the Arnoldian injunction, to a sense that we have a shared history, but I leave the discovery to the students. If I have a mission now, it lies in the direction of setting the kinds of self-historical discoveries I've been talking about in opposition to the fantasies of self and history that are now being acted out every weekend at midnight across the land in *The Rocky Horror Picture Show* and on disco stages.

Where theatre went to the streets in the 1960s, the street has now gone to the theatre, has gone theatrical. The shared and social aspirations of the Vietnam years have given way to an impersonation of self-transformation.

Theatre and theatrical gesture during the Vietnam years were aimed at a nontheatrical audience, were aimed at the audience of the dominant, middle-class culture, and these gestures imagined the possibility of real response and reform.

Futile or not, self-serving or not, the style of protest and radical pedagogy in the 1960s, however absurd, entered the lists against social injustice and unspeakable practices in Vietnam. The grotesqueries of immolation and napalm-bombing were mirrored in an often comedic politics.

Now we have only a protest of style: disguise, dress-up, cosmetics, and "easy listening" make-believe replace the social and political uses of the imagination. Where there were haunting slogans (Make Love, Not War) there are now a proliferation of T-shirt decal-mations: Disco Forever; I Survived the Blizzard of '77; Squeeze Me.

Where the 1960s wanted to obliterate the ego (in the service of a deeper narcissism, as it turned out), we have the Tux-Ego and Trans-Am Camaros with flame-flecked hoods proclaiming a ragtag grab bag of instant identities.

Was our experiment worth it? Because, as I have come to believe, we discover ourselves in relation to history, it was, of course, worth it. The self defines itself, achieves a possible form, through the encounter with history. Our experiment was a meeting with history. It couldn't have been otherwise for teachers who were alive to the times.

Can we carry *some* of our lessons forward? We must, especially the knowledge that love and rage are present in every classroom; that complex feelings surround all discourse, even the most polite and rational. Each teacher will deal with this knowledge in a different way.

I know that great teaching and learning—I saw some of it once—touch these passions. The question is still: "Who will love first?" But now I know that history—that real abstraction, that elusive river of time and style and belief that carries us off to tributaries and sinks us like silt—will always force us to ask again and again, "But, how?" And, "Is it still worth it?" So we beat on. . . .

Search for New Methods

Down and Out in the Sixties **2**

Within the fiction of a dramatic and Aristotelian ordering of time (beginning, middle, and end), we search for finer categories, intermediate structures through which to know ourselves. In America, the fiction is a decade. To some extent—speaking very much as a person of the mid-fifties—the fiction shapes life.

I remember with stop-action clarity my freshman roommate and me walking across the Town Common in the winter of '55 wondering what we would be in '65, as if we had only ten years in which to become. Even then, we felt '65 rushing towards us with a Fitzgeraldian urgency: Would we make it—once we knew who we were—in the decade allotted to us, or would we wake up on our thirtieth birthdays and say, with James Agee, that we had missed irretrievably all the trains we meant to catch?

Of course, '65 was a fiction. When it arrived and we talked together in New York, it became clear to us that '68, ten years after graduation, *the tenth*, was a meaningful end-tape; so we granted ourselves a reprieve. Because we knew—in the act of setting our watches—that the time we had condemned ourselves to was a fiction,

---

This essay first appeared in the Amherst College alumni magazine, *Amherst*, in 1968 and was reprinted in *The Voice Within: Reading and Writing Autobiography*, Knopf, 1973. It is reprinted here with permission.

we were able to keep our cool when '65 came. We were expert at pumping irony.

For us, '68 would be a harder rap to beat, fiction would edge towards myth; but we would make it, I was sure of that, because of the values of the decade in which we constructed our world view: irony and identity. So long as we believed in the self, time would never run out on us. The quest for identity has the redeeming quality of being a quest, and, as we used to say in the mid-fifties, the meaning of *Moby Dick* lies in the quest for meaning.

Our ironic awareness of the self looking at the self, and our understanding of the arbitrary symbolic structure the self uses to posit the world, would save us. Because we believed in the certainty of self and were schooled in the methodologies of uncertainty, the question we set forth from the Common—Who am I?—would never trap us in time, although there might never be a time when we are not trapped by the question.

The issue is relevant for me and, perhaps, for some of my teaching contemporaries, because the students we instruct share neither our concept of self nor our sense of irony. At one extreme, hippie culture, high on Leary and low on Freud, stands for the obliteration of self and consciousness. The tools of obliteration are LSD, pot, strobe lights, psychedelic art, and the photo-pornotopia of the Velvet Underground; the texts of annihilation are *The Tibetan Book of the Dead,* the lyrics of the Fugs, and numerous celebrations of madness: *One Flew Over the Cuckoo's Nest, Beautiful Losers,* and R. D. Laing's *The Politics of Experience.* For hippie culture, ego means "reason," reason means "authority," authority means "LBJ and the military-industrial complex"; and, together, these terms mean cop-out, death, or some such equation. In any case, the answer is—freak out!

At another extreme, we are teaching activists. The quest for the self, the self-reflexive tradition, is taken as a form of bourgeois idealism. Marx, C. Wright Mills, and Stokeley "tell it like it is," where Collingwood, Becker, and other subjective and relativist historiographers, tell us how we might go about imposing order upon what we have selected to know. Where we withdrew into the self in the face of social and corporate anomie (remember *The Lonely Crowd*?), this aspect of the new generation—symbolized by SDS (Students for a Democratic Society) and SNCC (Student Nonviolent Coordinating Committee)—wants to move through self-interest towards social justice. Demonstration has replaced introspection.

At the moment, an apparent field of concord exists between these two elements of the new generation at the *love-in,* an alleged selfless expression of a classless community. Beads, head-bands, and talismans can join hands with protorevolutionaries and celebrate the death of a dying culture. The cleavage between sit-in and drop-out, though profound, does not at this time seem to divide the young.

For both groups, the absurd is in, irony out: the prevailing mode of reality is rejected, not qualified in the self-reflecting mirrors of the mind. For both groups, the self is out, non-self in; only the routes of escape are different—*out* to the world, *down* to the collective, encoded history of the race.

In a word, those of us who are thirty are not prepared by generational disposition to teach those who are twenty; yet, in the nature of the academic world, those who are twenty will look to us, the young professoriate, for confirmation and instruction. Those going *down* and *out* will want to learn from us how to become in '78 what they want to be in '68. Perhaps this fiction of decade will get lost in the hippie-activist shuffle (both a good "trip" and utopia move beyond time), but they will want to learn—if they haven't flaked out to Haight-Ashbury, or Toronto, or gone up in smoke with their draft-cards—how to get to where they want to go.

In all of this I have created a fiction, to be sure. I use *hippie* and *activist* to emblemize centers of thought and feeling and do not imagine that one could go through a college dining hall and count heads in terms of flower power or black power. At the same time, no one in my generation would have walked out on McNamara during a commencement; and though a small band played at bongos and talked of pot, someone as "primitive" as Leslie Fiedler would have been laughed at, as he is not now (as he certainly wasn't last year at the University of Michigan as a writer-in-residence). The difference between the generations, though fictive in my categories, is real.

To some extent, the terms of our education, especially those of us who learned the catechism of New Criticism, put us in a position to understand the divide between the generations. Trained as we were to see the shape of our language systems, sensitized as we were to see the controlling metaphors of our discourse, we ought to be able first to define ourselves, or at least to know what we mean by self-definition. In my letters to friends and theirs to me, certain words reappear: sensibility, self, world, tension, irony, dislocation, paradox, ambiguity, alienation, dichotomy, and aloneness. These words point to a painful discontinuity between the individual and society and to an equally painful problem of knowing the nature of the self and the world. Like characters in the great nineteenth-century novels (I think of *Jane Eyre*), we curl into the self as a form of defense against an alien environment.

The language of our students is action packed, other-worldly, and takes its tone from James Bond and comic books: cop-out, flake-out, drop-out, trip-out. The verb, I suppose, belongs to the activists, the modifier to the hippies, and the whole verbal element is a meeting place like the love-in. Interestingly, the equation is reversed here with the beatific verb coming first followed by the activist "in": sit-in standing, as it were, for the Civil Rights and Peace Movements. Whether the hyphen will hold and whether the "ins" will continue to snake with the "outs" remain moot points, but it is clear that the road signs point in two directions for the teacher: towards sociology and mythology, towards N. O. Brown and Leary on one hand, Marcuse on the other—again, emblems.

We do, then, meet our students as spokesmen of an opposition culture. If the challenge is construed as student and teacher acting together as critics of society, not as student versus establishment, there is a chance that one may have a hearing, even if he is over thirty, has a wife, two kids, a VW, and still, guiltily, prefers the *New York Times* to the *East Village Other.*

And if we are prudent, we will not at first (now I speak out of my bag, English teacher) lay on our students those authors whose world views were consonant with the terms of our generation: Henry James, Jane Austen, E. M. Forster, and the shaped poems of the seventeenth century. We will turn as well to the prophets and radicals: Blake, Whitman, Thoreau, Hart Crane, Brecht, Dostoevsky—make your own list; we will include the world beyond the university as part of the meaning of education, and if we are still lugging around graduate school bibliographies and haven't tied into the gurus of this generation, we had better, as we used to say, get on the stick. We had better read *Understanding Media, Love's Body, Against Interpretation.*

Once we have turned on the students in their own terms, once we have established an atmosphere of trust, meaningful dialogue can begin. We can, for ourselves, possibly transform self-consciousness into selfhood by gaining access to the unconscious and social materials about which our students are so much sharper than we were. We will let our students push us down and out.

When my freshman roommate and I asked to know who we were on a winter night in 1955, we failed to realize that a new generation would make us see the question in new terms. We should, as Amherst men, have been aware of shifting cultural contexts, the Whorf hypothesis, Wittgensteinian language games—but, in a way, we lucked out, because now we have at least another decade to catch that train.

Composition and Group Dynamics 3

During a five year period of teaching freshman English at three large universities—Boston University, the University of Michigan, and Eastern Michigan University—I discovered that neither I nor my students had been prepared properly for an authentic experience of education. They appeared in class *to be taught,* and I came armed with a syllabus *to teach them.*

Although I had begun to learn something about what I was doing and to shift my approach to the students and the course by the fifth year, it wasn't until then—at Eastern Michigan University—that I understood the dimensions of the problem teachers face in the United States and the necessity for radical innovation.

Let me summarize my experience, describe the essential problem, outline a technique I used, and suggest a psychosexual analysis of the origins of the problem and the reason for the partial success of the technique.

First, the problem: it became clear at the outset of my teaching career that my students were writing papers that were, at best, neutral in quality and intensity and, at worst, uninteresting and tautological. I assumed, of course, that the problem lay in basic English—the

---

This essay is reprinted with permission from the December 1968 edition of *Paunch.*

students' experience in writing it and my unpreparedness in teaching it. As someone who had unthinkingly internalized the attitudes and methods of my former teachers, I addressed myself to drills, exercises, and the articulation of paper topics that were unmistakably clear, or so I thought.

Moreover, I tried to model class discussion of the texts we were reading after the best analytic minds, especially the ordinary language philosophers: Ryle, Wittgenstein, and Urmson; and after the current rhetorical and stylistic opinion: Strunk and White's *Elements of Style,* Martin and Ohmann's *The Logic and Rhetoric of Exposition.*

Using this approach, I managed to help some of the students who had mechanical problems, problems of grammar and syntax, write *correct* English, but despite this important step forward, their prose, and the prose of the class in general, did not become precise and personalized, accurate and clear in the only sense that is important: the unique expression of one's own experience. If the problem could not be understood as a failure of basic English, what was one to make of the flaccid and impartial quality of student prose?

At the end of the first semester of my second year at the University of Michigan—in which I had the best section that I had taught thus far—it seemed sensible to ask why *that section* had yielded superior results. Two inferences were inescapable: it had been a section in which two or three people took creative writing seriously, and it had been a section with a few activists in it. Significantly, both the creative writers and activists had this in common: the assertion of their selves and their world views. Looking back through this experience, it made perfect sense that a student would be able to write meaningful and expressive prose only if he could *actively* project his *self* in a *free* context.

When the next semester began, I saw unmistakably that most of my students were passive and afraid, perhaps passive because afraid: because they feared judgment—even mine (this came out in private conferences); they preferred, without thinking about it, to hide, as it were, to conceal the risks of autonomy behind a veil of neutrality. It seemed to me, then, that the problems of freshman English could not be separated from a culture that was *other-directed,* from a culture that broadcast acceptable and consumable self-images at every turn—on TV and in ads (the extension of the corporate view of human nature). What was one to do against such powerful odds?

In my last year of teaching at the University of Michigan, I tried to meet the problem by talking about it with the students, by working out essay topics with each student individually, and most important, by not letting the class know during a discussion exactly what I took to be *right* or *wrong.* Some students responded well to this; some withdrew further. It was not until the next year that I understood why some students withdrew more when given greater freedom, and it wasn't until then that I thought of a method to meet this particular dilemma.

At Eastern Michigan University, a rapidly growing branch of the Michigan system, I encountered students whose problems were, *in extreme,* the problems I had already encountered. Most of the students were first generation college students, and most of them had barely qualified to attend the university. For the first few weeks, many of the students were almost mute—by broad analogy, almost autistic.

At the time, I was reading R. D. Laing's *The Divided Self* and Bettleheim's *The Empty Fortress.* Laing's study of schizophrenia and Bettleheim's study of autism in children shared a common insight: when threatened, individuals withdraw. Most drastically, an individual may choose non-being so as not to be destroyed—the illogical logic of the mind.

Because they had not been encouraged in their earlier efforts towards freedom, towards autonomy, *the most threatening* situation for these students was a class in which they did not know *a priori* how the teacher would respond. Because they had not been encouraged to assert themselves in their prior educational and familial experience, they could function best when they knew what the rules of the teacher's game were, when their neutral and correct statements were sanctioned by the teacher.

I was not willing to renounce *my* commitment to an autonomous view of human development, and I was not willing to punish my students. I solved this dilemma by instituting a special kind of group dynamic. In each of my three sections, I divided the class into small groups in an informal way. I encouraged the students to cluster and talk to one another.

So that they would not face a void in this group conversation, I posed a question, one that was well within their reach and asked them to elaborate upon it. At this point, I left the classroom for about ten minutes. Occasionally, I would look into the classroom to see if conversation were flagging—energy is important here, as it is in all of education (the fixed fifty-minute hour is a Germanic convention we could well do without)—and if it was, I would re-enter the room and go from group to group, chatting in a casual way and answering substantive questions only. (It is crucial in this that the teacher not steal the insight from the group.) Then I would ask each group to appoint a spokesman who would speak for the group. After weeks of their silence, it astounded and pleased me that the group leader invariably did have something to say. Because he was speaking for the group, because he could say, "We feel . . . We thought . . . ," because he did not have, at that moment, to put his own identity on the line, the spokesman could be vocal. After each group had its say through the *mask* of the spokesman, I took the remaining five or ten minutes to integrate what the students had said.

Once again, I did not try to steal the power of insight from the students. I tried, rather, to show them how various comments that had been made might go together. I acted as a *synthesizer,* not an authority figure, and did not, in this sense, reinforce the fear that, once again, self-assertion would be denied. After attacking the problem of participation in this way for a few weeks, I went back to another attempt at free class discussion. For a meeting or two there would be more vital and dynamic discussions, but soon the silent passivity would settle in. And back I would go to the protogroup therapy with its role-playing spokesman, with its sanctioned scapegoat figure, if you will.

This method did not allow us to cover a great deal of material during the course of the semester, and it did not overcome a life's history of self-denial as a mode of dealing with authority (as it did not unbind the hostility that such self-denial inevitably entails), but it did give the students a more authentic sense of themselves. Moreover, the students' essays had the unmistakable imprint of individuals asserting their own being-in-the-world, their special sense of the world as it meets the eye and courses in the blood.

As I have tried to suggest, the students' failure to assert the self was based on a defensive, passive posture. Moreover, our culture seems oddly aggressive on the macrolevel and extremely passive on the microlevel. In *The Uncommitted,* Dr. Kenneth Keniston discusses the mother-orientation of the current generation and its attendant oral passivity. Dr. Malcolm Bowers, a Yale psychiatrist, who has confirmed some of Keniston's hypotheses, says:

> However, there are some male children who, because the father does not provide that role model, never develop that far. They remain at the earlier stage in which they still expect to be fed, to be kept warm, to be made to feel good.[1]

Keniston's hypothesis applies both to adolescents who have had drug experience and to normal children and should, because of its encompassing nature, be taken seriously. As a diagnosis of a pathological condition can teach us about normal constitution, so seeing the latent addiction to self-denial in the normal classroom can possibly avert a more extreme disaffiliation of young people from the world.

My technique, which coincides with some recent work in group dynamics, worked in part because the individual student was able to assert himself or herself indirectly through the dramatic device of the *spokesman.* Further, *in playing the spokesman* at one time or other, each student had an opportunity to test the limits of his assumed authority against my imagined authority.

Ultimately then, the problem of composition is political as well as psychological and pedagogic. Writing and freedom are intimately connected. Recent contributions to educational theory—John Holt's *How Children Fail,* Sylvia Ashton Warner's *Teacher,* Paul Goodman's notion of the minischool, the achievements of early school experiments in England (which Joseph Featherstone has written about in *The New Republic*)—all these point towards a greater degree of self-motivation in education. It is my conviction that, in a society where individuals can overcome passivity and assertively express their humanity, they will be less likely to compensate through indirect expressions of power. Freedom, rather than sublimation (*Bonnie and Clyde?*), may be the way to face the problems of aggression.

Finally, I should say something about the teacher. He can encourage freedom only to the degree that he can relinquish power and to the extent that he can face the materials that arise in a context of freedom. If the teacher is defensive, if he submits to a punishing superego (in its internalized form, or in the guise of principle, legislation, etc.) in its most punitive form, he will not be able to help his students. Without trust, there cannot be mutuality—as Bettleheim and Erikson have taught us. Without mutuality, education has come to the end of the road, the end of dialog.

The technique I have advanced cannot renovate the individual—indeed, it should not attempt to be group therapy—but it can enhance possibilities for free expression, and if every option towards free expression is exercised within institutions of learning, one may possibly imagine a society that has less need for psychotherapy, for psychotherapy addresses itself to inhibition. Existentialism, psychotherapy, and the best of contemporary educational theory are all in accord on one point: replace inhibition with increased freedom. Freedom can be frightening for both teacher and student; it can, para-doxically, make one feel less free. It may feel, at first, like a mael-strom in which one may be annihilated, like Conrad's "destructive element"; however, it is the irreducible risk one must take if one wishes to be human.

Teaching and Human Development 4

As a student and teacher at a diverse and representative sampling of American institutions of higher learning, I have found one unexpressed assumption held in common by them: learning and human development are disconnected.

In a sense, even this alleged separation of thought and feeling, cognition and affect, ascribes more intention to those institutions than is really the case, because it suggests that alternatives have been weighed and choices made.[1] I do not think, though, that the institutions and teachers who constitute them have made any such self-conscious judgment about the difficulty, inefficiency, and irrationality of an organic or unified approach to education.

It is rather the case that teachers in colleges and universities learn how to teach by internalizing the methods of their teachers, and only in a few instances have those "master" teachers *not* seen themselves as content-oriented transmitters of a body of knowledge — without the pulsating energy that the metaphor implies.

In only a few instances have one's master teachers been aware both of the effect and affect of what they taught. It has been an

This essay is reprinted with permission from *New Directions in Teaching,* Summer-Fall 1969.

essentially unchallenged assumption of educators and intellectuals in our print-biased, rationalistic culture, that knowledge is truth; truth, knowledge; and that is all you need to know: all of this despite the fact that almost anything one reads about contemporary American education—Kozol, Holt, Kohl, Coles, Schrag, Goodman—points to pain, repression, and the denial of feeling in both a psychological and political context.

Traditionally, the emphasis in *institutions* (is it any wonder that ordinary language links madness, the penal code, and education?) of learning has been cognition. American educators have failed to relate cognition to human development and social values and, in their own terms, have not kept abreast of the best cognitive theories—Piaget and Bruner, for example.

I do not mean to set up knowledge as a negative value against the positive attributes of a preverbal, McLuhanesque retribalization of learning, or the values of N. O. Brown's preliterate polymorphous perversity, or the sensualization of perception through Leary's sacramental drug.

I do not mean to set up this polarity for three reasons: (1) I believe in the ennobling and liberating power of knowledge; (2) my categories are reductive; and (3) what I stand for does not entail an oceanic loss of self or renunciation of the word, does not lead to a "space age primitivism," though there are, in a certain sense, primitive elements in my concept of a humane and developmental education.[2]

In my seven years of teaching, I have been forced by the needs of my students, as well as my own needs, to realize that education must, in some ontological sense, address itself to the *being* of the student, must encounter the more or less integrated self of the student. This is neither an easy task, nor a one-way street: both student and teacher must enact themselves in the process of learning and growth.

A full treatment of the problem at hand—adequate definitions of "being," "integrated self," "encounter"—would obviously necessitate a lengthy argument, so let me suggest some of the obstacles that

stand between the student and being, between the student and encounter, and some of the attitudes and techniques that may initiate
self-realization and freedom in the future.

Obstacles

• Most students whom I have tried to engage in an authentic
confrontation tend to be passive and dependent, deeply needful of
confirmation from their teachers and peers.

• Most of my students have been reluctant to express strong
emotions—either tender or aggressive—toward their fellow students
or teacher.

• In the main, my students have been uncomfortable with silence.

• Students tend to think in terms of courses, not experiences.

• Most of my students bring their bodies to class in only a
marginal sense and, as a result, are not prepared to face sexual impulses in themselves and others and the sensuous field of their perceptions.

• I have often been afraid, along with colleagues, to risk self-
exposure and uncertainty.

Techniques and Attitudes

In *Composition and Group Dynamics: The Paradox of Freedom,* I
discuss the relationship between passivity and what R. D. Laing in
The Divided Self calls "ontological insecurity," the relationship between passivity and the fear of non-being.[3] For student and teacher
alike, there is a fear that the presentation of self will lead to the
annihilation of ego-identity.

This is a particularly pressing issue for adolescents, and the college teacher pays a heavy price if he or she does not deal with the

defensive qualities of passivity, if he or she does not, in part, read passivity as a mode of forestalling the risk of being. Although there are strong tendencies in our culture towards the obliteration of ego-boundaries —and there is much that we can learn from our students about transcending narrow ego-boundaries—it is nonetheless true, I think, that the shaping of a self and the willingness to risk showing that self to the other is one of the necessary conditions of a complete life. In *The Paradox of Freedom,* I suggest that something can be done about passivity through a particular approach to group learning in the classroom. Related directly to the issues raised in that essay are the following examples of panic and non-being:

• A student I taught at Eastern Michigan University repeatedly handed in blank papers during class exercises, even when those exercises were *not* being graded. It became clear to me, after talking to her, that judgment of any kind was intolerable. Her "blankness" was a way of saying: "I will not put myself in a position where judgment is possible." She was able to support this fiction of safety even knowing that it would lead to failure. It reminds me of an irrational equation that Bettleheim ascribes to autistic children who seem to say, without saying it, "If I do not exist, then I can't be hurt."

• Another student at EMU would faint during exams. Needless to say, I only let it happen once. After I found out that it was a pattern of behavior for her, I excused her from exams and assigned some other task. Her fainting was another form of self-annihilation that had, I suspect, fear of performance at its base.

• A friend of mine at the University of Michigan, on the eve of his Ph.D. orals (a formality), also fainted, and when he regained consciousness did not know for a moment who he was. I suspect that given the pressures of the next day he didn't want to know.

• Another friend of mine often dreams that he must pass a Latin exam if he is to get his B.A. He *has* a B.A. as well as other degrees and has never studied Latin. Is he saying, in some way, *Even when I pass, I don't really pass?* This suggests that judgment can be internalized in a way that detaches itself from particular experiences of success and that the mere act of eliminating grades is not sufficient for freedom.

It is my feeling, based upon observation, personal experience, reading, and intuition that experiences of this kind often lie not too far beneath the surface in any classroom experience.

Because passivity is an inevitable response to latent fears of authority and represents a recreation of childhood feelings towards adults, because passivity may well represent an archaic mode of dealing with fears of reprisal, it is wise for the teacher, from time to time, to address himself to passivity in the classroom.

Although at this point I am not making a case for the fusion of psychoanalysis and teaching, there is a great deal to be learned from an understanding of and responsiveness to "transference" in teaching. A careful reading of Freud's twenty-seventh lecture in *A General Introduction to Psychoanalysis* will enable the teacher to take some profound steps towards freeing himself and his students from bondage to the past. Once the student knows that the teacher is a "stand-in," as it were, for past figures of authority, he may well be able to begin to assert himself.

The avoidance of strong feelings of a tender or aggressive nature cuts deep into the ontogenetic history of human development and the insights of psychotherapy, and it would be foolish to suggest that a teacher can overcome the denial of emotion easily.

Something can be done, however. For one, the teacher can by example demonstrate that love and anger are natural emotions, that one does not have to feel one at the expense of the other, that emotions change, that we can only feel with nuance and modulation and ease when we are capable of feeling strongly.

Moreover, the teacher can listen with "the third ear" and not become so lost in the discussion of content that the speaker's emotional attitude towards what is being said is not heard. If one listens in this way, it is sometimes useful and appropriate to call the student's attention to what the third ear has heard.

Great tact is called upon in knowing what to say and when to say it—one wants neither to drive the student into hiding nor to provoke emotions that cannot be controlled—but we are perhaps capable of greater subtlety than we imagine and, at any rate, we should be interested in working towards these sensitivities.

Too often, both teachers and students are uncomfortable with silence. It can be construed by the teacher as a form of passivity and by the students as a loss of control on the teacher's part. Silence can function in these ways; it can also be the seed-bed of discovery and responsiveness to oneself, toward one's deepest promptings.

> The trouble is that the human species is the only species which finds it hard to be a species. For a cat there seems to be no problem about being a cat. It's easy; cats seem to have no complexes or ambivalences or conflicts about them, and show no signs of yearning to be dogs instead. Their instincts are very clear. But we have no such unequivocal animal instincts. Our biological essence, our instinct-remnants, are weak and subtle and they are hard to get at. Learning of the extrinsic pulses in the human species, at the points where the instincts have been lost almost entirely, where they are extremely weak, extremely subtle and delicate, where you have to dig to find them, *this* is where I speak of introspective biology, of biological phenomenology, implying that one of the necessary methods in the search for identity, the search for self, the search for spontaneity and for naturalness is a matter of closing your eyes, cutting down the noise, turning off the thoughts, putting away all busyness, just relaxing in a kind of Taoistic and receptive fashion (in much the same way that you do on the psychoanalyst's couch). The technique here is to just wait to see what happens, what comes to mind. This is what Freud called free association, free-floating attention rather than task-orientation, and if you are successful in this effort and learn how to do it, you can forget about the outside world and its noises and begin to hear these small, delicate impulse-voices from within, the hints from your animal nature, not only from your common species-nature, but also from your own uniqueness.[4]

The teacher should acknowledge silence, sanction it, and, perhaps, when a particularly resonant silence is achieved ask the class *to experience* their silence and then to record some of their impressions and later to discuss them.

This will support the notion that there are emotive underpinnings to cognitive statements and will create an atmosphere in which everyone is participating even when they are not speaking. Students chronically feel out of it and inadequate if they are not verbal and articulate, and the sense of being out of it may be the very condition of their not getting into it.

If a student can learn to listen to his silence, he may well gain the confidence to make a contribution, he may discover that his silence is articulate.

Harold Taylor says in *Art and the Intellect:*

The intellect is not a separate faculty. It is an activity of the whole organism, an activity which begins in the senses with direct experience of facts, events, and ideas, and it involves the emotions.[5]

One of the easiest ways to avoid placing the "intellect" in the body of the "whole organism" is by making a distinction between *course* and *experience.* Nothing need be risked in a course, and the failure to participate in the process of human interaction can be written off as the logical limits of a course.

For students and teacher to think in terms of courses allows everyone to regard learning as a closed system with a beginning and end and examinations as markers along the way. In order for a class to move from course-consciousness to experience, there must be room for thought and feeling to probe undiscovered areas of the self and the other.

With the emergence of T-groups (sensitivity training groups) as a viable medium for learning through the experience of awareness and encounter, teachers can now, if they wish, move below the mind without getting lost in the backwaters of the unconscious. With emphasis on the latent awareness in the "here and now," the T-group strikes a line between the imagined world of the unconscious and the often defensive structure of the ego.

It is a mark of a significant deadness in our culture and a primitivistic reaction to this felt death that some people now choose to participate in sensitivity groups. What could, in a sense, be more absurd than having self-consciously to become aware of the body?

And yet many of us have experienced this loss of body-self, and we must learn again how to be complete, though we may well not, like Humpty-Dumpty, be able to put ourselves back together again. Some of the exercises used at Esalen (see Bernard Gunther's *Sense Relaxation: Below Your Mind*) can be experienced in a classroom as a prelude to discussion. If a class can, as a community, touch one another, they are well on their way toward meaningful communication. Bodily freedom is a prelude to emotional and intellectual freedom.

Just as a teacher can be a model with respect to the natural expression of strong feelings, so might he risk self-exposure and uncertainty in an exemplary way. I am not talking here about autobiography and confession, but rather about a willingness to pursue reasoning to the edge of coherence and the freedom to allow oneself to feel in new ways, in ways that grow out of experience and are not merely a replay of one's familiar emotional history. If the teacher is not willing to risk new feeling, surely the students will be reluctant to take similar risks. Risk is a contribution that existential analysis has made to traditional psychotherapy. It puts the emphasis on action as the best way of demonstrating to an individual that his expectations and fantasies about, and response to, his own behavior may be inaccurate.

As a teacher, I have found that I can be more open about my difficulties with a text, my discomfort in a particular atmosphere— say, of non-participation, and anxieties that literary insights provoke

—than I ever imagined. Indeed, I find that those classes are precisely the ones students appreciate most and are the ones in which students give most of themselves.

Most of us feel quite vulnerable when we do not have a firm and unwavering mask to present to the world, even when we know that such firmness can become rigid and stand between us and growth. It is as if we stand constantly on guard against a judgmental response to our feeling independently and authentically. If only someone we respect would say, "We must learn to be free and to feel freely," a great burden could be lifted. And when the burden has lifted, and we express how we feel without negative consequences (without destroying ourselves or the other), a basis may be formed that can take us deeper into trust.

In many ways, education must follow a pattern of de-creation and re-creation, must remove barriers to let a new self come into being. This is always a hard birth and takes much labor. One can feel at the moment of giving up an aspect of the old self that he stands on the edge of self-annihilation and death, but the fear is momentary, illusory. When one learns that he can survive this perilous journey, the quest for identity becomes less awesome.

All that I have said is a necessary beginning to a transformation of education in America, one that will doubtlessly take place only behind the needs of the black community, because it is that community whose educational needs at this moment in history are so intimately linked with human development.

We can learn a great deal from *Summerhill*, but, finally, if we are to be moved as a culture, it is unlikely that the enlightened texts—John Holt's *How Children Fail*, Sylvia Ashton Warner's *Teacher*, and others—will be a sufficient force. So I look to the black community for the revolution in American education, as I look also to the needs of youth: the music, theatre, literature, and dance that speak to young people all point in the direction of an integrated sensuous and intellectual field.

If one carefully reads Norman O. Brown, Leslie Fiedler, R. D. Laing, if one carefully listens to *Sergeant Pepper,* if one looks at the Merce Cunningham dancers and *Hair,* it becomes obvious that we are trying to move towards a community of complete involvement, to move against the alienation of self and world, mind and body. We are in many ways moving towards the East, and it may be that Vietnam represents, in part, a most grotesque resistance to an emergent sensibility in America, to a global fusion of lifestyle and sensibility.

Toward Therapy and Protest

From Course Consciousness to Experience 5

Teaching, as most of us know and have known it, is rather like proscenium theatre, with a clear line drawn between art and life, audience and performance. But unlike traditional theatre, the classroom situation does not have the saving grace of illusion, the willing suspension of disbelief, the projection or introjection of a self and world freer than the self-in-society that we re-create in drama.

We have had audience and performance, but little interaction. We have had, in some sense, a theatre of censorship. The performer-teacher as authority-figure, consciously or unconsciously, denies by role the very dynamism, process, and conflict inherent in the classroom. In order to oppose these tendencies, this stasis, I have tried a number of strategies and techniques in the service of freedom.

Some months ago I went into a classroom (a trailer here at Buffalo—apt symbol for the enclosed, mobile society) to teach Hawthorne's "The Minister's Black Veil." The night before I had seen *Far From Vietnam* and couldn't pry the story loose from my response to the film. I moved, it seemed, in a world of moral blackness. Had I been truer to my concept of teaching, I would have overcome this conflict. I would have dramatized the limits of objectivity, would

This essay is reprinted with permission from *Radical Teacher*, Spring 1969.

have moved from my own dilemma to a discussion, say, of the myths of cognition, the professional attempts to pry knowledge loose from its moral and historical implications. Instead, I concealed the conflict, though only momentarily, and acted as if we were engaged once again in formal analysis—the *bête noire* of my generation, of my literary training in the fifties.

But the moment a student, a somewhat uptight sorority girl, objected to the gloom and depression in Hawthorne, I untypically launched an attack upon her defensive blindness, her bourgeois inclination to see art as an adjunct of the living room, her desire to domesticate experience. I invoked as much destructive modern history as exploded and burned in my mind and set the disasters of war before her eyes. "Is this gloom or actuality?" I asked.

As soon as the class ended, the student—I will call her Cathy—came up to me and said: "Everyone in this room is Jewish." Then she was gone. I guessed what had happened. She had displaced her rage against me, the Buffalo English Department, the student activists, to her non-supportive, or so she felt, classmates. She had found her scapegoat and taught me something about the instantaneous access to myth that lurks beneath the social surface.

I worried about her because I knew, given past class behavior, that the feeling she had exposed would overwhelm her and need a hiding place. Perhaps she wouldn't come back—like a patient who can't bear the penetration of his defenses, or a politician whose rhetoric can't withstand the reality of protest.

She did come back but, poignantly, in *disguise:* white powder and wig. R. D. Laing's *The Divided Self* and *The Three Christs of Ypsilanti* were recently in mind, and I was frightened. Had she—like one of Laing's patients, or Bettleheim's children, or death camp survivors—chosen the gestures of non-being as a way of not being hurt?

There had to be a confrontation, a working through of conflict, but the situation was too volatile. I taught a subdued class and asked Cathy to come with me to my office. There, I apologized for acting out my rage against the war. In the next class, without, of course, making reference to the powder and wig, to the adoption of a false self to disguise a threatened self, I asked the group to describe and discuss what had happened.

Some students thought I had been too harsh; some, too soft; some, quite balanced. We talked about the relationship of thought and feeling, *Summerhill,* sensitivity training, encounter groups, detachment as a defense, the need to talk about the experience of a class as opposed to the content of the course. It was the best class of the semester.

Cathy continued to attend unmasked and was more willing to participate than previously. She emerged as a real person, however painfully, and I saw clearly that thought and feeling must be organically related. We had had, at least for one period, a living classroom, participatory learning, a sense of community. The oppressed and oppressor were demythologized, and, paradoxically, the primitivization of the classroom led toward greater objectivity. Along the way, we made Hawthorne live. Somewhere in all of this, there are notes towards a fusion of group therapy, psychodrama, literature, and education.

Classroom as Microcosm 6

If American universities are to become viable and life-supportive, students, teachers, and administrators should find ways to face and resolve conflict as an ongoing process. At the macrolevel of university organization, governance, and curriculum, this would mean decentralization, with groups having natural and diverse affinities (as well as individual students with a shared sense of selfhood) being allowed to create and implement their own programs, to project their own theoretical futures.

Most close observers of university crises over the past five years know that the scenario of militancy and reaction—with real strike demands and negotiations often obscured and damaged by police occupation and the inevitable confrontations and violence that follow —stems, in the main, from the irreconcilable opposition of dissident students and a hierarchical administration.

Dissident student groups often seem to have no choice other than to enact their beliefs through disruptive and violent means. Faced with what looks like a monolithic university structure and a hierarchical administration opposed to the values of the counterculture, students act desperately to seek redress for their grievances as well as

This essay is reprinted with permission from *College English*, December 1971.

salvation, however symbolic, for our perilously threatened biosphere.

I have little hope that the necessary decentralization will take place quickly, but I do believe that individual teachers and departments can begin to advance new educational concepts of human development and conflict-resolution. In an age of minimalism and psychic, as well as ecological, exhaustion, we must learn how to struggle with a sense of modesty. In trying to move towards a humanistic psychology of education, wholeness of self, and integration of thought and feeling, I have experimented in my teaching over the past four years with various modes and techniques of self-emergence.

Only after four years of apprentice teaching, though, did I realize, in a radical sense, that we reenact in the classroom our individual histories and our histories in groups; that we defend against the risks that authentic learning entails; that we will do almost anything to avoid the conflicts which must emerge—within ourselves and between ourselves and others—before we can claim knowledge as our own, interrelated, like breath and lung, to our deepest needs.[1]

For the first four years of teaching I had, like many of my contemporaries of the fifties, related to literary criticism as a neutral methodology and to the classroom as a clearing house where information and concepts were brokered from one person to a set of others.

I am indebted to the initially passive, recalcitrant, and innocent students of a small rural Midwestern university and the generational pressures of the age of rock for making me reexamine my assumptions about teaching, and to the integrative and mythic tendencies of contemporary youth and survival culture—with an assist from the writings of R. D. Laing, Freud, Marcuse, N. O. Brown, Robert Lowell, A. S. Neill, Erick Erikson, and Carl Rogers, to name some— for allowing me to think of myself and students as *persons,* not as archives or human retrieval systems.

My students have helped me to re-create myself, to break down the psychic and social boundries of the tranquilized fifties. They have made it clear that a policy of containment fits neither self nor world.

At the same time, the restraints and discipline of my own education enabled me, I think, to give structure to some modes of liberation in the classroom.

Having learned to wait for revelation during the silent fifties, I had, and have, somewhat more than most colleagues the patience to confront the passivity and alienation in the classroom that often disguises the dynamism of contemporary students.[2]

I would like to share an experience in which I and a group of twenty-five students at the State University of New York at Buffalo went beyond and below ordinary academic defenses during the fall semester of 1969. The course had been listed in the catalogue as the Literature of Mental Crisis and Madness and was an extension of a course I had offered the previous spring on the History of Madness in Literature from the Renaissance (*King Lear*) to the present (*Marat/Sade*). I had prepared an extensive reading list with a suggested bibliography: Freud's *Ego and Id;* Jung's *Two Essays on Analytic Psychology;* Gogol's *Diary of a Madman;* Dostoevsky's *The Possessed;* and Zamiatin's *We*—these were some of the texts.

During the first three weeks of the course, we read the assigned texts of Freud, Jung, and Gogol, but it was clear from the start that the students were restive with the psychological models I was advancing, especially Freudian theory. This restiveness grew more intense and centered on me as the embodiment of an apparently alien system: psychoanalysis.[3] Because I had had some experience with small group work in other classes and didn't feel uncomfortable with a nondirective, student-centered approach to learning, I opened the class to a discussion of why so much hostility was being directed at the materials and me, making it clear that I, in no way, construed the expression of hostility towards the course or instructor as unnatural.

By the end of the discussion, the group had decided that each member's own crises had been, and were, as important as the literary and psychological renderings of crisis they felt I had imposed upon them, and they suggested that *we take the group itself as subject.*

Although I had prepared myself emotionally and intellectually for an exploration of the texts, many of which were new to me (and knew that the new course would take us all into anxious waters), I decided to accept the challenge of the experiment.

I felt, intuitively, that coming to know this group would be valid in itself and would help me understand the prevailing discontent on our campus (which a year later expressed itself in a bitter, prolonged strike) and campuses across the country. I laid down two ground rules: that we should limit ourselves to verbal expressions of emotion; that people in the class should submit anonymous accounts of crises that I would mimeograph and distribute in class if they wished.

By the end of the month that we gave to these miniautobiographies, many interesting, complex, and touching documents had been submitted and discussed. A long monograph would have to be written to deal with these documents in their fullness, but let me cite one of the first crises that we discussed. Its clarity and directness lend it to exposition (many of the crises were characteristically dreamlike and surreal), and it stands somewhat typologically for issues and concerns that were recurrent in our experience together.

Since I couldn't think of any experience which seemed relevant to mental crises, which I would want discussed, I decided instead to relate a dream whch I feel is pertinent to this class. First, however, I feel a little background must be given. I was a student in one of Howard's classes last year, and I had a hang-up about speaking in class. I was very interested in the discussion and most always attended class, but I often hesitated to say what was on my mind, no matter how determined I was that I would speak. Class participation was one of Howard's pet peeves also, so it made the situation doubly tense. It seemed whenever I did speak, I was rebuffed or a reply was made that slightly embarrassed me, thus adding to the dilemma. Enough history. This semester when I tried to register for Howard's class, since I found him a fascinating teacher, and the course sounded interesting, I was closed out. This necessitated going to him personally and obtaining a class card, which I did. At this time, I had a dream one night which seems to capsulize my fears. I dreamt that I was the only girl in Howard's class and that during one session I was sitting on his desk carrying on an intimate and engrossed discussion with him for the benefit of the whole class. I don't know what the discussion was about or any other details, but I am sure there are psychoanalytic implications to several facets of the dream. For example, why was I sitting on the desk? especially since Howard never sits at one but rather in a regular chair. Also I'm sure there is significance attached to it being a predominantly male class. These things bother me—besides the obvious fact that I was carrying on a conversation with Howard which, in reality, is something I have difficulty doing. I think it would be interesting to hear someone else's view of this apparently simple dream.

This "crisis," however brief, contains materials that we discussed at length—such as the latent erotic components in the classroom that most students and teachers don't discuss and the educational dynamics of transference—but the elements I want to emphasize are this student's feeling of having been "rebuffed" and "closed out" and the appeal at the end "to hear someone else's view of this apparently simple dream."[4]

Throughout our experience, themes of loss and rejection appeared, as well as the desire to have these feelings shared and validated by the group. It seems in retrospect that *we were moving all along towards a position of trust in which rejection could be risked.* The anonymous crisis papers served as a masking device for self-revelation. As we demonstrated time and again that the crises were *collective* problems, deeply rooted in our historical and cultural position, it became easier for individuals to speak directly about their conflicts. This theatrical and ritual presentation of self freed us momentarily from real and imagined threats of rejection by the group. Those people who see student activism in nihilistic terms misperceive what I learned to see as a fundamental, humane quest for a context of closeness and trust in which self-expression would become possible.

Throughout our experience, I felt a need to make it clear to the group that we were involved in an experiment, that we were making tentative gestures towards a new mode of learning; I felt a need to relate what we were doing to literature—to what, after all, I had been trained to teach; so quite often I would prepare Notes on Class, brief recordings of my response to our experience. Here is the first one I wrote:

> We are hovering between a "class" and an Encounter Group. The hope is that we can bring a greater affective force to bear upon ourselves, the personal documents submitted in class, poems we read in class, and any outside material that we may read. We are literary insofar as we pay attention to language. To the extent that we pay attention to our own language and the language of our friends and classmates, and to the extent that we try to make sense of these languages, we become auto-biographers and biographers of a certain kind. Our class is an exploration in role-playing: What is a student? What is a teacher? What is the role of the university? Our class is an experiment in human development. How far can we go in helping ourselves and our friends to achieve understanding? These are immensely naive questions, but extremely radical in their implications. I think of our class, among other things, as a laboratory or theatre of a new kind of education. I hope all of you will make notes when important things happen and share them with the group; I hope some of you will make your project the documentation of our experience.

The question—what is a teacher?—became, I now realize, my crisis, which is not to say that I didn't contribute personal and immediate responses to what people were experiencing in the class. In fact, I presented the class with some of my rather autobiographical poems and made an anonymous submission of a childhood experience.

My sensitivity to the question about the teacher's role is illustrated in the following note I prepared. The context for the note was a moment during one of our discussions when one student made a comment about a crisis paper to which I didn't respond with appropriate intensity. Another student, feeling I had "rebuffed" the first student, said with anger, "Don't you respond directly to the person making a comment?"

I was visibly upset by the comment and after class Tom helped me see that I was reinhabiting the role of authority figure in a new way; that, although I had special responsibilities as a moderator, I didn't have to respond to everyone all the time, and I didn't have to assume that everyone making a comment demanded a dramatic response (though clearly the person who asked the question made these assumptions).

Unlike a group therapist, I came to see my role as primarily a reflector and mediator. I tried to limit myself to restating what people in the group said and to summarizing what we had experienced at the end of the hour. I didn't try *to interpret* what people were saying or to put pressure upon individuals to make interpretations.

Note: Tom pointed out two important things to me with respect to the question, "Don't I (Howard) respond directly to the person making a comment?":

• the assumption that Howard (or any authority) is capable of providing an "ideal" response and

• the assumption that every person making a comment wants an immediate and instantaneous response.

When Tom pointed out these assumptions to me, I realized that the question had put me uptight because

• I felt accused;

• I felt selfish;

• I felt I "ought to be" perfect; I felt I "ought to act" as the class and I both feel "authorities" should act.

What this suggests to me, among other things, is the notion that both teacher and student tend to relate to a *third* entity—a mythic entity: *the idea of authority.* That is to say: I am as much tyrannized by authority as any student.

This means to me that our class is alive; that we can move towards clarity; and that we are learning something about literature, *i.e.,* drama. I mean that kind of drama that deals with "unmaskings," with acts of confrontation, as in *Long Day's Journey Into Night* and *Death of a Salesman.*

Most teachers understand that they must not tyrannize students through the misuse of their power, but they rarely understand that they themselves can assume a posture of self-tyranny. Tom helped me to learn something about myself, and, if nothing else, the sort of classroom we were creating—with a new psychic space—made it possible for everyone to be a learner and a teacher. As a moderator I had to sense which contexts could be used for learning and teaching by different members of the group. Predictably, I made an effort in my note, as I did all semester, to bring in literature, to push our insights towards wider areas of cognition.

The role of *written* crises became central to our experiment towards the end of the month in which they were written. Then early in November, there were some in the class who felt we should abandon the crises, that, though they had been useful at first, they were serving as "shields." I held the line on this issue.

The session after I held this line, one of the people in the group—taking a cue from a crisis paper—opened up more than anyone else had all semester. He discussed in depth, with feeling and insight, the complication of a love affair that was causing him great pain. I felt vindicated and wrote the following note outlining the role of "documents":

Wednesday's meeting (5 November), so far as I could tell, was not so much an encounter group—leading towards individual confrontation—as it was a subject-(person-)centered experience. It had, from my point of view, focus and depth, and moved towards some kind of clarity for Richard. On the subject of "documents," it would seem clear that having something "out there" at least helped Richard to say something he wanted to say. In a smaller group, such a document is probaby not necessary, but in yesterday's group it seemed to serve the function of allowing one person to relate initially to at least one other person. Knowing that someone else has had an experience similar to one's own makes it easier to talk about that experience. In general, literature can serve the function of making subjective experiences external, of undoing our isolation. It is all too easy, I think, to be naive about defenses, about the difficulties of communicating honesty. As much as we want to be honest about ourselves, about our relationships with others, there are often deeply imbedded resistances to such honesty. It is not always easy just to say: *be open.* We have to find *ways* of being open. That is one thing that our class is "about." What Don calls "shield," I would call "vehicles." This is a subtle issue—one each person has to come to terms with for himself.

The group was not terribly convinced by my analysis and felt that Richard's "opening up" had marked a turning point in our experiment. Although he had been prompted by a crisis paper, he had gone so far beyond it that papers no longer seemed necessary. Moreover, the students suggested we leave the sterility and rigidity of the trailer we were meeting in and use someone's apartment. I felt uncomfortable with these attitudes, but I had a responsibility to the group. Besides, all our decisions had been intuitive and right, so why not risk more?

We met in someone's apartment for two meetings, which lasted three hours each, and we continued to probe Richard's situation. During these sessions, I experienced anxiety for a number of reasons: (1) I found it difficult to decide when we should *end* our meetings. It became dramatically clear that the fifty-minute hour obscures profound questions about the authentic rhythms and duration of human interaction. (2) I also found it difficult to maintain my role as moderator: at times I wanted to dissolve my role and at other times I felt a need to control the group. Both options seemed to me an irresponsible extension of our experiment. After the second meeting, I went home to rest and lay in bed shaking slightly and half-dreaming that the next time the group wouldn't let me go.

It took me a few weeks to figure out that the group had become a *body* itself, that one could feel overwhelmed by it as much as by separation from it. My relationship to the group wasn't unlike a child's relationship to a parent figure. The developing self needs to be protected, but it also needs separateness and autonomy. This insight had not come to me in full force, so I presented the group with the following note the next time we met:

> As many of you have doubtless noticed, I have been unsure of the movement of our class during the past two meetings. It now seems clear to me that I want to do three things:
> - hold our meetings in trailer 8;
> - limit the time to an hour;
> - and use personal documents, poetry, or any other kind of written material as *touchstones* (stimuli, catalysts) for discussion.
>
> My reasons are:
> - I find the apartment atmosphere too difficult for the focusing of attention and dialogue.
> - I find the open-ended time situation too anxiety-provoking. When one knows that there is a limit set to self-revelation, one feels free to express oneself and also to use the time to get something done.
> - By using some kind of written material as a touchstone, I feel that we can remain literary in some essential way; and I find that my identity as an English teacher and writer is very important to me as it is hopefully to a group of people interested in literature.
>
> What I have realized for myself over the past week is that there is an essential difference between an encounter group (or group therapy) and a class interested in self-awareness, the expression of emotion, and relevance. I see my position as one committed to *synthesis,* not *compromise.* It is one kind of experience and does not take its value from the rejection of other experiences. Under certain conditions I would like to participate in encounter experiences (as in fact I have over the past two years), but *without an effort to be literary:* without having to impose the role of teacher upon the role of encounter participant or leader.
>
> I am especially interested in reestablishing the course in the above terms because it has been for me thus far my most exciting semester as a teacher, and I do not want to blow it by taking on more than I can handle. And I do not see the structure we had evolved together as limiting or narrow—quite the opposite. Those people who find my position too limiting can either continue to meet in addition to the course or separate from it. I have made a choice, and I can only ask you to do the same.

To my surprise and relief, almost everyone in the group was pleased I had come to my decisions. I seemed to express an anxiety about going too far that most of them had felt but had been unable to express. As it turned out, for the remaining seven or eight weeks of the semester, we rarely used a crisis paper; but knowing that I *could* introduce one if our spontaneous energies gave out helped me deal with the newness and experimental aspect of our situation. Almost all of our meetings were intense and fruitful, and they continued to be person-centered rather than interactional.

By this I mean that our style was one in which someone would say something that revealed guilt or discomfort about a particular situation; then other people in the group would *share* the experience, indicating that they had been through something comparable. In this way the person who had risked exposure would feel comforted, less guilty and alone, and would often see some aspect of his situation in a new light.

Our experience seemed to be characterized by moments of *clarification* and *validation* rather than by depth interpretation. Contemporary students need less to examine their motives than to learn that what they feel is *authentic* and relatable to *others*. We rarely focused on interaction between persons, and people were seldom attacked. I knew that encounter groups and group therapy have focused on those dynamics, but I felt that it was important for us to be true to our own styles and needs.

Towards the end of the semester, I knew the group would become somewhat mournful.[5] We had created an atmosphere of trust together, and where people had already begun to express anxiety when I came five minutes late to our meetings, they would now feel something like sorrow. This happened. I don't have documentation of these last meetings—we only talked—but a crisis paper of a month before may give some indication of how sensitive people in the group were to matters of separation:

I hitchhiked from Copenhagen to Paris with an extremely beautiful Swedish girl. I felt very proud to be with her because of her good looks. I liked showing her off in public places, but usually I avoided unnecessary contact with other people for fear of losing her. Often I felt uneasy in the company of other males because I would suspect them of trying to steal her away from me. I noticed every glance she shared with them and my suspicions would heighten. Once, when I was with her, in a dark room, in the company of some other people, I heard some noises. These, in conjunction with some earlier observances, gave me a picture. I was convinced that she was making love to another guy. I was too shocked to move so I just lay there in the dark. My only thoughts were how I was to maintain face and how to punish the girl the next morning.

The next day I realized that I had fantasized the whole thing. I didn't make my suspicions known to her and thus our relationship didn't suffer (at least on her part). However, in the next two weeks a similar occurrence was repeated three times. These times, I acted upon my fantasies and our relationship rapidly deteriorated. I accused her of lying and once while she was admiring a bracelet in a store window, in Paris, I accused her of trying to con me into buying it for her. She was shocked at my accusations and informed me that she would return to Sweden the following day.

That night, in a café, in the latin quarter of Paris, after numerous glasses of wine, I left her. I couldn't bear the thought of *her* leaving me. I had to be the first.

The group had become like the girl in the crisis paper, and it wasn't easy for any of us to think of being left.

We spent the last week of our meetings talking about the group's importance to the participants. Our bonds to one another became clear in the next-to-last hour when someone who had enrolled in the course, but who hadn't attended at all, came and expressed cynicism about what we were doing (i.e., relating to one another). Intense anger was directed at him, and it took some diplomacy to ask him to leave so that we might finish the semester with a feeling of closeness. Almost everyone in the group trusted the other members. For some it was the first time they could remember experiencing trust in a group.

Because of my role in an experimental college at the university, I was, in the second semester, able to get class cards so that those in the group who wanted to could continue. My schedule and desire to teach modern poetry didn't easily permit me to meet with them, and I was eager to reevaluate our experience before I went on with it; I also thought it would be good for the group to meet without their original parent-figure whom they had hopefully outgrown.

A group did meet, and they were alive and well in Buffalo on their own. I felt sometimes that I had lost a large family, but then I know that I, like other members of the group, am sensitive to loss. I also know that I hadn't completely come to terms with the need to be an authority and parent figure to my students.

Conclusions

- The hierarchical and impersonal university makes it difficult, if not impossible, for trust to be established in the microcosm of the classroom.
- Teachers who attempt to create an atmosphere of trust will have a difficult and conflicted experience if they are committed to transmitting another discipline at the same time. It is impossible to teach a traditional course and to pay serious attention to the developmental needs of the students. The inevitable first phase of experiments like ours—given the educational histories of most students—tends to be regressive, to recapitulate stages of growth and learning that have been neglected in primary and secondary schools.
- Some commitments to time and place will help the group control inescapable anxieties. Because we discovered our interest rather spontaneously and hadn't consciously chosen a group experience, spatial and temporal guidelines were especially useful.
- Both teachers and students tend to relate to a third entity: the image of authority. Until this is recognized, most exchanges will be

inauthentic.

● It is possible to have a person-oriented experience that is neither an encounter group nor group therapy, but which nonetheless touches the person deeply and which can be facilitated by a caring, intelligent teacher *without* special training.

● American students are especially sensitive to expectations of loss and rejection, and it is vital to the survival of the university that we come to understand the psychocultural origins of these expectations.

● Students who participate in groups like ours should be able to pursue these explorations and to receive credit for them, so that it will be clear to everyone that human development is at least as important as orthodox course work.

● Only in the context of radical decentralization—touching all aspects of our ecosystem and university structure—will the kind of experiment in living we conducted be able to flourish and extend itself.

● Given our needs, the experiment we carried out forced us to let go of content as it is ordinarily understood, but there is no theoretical reason why a choice has to be made between cognition and affect. If American education now forces this choice upon certain teachers, it is a comment about our divisive culture and its institutions.

One can imagine a new intellectualism based upon wholeness of being in which thought can once again—if such moments of telelogical harmony ever existed—be felt, in which our sensibilities will not be disassociated. For the moment, however, there will be serious conflicts between teachers who see themselves as traditionalists and those who see themselves as, I suppose, radical romantics.

In my futuristic setting, these teachers would come together and explore the assumptions that divide them.

Freud and Marcuse: Transference and the Demystification of Authority in the Classroom

Because psychoanalysis cannot claim for itself the theoretical elegance of relativity theory or calculus, it is difficult to seize upon a major premise from which all else follows within the theory. Even its most ardent advocates would admit—even advance as one of its virtues— that psychoanalysis approaches art in its explanatory power and resembles history more than it does science.

Many of the controversies that surround psychoanalysis cannot be resolved because both advocates and antagonists claim both more and less validity for Freud than is appropriate. If Freud had called *The Interpretation of Dreams* an *Autobiography of Dreams,* and if he had presented his case studies as fictive biographies, he might well have gained a greater consensus for his life's work than is now the case. We can, it seems, accept mythology or wholly testable theories (if any exist) more easily than most of us can accept the often mythological empiricism of Freud's contribution.

So let me be the first to admit that my remarks about the relationship between psychoanalysis and education are speculative and appeal, more than anything else, to common sense for their possible

This essay is reprinted with permission from *New Directions in Teaching,* Winter 1971.

truth-value. Those familiar with Dr. Johnson's literary criticism will not, however, find this appeal inconsequential; though I recognize at the same time that the apocalyptic character of much contemporary discourse—whether in R. D. Laing's *The Politics of Experience* or Abbie Hoffman's *Revolution for the Hell of It*—makes the appeal to common sense seem undramatic.

As I have tried to make sense of my own teaching experience, it has become clear to me that most teachers and students either uphold content and cognition at the expense of interpersonal and intrapsychic dynamics, or they promote the expressive implications of humanistic psychology at the expense of rationality. Because there are more defenders of content, I want to speak on behalf of process and the *act* of learning rather than of *what* is learned.

The most neglected developmental issue is, in my opinion, the terror of judgment and the attendant risk of self-assertion that characterize so much of contemporary learning behavior. There can be, I would imagine, few teachers who have not noted some disparity between passivity in the classroom and self-assertion in the politics of confrontation. It is not at all clear to me why the classroom has become such a threatening ambience to so many students, but it is clear to me that it has.

Just as multimedia and environmental aesthetics have overtaken the novel, so various modes of sensitivity training and tribal sharing have replaced the classroom in the imaginations of most students. It is precisely for this reason that those teachers who wish to preserve the classroom as a place in which value can be examined and criticized should begin to pay attention to the experience of being a student and teacher.

If one were to name the discoveries to which Freud would have assigned the most significance, they would be: the Oedipus Complex and its relationship to unconscious processes, infantile sexuality, and the therapeutic phenomena of transference and countertransference. Freud defines transference as follows:

Transference (in analysis)—the patient sees in his analyst the return—the reincarnation—of some important figure out of his childhood or past, and consequently transfers on to him feelings and reactions that undoubtedly applied to this model. It soon becomes evident that this fact of transference is a factor of undreamed-of importance—on the one hand an instrument of irreplaceable value and on the other a source of serious dangers. This transference is *ambivalent*: it comprises positive and affectionate, as well as negative and hostile, attitudes toward the analyst, who, as a rule, is put in the place of one or the other of the patient's parents, his father or his mother. So long as it is positive it serves us admirably. It alters the whole analytic situation and side-tracks the patient's rational aim of becoming well and free from his troubles. Instead of it there emerges the aim of pleasing the analyst, of winning his applause and love. This becomes the true motive-force for the patient's collaboration; the weak ego becomes strong; under the influence of this aim the patient achieves things that would otherwise be beyond his power; his symptoms disappear and he seems to have recovered—all of this simply out of love for his analyst. . . . Therapeutic successes that take place under the sway of the positive transference are under the suspicion of being a *suggestive* nature. If the negative transference gains the upper hand, they are blown away like spray before the wind.[1]

If one thinks of the teacher as therapist and of the student as patient, he can find many similar dynamics in the classroom. I use the word "patient," of course, in an analogical sense. My intention is to illustrate a dynamic element in all human relationships in which at least one party is seen as an authority figure. Moreover, Freud approached neurosis not as a specific "disease," but as a general condition of man:

Neuroses (unlike infectious diseases, for instance) have no specific determinants. It would be idle to seek in them for a pathogenic factor. They shade off into what is described as the normal by a series of transitional steps; and on the other hand there is scarcely any condition generally recognized as normal in which it would not be possible to demonstrate neurotic traits.[2]

If any students still feel they are being maligned in this analogy, I might mention another phenomenon—countertransference—in which the student becomes the therapist and the teacher, the patient, but that is another, somewhat more taboo, subject. Because professional training in the humanities centers on scholarly methods, the "products" of such training tend to transpose their textual methods into classroom pedagogic methods.

I would argue that this is a risky and potentially dehumanizing transposition. It is important to find out in what ways teachers deny, in their research and teaching, anxieties that are threatening to them; to find out in what ways teachers project onto students and texts their own unresolved and unacknowledged archaic fantasies.

The dynamic similarities of transference are:

- an unwillingness on the student's part to accept anything the teacher says;

- the extraordinarily complex possibilities of seeing the teacher, the material, and other students "as a return of some important figure out of his childhood or past"; possibilities for complex projective and introjective mechanisms that R. D. Laing has tried to code and record in *The Self and Others* and *The Politics of the Family;*

- the difficulty, in this context, of the student "freeing himself from the parents";[3]

- the difficulty of transforming repetitious responses into recognitions which can then allow the student to learn from a position of freedom;[4]

- the dissolution of the transference itself at the conclusion of the learning experience;[5]

- the aim of pleasing the teacher and winning his applause and his love.

Although these are simple enough statements, they take as their appropriate context the earliest needs of the child and the persistence of those needs into adult life together with that paralyzing duo: the terror of judgment, the risk of self-assertion. Joining Freud's account of transference with the passive quality of the classroom, one can say, I think, that passivity and silence can be defenses against the fear of not pleasing the teacher and winning his applause and love (remembering, as I say this, that the teacher is a surrogate, a stand-in for parent and sibling figures from early childhood).

The fear of rejection in the classroom re-creates an archaic fear of rejection and reprisal by parent figures. Self-assertion can feel like aggression—especially in our competitive society—and it may evoke fantasies of aggressive retaliation and rejection. Depression and withdrawal often conceal this matrix of fantasy and feeling. Freud's essay, "Mourning and Melancholia," would be a useful text for most teachers and students to read.[6]

For these reasons, I believe teachers should in some way face the implications of transference in the classroom, for political as well as educational reasons. An enlightened curriculum would provide a variety of options in which process-oriented classes, as well as sensitivity training, could fulfill the regular distribution requirements.

If students could receive credits for these kinds of experiences, we might find that "content" courses would be perceived in their proper context. If higher education addressed itself more to the whole person, there would be fewer attempts to reclaim the whole person in areas where such reclamation is difficult, if not impossible.

So long as student and teacher are contained by the unexamined authoritarian structure of transference (whether positive or negative), the possibilities for learning will be reduced, and the student will be put in a double-bind because he will hear the teacher saying: "realize your potential to the fullest" and—simultaneously and silently—"but do not challenge my authority." More often than not, teachers are not aware of transmitting these contradictory attitudes. If left unexamined, the transference will, to reword Freud, "alter the whole educational situation and sidetrack the student's rational aim of learning."

The subjectivity of transference in the classroom needs to be examined before meaningful objectivity can be claimed, at least an objectivity different from the one Roszak describes in *The Making of a Counter-Culture*. The specific ways in which transference can be faced in the classroom would take some painstaking analysis, but let me suggest a few guidelines:

• Teachers should ask students how they feel about what they are asked to do.

• Teachers should tell students how they (the teachers) feel about what they are asking students to do.

• Teachers should be more restrained in approving or disapproving of student comments.

• From time to time this restraint should become silence—so that deep feeling can gain access to consciousness.

If the problems of transference are faced by teachers and educators, if the ambivalent feelings towards authority figures are recognized, there might be less nonspecific positive and negative magical thinking towards authority figures on the campus and in the culture.

If the re-creation of family patterns in the classroom is seen for what it is, it may be possible to demystify the relationship between student and teacher (and, by extension, authority figures in general); to extricate both student and teacher from the labyrinth of infantile projections that can cast the teacher in the role of *oppressor* and the student in the role of *oppressed*.

Just as it is difficult for families to give up a neurosis of one of its members—what Laing would call a "collusive" relationship—so will it be difficult for student and teacher to give up the latent authoritarianism of the contemporary classroom.[7]

At this point, I would like briefly to compare Freud and Marcuse. Let me first point to one of Freud's many comments on education in the *General Introduction to Psychoanalysis*:

> The sexual instincts are less easily moulded; for in the beginning they do not know any lack of objects. Since they are connected parasitically, as it were, with the other physical functions and at the same time can be

autoerotically gratified on their own body, they are at first isolated from the educative influence of real necessity; and in most people they retain throughout life, in some respect or other, this character of obstinacy and inaccessibility to influence which we call "unreasonableness." Moreover, the educability of a young person as a rule comes to an end when sexual desire breaks out in its final strength. Educators know this and act accordingly; but perhaps they will yet allow themselves to be influenced by the results of psychoanalysis so that they will transfer the main emphasis in education to the earliest years of childhood, from the suckling period onward. The little human being is frequently a finished product in his fourth or fifth year, and only gradually reveals in later years what lies buried in him.[8]

This suggests that education might both initiate learning processes at the earliest stage of life (which has begun to happen to some extent both for privileged and underprivileged children) and provide a meaningful field of *eros* for later education.

If this is not done—if thought and feeling, affect and content, sight and sound, work and play are separated—we will find students turning, as we now do, to modes of regressiveness in an attempt to reclaim the sensuality that one never really loses or is willing to lose.

We will find prevalent fantasies of oral fusion in which self and world are obliterated as a way, in part, of annihilating the possible rejection by the Other. Teaching will become an "erotic irritant," as Philip Slater calls it in *Microcosm,* and there will be an attempt to give up ego in all its positive manifestations. R. D. Laing's *The Politics of Experience,* N. O. Brown's *Life Against Death,* and Marcuse's *Eros and Civilization* are sacred texts now precisely because they provide a rationale for such "prophetic" regressions.

The following passage will suggest this aspect of Marcuse's thinking:

Under optimum conditions, the prevalence, in mature civilization, of material and intellectual wealth would be such as to allow painless gratification of needs, while domination would no longer systematically forestall such gratification. In this case, the quantum of instinctual energy still to be diverted into necessary labor (in turn completely mechanized and rationalized) would be so small that a large area of repressive constraints and modifications, no longer sustained by external forces, would collapse. Consequently, the antagonistic relation between pleasure principle and reality principle would be altered in favor of the former. Eros, the life instincts, would be released to an unprecedented degree.

Does it follow that civilization would explode and revert to prehistoric savagery, that the individuals would die as a result of the exhaustion of the available means of gratification and of their own energy which could promote material and intellectual production on a higher level and larger scale (Freud answers in the affirmative)? His answer is based on his more or less silent acceptance of a number of assumptions: that free libidinal relations are essentially antagonistic to work relations, that energy has to be withdrawn from the former in order to institute the latter, that only the absence of full gratification sustains the societal organization of work.[9]

Even if Marcuse is right (and it would require the realization of utopia to confirm his forecasts about utopia, as he himself suggests in "The End of Utopia"), he must be faulted for not weighing seriously enough the potential dangers and schizophrenic possibilities of ego-loss experiences. He does not face many of the necessities of the adaptive ego-functions that David Holbrook discusses in his essay, "R. D. Laing and the Death-Circuit."[10]

One wonders if the very criticism of the war in Vietnam, of the university, of the concepts of surplus repression and repressive de-sublimation, one wonders if any of these moral stances would be possible within his own system—for the aims of morality are clearly not in the absolute service of the pleasure principle.

Where Freud argues against culture, he also esteems it highly, as his treatment of art and artists makes clear. Marcuse, on the other hand, only condemns it:

Whatever the implications of the original Greek conception of Logos as the essence of being, since the canonization of the Aristotelian logic, the term merges with the idea of ordering, classifying, mastering reason. And this idea of reason becomes increasingly antagonistic to those faculties and attitudes which are receptive rather than productive, which tend toward gratification rather than transcendence—which remain strongly committed to the pleasure principle. They appear as the unreasonable and irrational that must be conquered and contained in order to serve the progress of reason. Reason is to insure, through the ever more effective transformation and exploitation of nature, the fulfillment of the human potentialities. But in the process the end seems to recede before the means: the time devoted to alienated labor absorbs the time for individual needs—and defines the needs themselves. The Logos shows forth as the logic of domination. When logic then reduces the units of thought to signs and symbols, the laws of thought have finally become techniques of calculation and manipulation.[11]

Who can know which "laws of thought" are not "techniques of calculation and manipulation"? It is a difficult question to answer and perhaps that is why repressive tolerance is an important but self-serving concept in Marcuse's system. Like Freud's concept of resistance, it can be used to deny criticism.

Even though the application of psychoanalysis to teaching methods might help us create the humane future we all want, it is probably true that—because of the misuses of "rationality" by the technocracy and the repressive power elites that seem to control our lives—psychoanalysis has come to be seen as part of the problem and not as the solution. The commitment of psychoanalysis to privacy and dialog, verbal analysis, integration and strengthening of ego, determinism, linearity, and sanity finds strong, opposing voices among students.

This opposition takes many forms: tribalism (from rock festivals, e.g., Woodstock, to the commune movement), McLuhanism (with its antiprint and antiperspective biases), ego-loss tendencies (ranging from psychedelic drugs through collectivist politics to transcendental meditation), a preference for the random and aleatory elements in art (the music of John Cage and Happenings come to mind), and a renewed interest in the visionary aspects of madness, magic, and hallucination (see *The Teachings of Don Juan, The Politics of Experience,* and *One Flew Over the Cuckoo's Nest*).[12]

It may be that before Freud's rationality can be appreciated—a dialectical balance between conscious and unconscious processes—there will have to be a conversion of the human spirit, a reform of all our institutions, and a social, as well as political, revolution.

Marcuse will displace Freud in this vanguard because he puts significant emphasis on what Freud called the *polymorphous perverse,* and in doing this, Marcuse points back through ego-development to origins, leaving the return for a utopian future; and the quest for an "original" state of consciousness is very much in the air, as we know. Freud, contrastively, looks to origins as a prelude to the possible psychic reintegration of the individual in the particular terms of that individual life. Freud acknowledges the bliss of oceanic feelings, but he also acknowledges its dissociative and tragic possibilites.

The question is, then: will we, on a day-to-day basis, try in our studies and actions, to integrate eros and rationalism—by recognizing the transference as a structure of human relationships and by sanctioning regressions in the service of the ego—or will we polarize rationalism and eros and chose one over the other?[13]

I believe the integrative approach is the more meaningful one and that Freud, not Marcuse, can be more helpful to the teacher in this regard. Because Freud's theory is rooted in the psychology of the individual within the context of the family, he gives us a set of concepts applicable—through a series of transformations—to the classroom. Marcuse's vision takes us *out* of the classroom into an imagined perilous future.

The Role of Countertransference in Teaching 8

We have become so accustomed to looking at the student's response to the teacher as the center of the learning experience—from the points of view of both traditional scholarship and humanistic psychology—that we often overlook the equally present, however repressed, dynamic of the teacher's response to an individual student, a group of students, or the whole class.

This limited perspective, however benevolent it may *feel* to the teacher, is nonetheless an aspect of the hierarchical structure that the contemporary American student—often without understanding and clarity of purpose—is trying to change.

If the American university is to remain viable and to survive as perhaps our most important vehicle for personal growth and reconciliation of the generations, we might try to begin to see the classroom as an interpersonal context—in which the teacher, like all the members of the group, is involved   that calls for multiperspectives.

We might begin to develop what R. D. Laing calls a notation for *dyadic perspectives:*

> Only if two people carry out reciprocally "successful" acts of attribution can any genuine relationship between them begin. Interpersonal life is

This essay is reprinted with permission from *The Psychoanalytic Review*, Winter 1972.

conducted in a nexus of persons, in which each person is guessing, assuming, inferring, believing, trusting, or suspecting, generally being happy or tormented by his phantasy of the other's experience, motives, and intentions. And one has phantasies not only about what the other himself experiences and intends, but also about his phantasies about one's own experiences and intentions, and about his phantasies about one's phantasies about one's experiences, etc. There could be no greater mistake than to suppose that these issues are mere "theoretical" complexities, of little practical relevance. There are some people who conduct their lives at several phantasy steps away from their own immediate experience or their own intentions. Family interactions are often dominated by these issues. An analyst or psychotherapist is constantly using his capacity to make, it is hoped, valid inferences about the patient's phantasies about him.[1]

I want to focus here on one aspect of a dyadic perspective, the phenomenon of *countertransference*: because of the difficulty of gathering hard and statistical evidence in this area, I will re-create and summarize one of my own experiences in the classroom both to articulate a model with clear outlines and to draw from that experience some general implications for education.

I hope in time that researchers will begin to approach the classroom as a laboratory of human development (not unlike new modes of family therapy in America and England) and to confirm and disconfirm inductive hypotheses based on any one dedicated teacher's intuitions.

By taking a model (countertransference) from one context (psychotherapy) and applying it to another (the classroom), I am trying to correct what has been a lack of self-consciousness on the parts of students and teachers about the affective and interpersonal dimension of the classroom as a laboratory for human development. This is not to suggest that therapy and the therapeutic possibilities of literary study are equivalent. From one perspective, however, psychotherapy and its applications can be seen as part of the broad humanistic attempt to achieve self-knowledge and knowledge of others, and, as a teacher and educator, this is my leading interest.

During the summer of 1970, I taught an Introduction to American Literature, a course which in our department may pay as much attention to the critical as to the historical possibilities of the subject. Because many, if not most, of the students choose this level course either to fulfill a distribution requirement, or as an elective mode of "having some but not too much English," many teachers, including myself, take on this assignment with a sense of trepidation.

The teacher never knows beforehand if he will be able to deal with the situation of the "captive audience" or to engage the tentatively committed student without pretending that both students and teacher have freely chosen their roles. Most teachers want to believe, after all, despite the realities and tacitly understood initial premises of such a course, that their dedication and the power of the material can obliterate the intellectual and emotional difficulties of such an introductory course.

Because I have experimentally applied humanistic psychology and group dynamics to the classroom, I may experience less obvious anxiety with the captive audience than some of my colleagues; in another way, however, I may be more aware of the serious problems of response in a context where the teacher is perceived as the *knower* and the students are seen as —and feel like—the *unknowing*.

The seriousness of this cognitive imbalance became especially evident in the summer course as a result of the phenomenon of countertransference and its particular manifestation in terms of my private life. The conventions of traditional education and academic decorum force one to introduce one's "private" feelings self-consciously (with quotes), as if the teacher and the person could be separated easily; yet we might do well to follow the example of William James in some instances:

> Since these experiences of melancholy are in the first instance absolutely private and individual, I can now help myself out with personal docu-

ments. Painful, indeed, they will be to listen to, and there is almost an indecency in handling them in public. Yet they lie right in the middle of our path; and if we are to touch the psychology of religion at all seriously, we must be willing to forget conventionalities, and dive below the smooth . . . conversational surface.[2]

While I was teaching, I was also getting ready to go West to visit my daughter whom I had not seen since Christmas vacation. The interval between January and the end of July represented the longest separation between us. Like most parents who are separated from their children—especially parents who are sensitive to the sense of loss and anger children feel when they are "left" at an early age (my daughter is now five and a half) without a clear and firm understanding of the meaning of visits and departures—I was not at all sure if my daughter would accept me easily and openly,[3] and I was not sure if my feelings would unfold easily.

Adults are not exempt from defending against loss or withdrawal of love by denying their own feelings. At the same time, my ex-wife was about to give birth to her second child, and insofar as the bonds of the first marriage had not been completely severed psychically, I felt that I was being definitively excluded from my former wife's life: the birth of the new child expressed literally and symbolically the sealing of her new marriage.

The dynamics of these feelings can be pursued further because, to the extent that I identify with my daughter, it was also as if I had a new sibling rival in the birth of the child, and, at other deep levels, my oedipal anxieties were, of course, mobilized in this poignant symbolic demonstration of "parental" sexuality.

But before these realizations became clear to me, I found myself going to class during the first half of the summer session with an uncommon degree of anxiety and—after a minimum of dialog and response—leaving feeling depressed and alone. No matter what the students said in response to the fiction and poetry we were reading (Willa Cather, Sherwood Anderson, Ernest Hemingway, Wallace

Stevens, T. S. Eliot, F. Scott Fitzgerald, and Gary Snyder), I felt as if we were letting one another down, as if no real communication and understanding were being shared in the class. Moreover, it did not allay my anxiety to know that the atmosphere in the class was not atypical for students enrolled in this level course.

At the end of the third week, when I wasn't sure if I could help myself and the class to vitalize our experience, I decided to immerse myself in the "destructive element" and spoke to the group openly about my feelings. As I spoke, *discovering connections,* it became clear that my feelings about going West and going to class—improbable as it seemed—were related.

Seeing the connection—the "talking cure"—came as a relief to me, and only then could I ask the class—once the weight of the two situations was separated—how, in fact, they felt about our group and my role as teacher. I knew I was risking a confirmation of my feelings of rejection (even though it would now be located in the present, not past; in the class, not my private life), but I took the risk.

If I had not realized that I was making the class bear the inappropriate weight of *my* fantasy life, that they had come to represent through countertransference a possibly *rejecting* body, I do not think I would have had the insight or courage to ask them directly if I was engaging their interests. Where, as a teacher aware of the inherent difficulties of the course, I would have been able to accept their failure of interest, I might not have been able to accept this failure of interest in the context of my fantasies and fears about going West.

In the discussions that followed over the next week, before we returned to the subject matter, the class convinced me that they *were* interested in what I was saying, that they often wanted to participate, but that, in the context of what they perceived as their inadequate position as the unknowing, they had nothing of value to say.

So it seemed, in Laing's terms, *that their misperception of my attitude towards them mirrored my misperception of their attitude towards me.* Only through intensive discussion of our feelings were we able to begin a process of de-mystification and de-projection. Where the class looked at me—through a process of transference—as the male embodiment of intellectual authority, I looked at them— through the process of countertransference—as both my *imagined* rejecting child and the rejecting former wife-mother figure.

The crucial question for me is how I might have gone about enhancing the process of de-mystification and how I might in the future allow a class to see me and themselves more clearly. In the example I have given, the class was not in a position to respond to my need to be accepted because, among other factors, the need had an *infantile* dimension that would have called upon the group to have an *adult* response to my situation.

British psychoanalyst D. W. Winnicott provides a compelling point of view and a possible direction for educational theory. His "Mirror-role of Mother and Family in Child Development" suggests one resolution to the problem of how I might have helped the class to gain the self-confidence they would have needed to reverse the roles of helper and helped. If I, in his terms, had allowed the class to see themselves reflected in me, they might have seen themselves in sufficiently strong and positive terms to have responded to me. If I had understood more clearly, along with Winnicott, that the formation of self is dependent upon the child's—and by extension the student's— seeing his face and self reflected in the face of the mother (and in my paradigm, in the face of the teacher), I would have been better able to help the students establish their "own mood" and confidences.[4]

If I had understood better the possible analogy between the educational and therapeutic task by focusing on the relationship between the sets of child-mother and student-teacher, I would have been in a better position to help my students to feel "real" and "to relate to objects as oneself."

> This glimpse of the infant's and the child's seeing the self in the mother's face, and afterwards in a mirror, gives a way of looking at analysis and

at the psychotherapeutic task. Psychotherapy is not making clever and apt interpretations; by and large it is a long-term giving the patient back what the patient brings. It is a complex derivative of the face that reflects what is there to be seen. I like to think of my work this way, and to think that if I do this well enough the patient will find his or her own self, and will be able to exist and to feel real. Feeling real is more than existing, it is finding a way to exist as oneself, and to relate to objects as oneself, and to have a self into which to retreat for relaxation.[5]

Given the nature of the countertransference that developed in our class, in which I, *like* a child, became dependent upon the approval and acceptance of the class as mother, and, given the predictable nature of the transference in which the students, as children, did not feel that they could support me, it followed, of course, that we as a group were in a double-bind.

It was only when out of necessity I bared my feelings and, in that regressive sense, dramatized the infantile component in my role that it became possible for the class to work against the force of the transference and to play a more adult role.

If I had been clearer about the dynamics of our situation from the beginning—with Winnicott's specific attitudes in mind—I might have been able to encourage, through a *reflective* and mirroring mode, an increased sense of selfhood and maturity on the part of the students that would have allowed for a reduction of the anxiety produced by the double operation of transference and countertransference in our class.

What this experiment argues for, in a broad sense, is the fusion or multiple awareness of Freudian and Winnicottian dynamics in the classroom.

As a teacher, I must move cautiously in this area because of my ongoing commitment to ideas *and* content and because of my unwillingness to make a classroom a clinical context. Still, the event I report has experiential validity, and I think most university teachers, including myself, have waited too long to begin to formulate aspects of teaching to which better teachers in primary schools have paid attention for some time.

As a teacher educated in the fifties, whose concept of teaching has been shaped during the difficult and transformational decade of the sixties, I find that some of my writing about teaching has become *autobiographical* for two reasons: because the intellectual assumptions of my students are so different from mine, and because my students have forced me, without their knowing it, to consider the classroom as a theatre of human development. The first reason compels me to reexamine my assumptions about education that were shaped during a "silent" generation, and the second makes me keenly aware that I, like my students, am present in the classroom in the fullness of my subjectivity: a subjectivity that must be explored if I am to make any claims, finally, about the objectivity of literary study.

Education and Social Discontinuity:
The Critical Price of Vietnam   9

In "Classroom as Microcosm," I summarize a humanistic experiment in education and relate that experiment to the anguished and prolonged strike that dominated the SUNY-Buffalo campus in the late winter and early spring of 1970:

> Most close observers of university crisis over the past five years know that the scenario of militancy and reaction—with real strike demands and negotiations often obscured and damaged by police occupation and the inevitable confrontations and violence that follow—stems, in the main, from the irreconcilable opposition of dissident students and a hierarchical administration.[1]

Further reflection in light of the persistence of the war in Vietnam and the invasion of Cambodia has now made me realize that what I took to be self-evident generalization is mildly stated and couches a larger and more significant generalization: *that there is a radical discontinuity between the microcosm of the university (and the sub-microcosm of the classroom) and the macrocosm of the prevailing mystifying power structure in America.*[2]

If the issue is redefined in these terms, one can see that the

---

This essay is reprinted with permission from *Soundings*, Spring 1971.

campus "crisis" represents a seemingly terminal point of alienation: divisions within the self, estrangement of the individual from the group, and separation from society *as a whole*.

The consensus among students about the immorality and the illegality of the war in Vietnam—and the total failure of the Nixon administration to address itself in direct and human terms to this consensus—exemplifies in a tragically concrete way what enlightened cultural critics have been saying in various terms since the midnineteenth century: that our lives are characterized—to use David Bakan's phrase—by *telic decentralization*.[3]

At every level of psychic and social organization, we suffer radical discontinuities and fail to achieve wholeness of being. From Wordsworth, Marx, and Freud through T. S. Eliot to Marshall McLuhan, the message—if not the medium of analysis and the historical moment—is the same: Man's inner life is not projected outward in its full affective and symbolic wholeness, and the world we move through does not reflect and support our deepest intrapsychic and transpersonal needs.

Our lives have become increasingly fragmented and splintered in response to which the burden of modernism—in psychoanalysis, cubism, Marxism, and the important literary works of the age—has been an attempt at reconstruction. The war in Vietnam, however, has made it virtually impossible for students and teachers who are alert consciously or unconsciously to this historical predicament to carry on, in whatever minimal ways that are still open, the task of reconstituting, in the tradition of Eliot, Yeats, Pound, and Joyce, some sense of harmony in our lives; of reconstituting some continuity between the ego and the deepest reaches of the self; between self and others; between self and society; between history and myth; between the existential present and the impulse towards transcendence.

As a teacher interested in bringing together humanistic psychology and the study of literature, I have experienced the Vietnam War (in a Laingian sense) as a devastating impingement of an alien reality upon experiments and explorations in humanistic reconstruction.[4] Let me cite directly and somewhat propositionally the implications of this violent impingement for me and my students.

Implications for the Study of Literature

If one takes T. S. Eliot—poet, dramatist, and critic—as emblematic of the modernist approach to personality and culture, it is clear that the relationship between *tradition* and the *dislocated present* becomes the most pressing claim for a possible humanism. Teachers of literature like myself, who came of critical consciousness in the post-World War II years, whether they are committed to psychoanalysis, Jungian psychology, New Criticism, mythology, or structuralism—have shared a belief, however divisive "opposing" schools may seem, in the possibility of reestablishing a communality of the deepest sources of the experience of man in Western culture.

The war in Vietnam—not as an isolated event, but as the culmination for American students of the modern history of violence and the denial of the claims of humanism—serves to invalidate this study. To pursue the study of rituals of death and rebirth in *Sir Gawain,* Shakespeare, Henry James, or John Barth (relevance is not a matter of period interest) in the face of Kent State can make sense only as a gesture of cosmic nihilism. Without a potentially viable present and a possible or theoretical future, the Eliotic approach to personality and culture must lead us to say:

> Because these wings are no longer wings to fly
> But merely fans to beat the air,
> The air which is now thoroughly small and dry,
> Smaller and dryer than the will,
> Teach us to care and not to care;
> Teach us to sit still.[5]

But we cannot, with conscience, teach our students "to sit still."

The commitment to tradition and humanism—insofar as they inescapably embody Renaissance and Enlightenment values—goes hand in hand with a set of intellectual preferences that the war in Vietnam has made it difficult, if not impossible, to sustain in the university. These include commitments to rationalism, skepticism, and rational language.

Because of the logistical and statistical rationalizations of the war in Vietnam—the logic of "body counts"—it is difficult for a young person, faced with specific moral responses and choices, to separate the rational from the rationalized; just as it is difficult for a young person to separate theories of computer analysis from the application of this technology to the success or failure of "hamlet pacification."[6]

In ways that often frustrate, confuse, and anger the teacher of literature, critical methods and analyses take on the qualities, in the minds of outraged students, of inhuman methods of annihilation. Literary and other humanistic programs and programming are often felt as part of an evasive pattern, a failure to confront reality in all its particularity. Rather than accept the limits of Cartesian categories, this generation prefers the minuteness of psychedelic perception as a symbolic substitute for terror on a grand scale—if not as a conscious choice, then as a psychological necessity.[7]

Literary critics, whatever their differences, hold in common a respect for complexity. The New Critic may call it *ambiguity;* the psychoanalytic critic, *ambivalence,* but there is a common recognition that human experience and the symbolization of experience are many sided, multilayered, overdetermined. Understanding the work of literary art is unimaginable without sensitivity to *metaphor,* and only a narrow intellectualism would insist on *exact* limits and resonance of metamorphic range. This respect for complexity in literary criticism is only one academic manifestation of a broader sceptical tradition, the Socratic one, just as liberal politics (with its commitment to free speech, the right to dissent, and protection for minorities) is another part of that broader tradition.

Students have discovered that they must violate this tradition of balanced ambiguity in order to get an effective response to their objection to the war in Vietnam. Because he seems to provide an intellectually honorable alternative to this liberalism, Marcuse has become a cult hero. As a teacher and critic, I find myself often appalled at the willingness of students to deny complexity of judgment and value, but it seems clear that we must end the war in Vietnam and all that it stands for, and not merely lament the excesses of the New Left or any political faction if we are to remake the university and the classroom into a structure where complexity and amorality do not seem to be equivalent.

Orwellian prophecies have become all too true in our day, and the language of the United States government often resembles Newspeak. It is no wonder, then, that students find "official" rhetoric unacceptable; nor is it difficult to understand that if there is a radical discontinuity between a student generation and the adult culture, language as well as value system will be rejected.

Antilinguistic, as well as pre- and nonverbal, tendencies are evident on all campuses (e.g., the "No Words" on the side of the plane in *Zabriskie Point*), but the sources of this attitude are deeper than the perversion of language evident in phrases such as "body count" or "clean bomb" or "defoliation." One sees in the writings of N. O. Brown, the later R. D. Laing (*The Politics of Experience*), Leary (egregiously), and McLuhan an attempt to reconstitute man in his multisensory field of experience. So long as the official culture not only denies pleasure but inflicts pain, teachers in all disciplines, but most noticeably in literature, will find that the act of rational discourse itself, to say nothing of content, will be suspect.

Implications for Humanistic Psychology

If one tries in teaching, as I have, to draw together process and content by extrapolating from the concepts of encounter groups, sensitivity training, group therapy—all of which are modes of exploration calling for a risk of greater belief in the possibilities of trust—one will find students apprehensive about *what comes afterward.* If one learns to express oneself more fully in a classroom, what becomes of the increased measure of openness?

In order for various modes of "laboratory" training to be useful, it should be possible to imagine the translation of the microstructure into a macrostructure, to imagine that the small world remade could become a paradigm for a larger social experience.

If this is not possible, then sensitivity training, like the pastoral life, becomes a form of escape, a context for repairing but not remaking the self. So long as conscription and the war in Vietnam represent the reality to which students must always return, one can expect minimal results from new approaches to education. Increased disappointment, after new knowledge, may be the only result.

Related to this first implication for humanistic psychology, but different from it, is the present danger of regressiveness. Most modes of humanistic and depth psychology ask the individual to recapitulate his development in some way, to reexperience the first experiences of life that may have set the individual on a painful course. These psychologies also assume that there will be a "return," in somewhat mythic terms, to an expanded sense of selfhood.

A cursory glance at the contemporary American university and the prevailing life-styles makes it unmistakably clear that a return is unimagined and unwanted. A closer look at experiments in education, which ask for reexperiencing early childhood feelings, reveals that regression, not return, is the most appealing aspect of the experience.

If a teacher has commitments, as I do, to content, normative values and nonmagical thinking (demystified thinking, in Laing's terms), he will find that—because of the difficulties of everyday realities for the contemporary American student—the satisfactions of regression will outweigh the impulse to return. The loss of self, not the remaking of self, will be a constant risk for the progressive educator if our society insists on acting out violence on a global scale.

In any educational experiment involving humanistic psychology, exploration of the role of authority becomes extremely important. The intention of this exploration is to work through latent fears of punishment and retaliation to a more open, mutual, and dialogic relationship between student and teacher. If the teacher, like the presidents of so many universities, comes to be perceived as the incarnation of the power structure (so that assigning a paper is like all other acts of repression), if the teacher is endowed with magical powers through the magic of projection, then a meaningful exploration does not seem possible or plausible. The assaults upon defense-funded research are mirrored in a thousand classrooms—in teachers who are and are not complicit—and it is unlikely that education can become authentic within this political and military context.

My point throughout this essay has been to dramatize how the war in Vietnam makes the translation of humanistic values, both literary and psychological, difficult if not impossible; to show that unless there is an aspect of *correspondence,* to use a Renaissance word, between a world of discourse or a model of society (the classroom) and the society as a whole, then one's best efforts serve only to define the extent to which our lives are lived in the service of *telic decentralization* and the extent to which they are encapsulated and can become private hells.

Although I have summarized my experience as a teacher in general terms, what I have said is based on the specific events of the classroom; and I would like to conclude with an account of a dream submitted by one of my students to suggest the inseparability of inner processes and political events:

> Flarelit battlefield. Scarred land and dead bodies. I am in uniform, with rifle. Others like me, trapped, fire machine guns across the field. The only possible way out is to put an end to the attack. I jump out of the foxhole, firing wildly at all of my enemies. They fall and die, and I find

this all like a shooting gallery, with the same satisfaction of hitting every elephant, lion, and bear. Now at the machine gun nest, one blast from my weapon and they all die. I know I am a hero, but it's not a simple thought; it's a goddamned political experience, all of me knows it. I run back to my own lines, firing, and a second later one more of the opposition is out of the way. Until . . . now it seems incredible to me, but I am face to face with one of the enemy. And my gun is out of bullets; I panic inside, smashing his skull with the butt of my rifle; and then, when he falls, I kick and knee him in the face, in the body, until he lies helpless at my feet. I have not, cannot put an end to his existence. I finish that passage back to my own side of this particular war. I am greeted by my standing comrades as a hero. I feel simply god-like, or as close as a man can get. And then . . . there he stands, being held up by his sad-looking fellows, the one I could not kill; he is bleeding, badly wounded. And for a moment, so am I.

Encounter and Humanism **10**

Like many English teachers of my generation, especially those trained in New Criticism during the 1950s, I find that I am inescapably a print-man and am most comfortable when I have written out some kind of essay *to present* to an *audience,* but I cannot go further than this sentence without realizing that I may have already put some distance between myself and you.

As I look at these opening sentences—regarding them for a moment as if they were a statement written through me—I see that I move through a state of consciousness probably not shared by many of you and towards which I have become somewhat skeptical myself.

The word *generation,* as I use it, suggests an historical awareness and is very much an anti-Nowist stance. Perhaps I am aware of generations because I have been reading a good deal of biography lately: Nancy Milford's *Zelda,* O. Mannoni's *Freud,* Edmund Wilson's *The Shores of Light* (which includes a tribute to his former teacher: "Christian Gauss as a Teacher of Literature"), and Lytton Strachey's *Eminent Victorians,* where four Victorian sacred cows are sacrificed. Most notable for our purposes here, he draws the blood of Dr. Thomas Arnold who became headmaster of Rugby in 1828.

This essay is reprinted with permission from *Symposium Humanities,* Winter 1972.

More profoundly than anything having to do with recent reading, I use the word *generation* because my own literary education planted a sense of *period* in my mind and because the radical shifts of style and thought in the university during the past ten years have made my own undergraduate education seem part of a world I hardly can remember. And I suppose there will come a time when you will—defying Bob Dylan—look back and see yourself and your contemporaries as having lived *in* time and history. For the moment though, you are probably uncomfortable with my using a word that speaks for historical progression and closure rather than mythological simultaneity and evolution, for a serial (diachronic) approach to time, rather than an electronic sense of historical circuitry (synchronic).

Then there is *criticism*. In my nine years as an English teacher, I have found an increasing unwillingness on the part of students to subject texts—especially texts that are endowed with any sacred quality—to analytic scrutiny: as if verbal analysis could somehow leave its imprint upon the work and make it live less as a vibrant object; as if the act of rational discourse itself were another embodiment of the mind-body, sense-intellect, and subject-object split to which so many of you and so many leading critics of culture object.

This skepticism towards criticism and analysis is closely connected, of course, with a suspicion of language and a contempt for its misuse. It is no wonder, in an Orwellian age of advertising pollution and political rhetoric ("clean bombs," "body counts," "defensive actions"), that many of you—and myself—may want in extreme moments to paint on the side of our lives a sign that says, as in *Zabriskie Point,* "No Words."

This brings me to another phrase I used that tips my hand: *to present* to an audience. At a time when participatory democracy, street action and theatre, and environmental happenings are so much a part of our lives (to say nothing of Richard Schnechner's Performance Group in New York or Grotowski's Poor Theatre), the separation between the presenter and the audience may seem anachronistically antitribal and antiglobal: part of the world of product, not process; part of proscenium, not living, theatre.[1]

And, as I have said, I myself have become somewhat skeptical of my attempts to be, in the language of baseball, a "control" teacher; but you will forgive this linear presentation of a nonlinear argument —to which I will move in a moment—by remembering that ordinary language may serve us best when we are trying to invent a future that is difficult to imagine in even the simplest terms.

I have already edged towards my subject, a summary relationship between group psychology, family drama and film, and humanistic education, and I have suggested, both in tone and content, that I have somewhat mixed feelings towards the case for freedom and openness that I am going to make.

In "Such, Such Were the Joys . . . ," the autobiographical account of his student days at the English boarding school "Crossgates" in 1910, George Orwell, essayist, novelist, and Loyalist combatant during the Spanish Civil War of 1936 to 1939, writes:

> Part of the reason for the ugliness of adults, in a child's eyes, is that the child is usually looking upwards, and few faces are at their best when seen from below.[2]

This *lowly* feeling of being a student in the earlier part of this century is all too true even now as we speed towards the twenty-first century, and it is precisely the structure of the teacher being *up* and the student *down* that has precipitated so much conflict in the contemporary American university.

Before I move on and suggest how this situation might in part be changed, let me say that insofar as there was a time when the teacher-student relationship carried the weight of a parent-child relationship, this up-down structure made some sense. It could be benevolent as well as cruel; it also carried the possibility of transferring wisdom from one generation to the next.

But rapidly accelerating technology has made the transmission of information from generation to generation difficult, if not sometimes an actual impediment to growth. Even if one believes in the value of maintaining the up-down structure, students do not view this structure as viable, a reality of university life which should be faced.

In "The Joys and Terrors of Sending the Kids to College," Harvey Swados, the American novelist, describes a theme that asserts itself in all his writing classes: "the discovery of the vulnerability or fallibility of the writer's father."[3]

He goes on to say:

> It is curious and interesting that in the last year or two I have found such tales being supplemented, if not supplanted, by stories which portray the professor rather than the parent as a sorry figure. . . .[4]

Swados could, I believe, have traced this decline of the father back to the rejection of the authoritarian nineteenth century *paterfamilias,* but what he claims as the consciousness of youth I take to be accurate.[5] What Swados says is reflected in *The Whole World Is Watching,* the autobiography of Mark Gerzon, a contemporary student. In the chapter "Youth and Identity," Gerzon writes:

> Gone completely is the word "comrade" from the radical groups of the 1930s. Gone too is the word "buddy," carried over from army language. The young people today who recognize the meaninglessness of old definitions of self, of old concepts of loyalty and authority and belief, must search for a new concept of family and community. They must call men brother not because they have the same "dad" as father, or because they believe in the same God as father, or even because they have the same fatherland, but because they share the young awareness of being symbolically fatherless. Orphaned by a world of technology, they find in the poetic phrase "the family of man" a very deep and meaningful allegiance.[6]

If students feel orphaned by a world of technology (a theme

echoed in Roszak's *The Making of a Counter Culture*), and if the fathers—real and pedagogic—aren't seen as viable transmitters of knowledge and tradition, what can be done to avoid classroom manifestations of the double-bind situation described in the writings of R. D. Laing and in contemporary film and drama?

What can be done to undo the anguished and contradictory situations of "patients" and characters (like Biff in *Death of a Salesman,* Edmund Tyrone in *Long Day's Journey Into Night,* and Mark in *Zabriskie Point*) and the contemporary student who says, in effect: "I cannot accept my role as son with respect to your role as father, but if I do not play my role and let you play your role, one or both of us will be destroyed"?

How can a teacher of the humanities see the *collusive enterprise* of the teacher-student roles for what it is and not try to change it? And, as vexingly, how can he change it and not relinquish his vision of the humanities as an inherited body of *knowledge,* contained in *words,* that must be critically examined and imparted to an impersonal *audience* of students? How can he escape the double-bind of serving two masters: human development and cognition?

Although there are many modes of moving towards a sense of feeling *real* and *authentic* prevalent on the American scene today, we can find an apt description of the situation in Carl Rogers's *On Encounter Groups.* In "The Lonely Person—and His Experiences in an Encounter Group," he says:

> Loneliness verges in despair when a person permits himself to realize that the meaning of life does not and cannot reside in the relation of his outer facade to external reality. . . .[7]

Rogers is saying, in effect, that when one realizes that there is a discontinuity between one's *role* and one's *self,* then one will feel *angst,* loneliness.

So loneliness exists at many levels and in many degrees, but it is sharpest and most poignant in the individual who has, for one reason or another, found himself standing, without some of his customary defenses, a vulnerable, frightened, lonely, but *real* self, sure of rejection in a judgmental world.[8]

For Rogers, the way out of this situation is the risking of the real self to others and the discovery that one's real self will not, after all, be rejected.

In *Rachel, Rachel,* this moment comes when Rachel is willing to accept her sexual feelings and give herself to a young man she has unquestionably idealized. . . . She has learned that it is only by taking a risk that she can genuinely encounter another human being.[9]

Teachers and students, then, who wish to make the disparity between self and role creative must be willing to risk exposure of the self: to enter into an act of unmasking that lies at the heart of modern drama and group psychology. Teachers and students must be willing to demystify (in R. D. Laing's sense) their roles; to enter into acts of self-revelation and responsiveness that may even approach the intensity of Edward Albee's "Walpurgisnacht" in *Who's Afraid of Virginia Woolf?*

The hope is, of course, that *after* encounter one person will be able to say to the other, as Edmund says to his father Tyrone in *Long Day's Journey:* "I'm glad you've told me this. . . . I know you a lot better now";[10] that one will be able to say with Biff in *Salesman,* "Will you take that phony dream and burn it before something happens?" and survive intact, whole.[11]

I do not want to underestimate the risks involved in this educational project, nor suggest that a special kind of sensitivity and training may not be in order for the teacher who takes on this project, but these issues exceed the bounds of this essay.[12]

What I espouse—seeing a connection between group dynamics, family drama, and the classroom, and the possibility of making all three contexts for unmaskings of the self—does not preclude a structure and order of awareness that can take its place in the humanistic tradition.

I would argue, in fact, with L. L. Whyte that

> this is the century of structure and as we pass into its last third, research is moving from the study of stationary equilibrium structures to the processes by which they are formed and the changes they undergo. This is the fascinating world of *ordered processes* and it will be marked by unexpected insights.[13]

The ordered processes referred to here are "morphic":

> So we select a short, Greek, unspoilt, and scientific-sounding term: *morphic,* and call "morphic" all processes generating spatial form. "Morphic" is the modern name for the spatial expression of the tendency towards unity, order, and intelligibility which Plato recognized in nature.[14]

Whyte's attempt to synthesize with contemporary biology a Platonic concept of form is echoed by Alvin B. Kernan of Yale, who says in "A New Context for Literature?":

> For example, Susanne Langer has thrown considerable light on the nature of comedy by comparing its celebration of the ongoingness of life and the ability of individuals to adapt and thrive in changed circumstances to the ability of organic life "to maintain the pattern of vitality in a non-living universe . . . to keep its equilibrium amid the bombardment of aimless forces that beset it, to regain equilibrium when it has been disturbed, and to pursue a sequence of action dictated by the need of keeping all its interdependent parts constantly renewed, their structure intact."[15]

I have faith, then, that we can let go of many of the traditional constraints of education, especially the rigidly defined roles of teachers and students, and still discover structures of awareness and cognition and imagination that refer both to the humanistic tradition and to the immediate pulsations of our inner selves.

As a matter of fact, many of the most acute and rational critics of contemporary art and culture (e.g., Hilton Kramer, Harold Rosenberg, and Lionel Trilling) have pointed to the profound relationship between humanism and openness, between the image of man and mythical thought *processes*.[16]

So if we lose our equilibrium for awhile, as we must, it will return. But we must not mistake *ordered processes* and our engagement with them as *merely doing your own thing*. At this point, we will probably disagree, so I will—being someone conditioned to an Aristotelian sense of beginning, middle, and end—stop. . . .

A University in Time of War 11

Richard had grown up on the eastern shore of Lake Michigan, fifty miles from Horton's Bay, where Hemingway spent the famous summers he wrote about in *In Our Time*. Richard's father, who wanted to write, was derailed by the depression and World War II. He ended up selling books on the road until he returned to high school teaching and writing in the late 1950s.

Given his father's literary ambitions and Richard's natural gifts as an athlete, it was appropriate that he had grown up in Hemingway country. He looked like Hemingway, too: broad-shouldered and barrel-chested; he nonetheless had a miler's legs. His face was classically handsome but curiously more sensitive and subtly passionate than I'd thought possible for a midwestern high school kid. Hemingway had furnished the adolescent Richard with a necessary mythology. When I told him of my having had a few drinks at Hemingway's haunts in Paris and Venice in the 1950s, Richard naively looked to me for answers. For one, he wanted me to make all the books we read in class "relevant" to the war in Vietnam.

"I can't do it."

This essay is reprinted with permission from *Forgive the Father: A Memoir of Changing Generations*, New Republic Book Co., 1978.

"You were at the Ritz Bar and Harry's; you can."

"This isn't a game, Richard. I can't."

"Well, I can." He goes on to tell me about Orwell's "Shooting an Elephant."

"I've made my decision; I'm giving up football and joining SDS [Students for a Democratic Society]. It came to me clearly last night while I was reading the Orwell essay. What we're doing in Vietnam isn't different from what the British were doing when Orwell was in Burma. Don't you think I'm right?"

"I haven't thought about that connection very much," I say, though in fact I'm not eager to pursue an analogy that will require me to discuss imperialism. By training and temperament, politics always feels strange to me. I've mastered most of the correct liberal responses but would rather talk about language. "Anyway, I'm too busy being a father and getting a Ph.D.," I add.

"Maybe you can hang back," Richard says, "but my generation doesn't have that much time."

"Aren't you being a little apocalyptic? We don't know what's going on over there."

"I heard someone speak on the steps of the library last night. And he does."

"What differences will it make in your life, though?"

"If you're from Muskegon, giving up football is a pretty big change, but it's more than that. There's no such thing as an individual effort. I can see that now. Everything we do has been programmed in some way. The only answers are collective ones. I know I must sound like an SDS organizer, but it's what I feel. It's what Dylan is singing about. He's very important. He's showing us how to put our private and public lives together."

"Are you sure that's possible anymore?"

"Dylan is a poet, right? He's a symbolist, a surrealist. He has an unmistakable style. He has found his own way of speaking about the larger issues. He speaks for us; no one owns his language. I want to be like him."

"Isn't that a contradiction?"

"I don't want *to be* him, just *like* him. I want to discover the secrets of language that he knows and use them in my own way."

"Why can't you just write in your own voice straight out? Why imitate Dylan?"

"Why do you imitate T. S. Eliot? Or Henry James? Dylan is out in front of us. It's almost arrogant not to imitate him in some way. Imitate him and then forget him. I want to go through the same process as him, to experience as closely as possible what he experienced when he wrote his songs in his style, and then write my own songs. . . if there will be anyone around to listen to them by the time this war is over."

It was hard to keep up with Richard. He would be in town for a week, then away. It wasn't always clear whether he was enrolled or not, whether he was working toward a degree. It became a matter of pride on both our sides not to ask these questions, but I was always interested in how his quest for Dylan was going and where he had been to authenticate the search.

On and off for the year I knew him in Ann Arbor, postcards came from San Francisco, Nashville, Minneapolis, and, of course, Brooklyn. His cards were spirited and depressive: "Burnt out on you know what, but what a view from the Brooklyn Bridge."

It pleased me that he continued to write through the mounting protest, that he didn't let too much rhetoric get between us. As he said in one card, "Maybe you are paid by the state, but we've both read the essay 'Politics and the English Language.' "

When he returned once, he sat in the Michigan stadium, the only place in town we could count on to be nonpolitical.

"I might pull an eighty-yard run."

"What's that?" he asks.

"You know, the Irwin Shaw story, where an aging athlete tries to relive his youth."

"That would be embarrassing. I'd have to tackle you."

"I thought you'd given up sports."

"I have, but I'm still enough of a Big Ten jock to put politics aside, even dangerous politics."

"Maybe you've just decided to embrace your brothers instead of flattening them."

"I'm tired of all this male superiority anyway, aren't you? We've been exploiting women long enough. It's time to 'off' male oppression even if it means loving men, too."

"Tell me what you've been doing."

"We make sure that certain people get from here to there. Often 'there' is Canada, but I can't really talk about it. You played football, didn't you?" he asks, changing the subject.

"That's true, I could catch anything, but I couldn't run to save my life. My coach couldn't understand it. He was Irish. When things got really bad, he'd remind us that we had a proud tradition behind us, that we once even brought in ringers from New Jersey and Massachusetts. Guess what? I learned later that Jack Kerouac had played for the school in the late thirties. How's that for a connection?"

"I'd like to meet your old coach. I'd really like to find out if you *could* catch anything. Maybe I'll look him up in a few weeks."

"Where are you going?"

"I'm going to take a break. I've had enough Civil Rights and antiwar stuff for awhile. I'm going to the Cape. But I'm not giving anything up. I'm just taking a break."

We walk around the field. It smells rich and pungent.

While Richard was working in Provincetown—"they're boiling my tail at the Lobster Pot, the pigs," he'd written—I moved into a Buffalo apartment without furniture or electricity. I had only a phone and a double mattress. I'd barely opened the windows when his brother called.

"He's dead."

"Who, for God's sake? Who are you talking about?"

"My father—my father's dead. Who'll tell Richard? You've got to tell him."

"You've got to tell him, Bunny. You're his brother."

"I wouldn't know what to say to him, and Spike, our older brother, is too drunk most of the time to know what to say. Besides, he is a little crazy about it right now."

"What will I say to him, Bunny? Isn't there a close uncle or a minister?"

"There are just the three of us. Mom died two years ago, and Richard doesn't believe in God anymore. He wanted to be a minister once, though."

"Okay, Bunny, I'll tell him. I'll tell him something. He should be here in a few hours. I'll have him call you after I've told him and we've talked about it. How are you Bunny? You sound all right."

"I've known for six months, I could see it in his face. When you live at home, you know these things. I knew it with Mom. I'm all right. I believe in God. I know this had to happen. Richard's different, though."

"What about money, food, do you have everything?" I imagine Bunny standing alone somewhere in Michigan. I've never been to their home, but I see it as a desolate bluff overlooking Lake Michigan, an empty lot, with a few scrub pines, near an ESSO station on a side road.

"I'm okay. I've spoken to a lawyer already. There's a high school pension fund. Dad was lucky to get back into teaching five years ago. He was writing too. He was coming along. Richard wants to write too, you know. I wonder how this will affect him. So there's the school pension and social security. We'll each get some of that until we're twenty-one. The house is almost paid for. We'll do fine.

"What about school for you and Richard?"

"He's got a scholarship to the U of M; I'll get one. There are loans, I guess, if we need them."

"If I can do anything, Bunny, call. Richard will call later tonight.

He'll have to tell you when he'll be back. I'll give him airfare if he's broke. He's probably broke. He's always pretending he's Dylan."

Before I have time to imagine what I will say to Richard, the phone rings, and he tells me that he is in Lockport.

"I can hitch to your house from here in an hour," he says.

"Lockport's still pretty far away. Don't be so cocky!"

"Is that what I am? I don't know half the time."

"By the way, I have no electricity. Niagara Mohawk doesn't trust me yet."

"Those power-hungry bastards," he says. "They own Niagara Falls, don't they? It doesn't matter, I have a present for you from Provincetown."

Richard has never brought me a present before. I've given him an old typewriter, a field jacket, a second-hand electric fan, but he hasn't been old enough to give me anything. When he does arrive, it's early twilight. I haven't had to light any candles yet as I've been doing for about a week. When Richard appears at the door, we embrace like Russian comrades.

"Look what I have for you."

He swings an old railroad lantern into view. It has been freshly painted black and has a ruby colored glass. It's beautiful.

"I've always wanted one, ever since I went to Florida on the Seaboard Express."

"I won't get there this trip. If I go south, it will be to Selma, not Miami Beach." We laugh.

"You look good." He actually looks thin and played out, as if he has been smoking too much pot and not eating.

He looks around the apartment, leading his way with the lantern that he has lit. A pleasant copper-amber radiance spreads into corners.

"This is quite a football field," he says. "We could make it into a Summerhill school."

He runs through the large living room as if it were a football field, dodging imaginary tacklers, giving chimerical straight-arms and bringing his knees up to his stomach.

I bring some wine out to the porch where there is still some light.

"I want to tell you about the trip," he says.

"Tomorrow."

"You look sad. What is it? What's wrong?"

"I've got to tell you something."

He stares at me. I think he knows what I am going to say.

"Your father died. Bunny called. You've got to call Michigan and go home."

He runs into the living room and falls on the floor.

"The lousy bastard, he left me alone. I knew he'd do it. The goddamned lousy bastard. I could kill him."

He beats his hands against the floor.

"The lousy bastard."

He weeps for half an hour, stopping only to ask me what else Bunny had said.

When he comes out on the porch again, he is calm. "I guess I knew it was coming. I thought about going home a few times from P-Town."

"Maybe it's better that you didn't see him die."

"How's Bunny? Is he all right?"

"Do you want to go back tonight?"

"No. I'll call Bunny and stay here."

After Richard calls home, we sit on the porch around the lantern and talk late into the night. We do not mention his father at all. We talk about his going back to Ann Arbor, how the campus is going, and his growing impatience with SDS: "We've got to go further left; they'll kill us all in Vietnam if we don't."

I believe him and can imagine a whole generation being wiped out. It's a nightmare I've had. But a reflexive inability to think in such impersonal terms impels me to focus on his safety.

We finish the bottle of wine. It's clear that we don't want to talk anymore. "There's a large mattress and lots of floor," I say. We set the lantern at the foot of the mattress and put the sleeping bags and blankets, fixed now as a bedroll, side by side. "It reminds me of summer camp. What a farce that was," I say and recount some tales from the Berkshires in the late forties.

"Nothing like that ever happened to me at the 'Y' camp. Is it too late to go to yours?"

Sleep comes the way it often does in the army: obliquely, unresisted, voices trailing off one by one and, then, total silence.

I didn't see much of Richard again until 1969 when he came to Buffalo as a graduate student. But it became clear, in letters, as he recounted protests, marches, arrests, and cited quotations from the Left and Right, that he had become more radical, more heedless of consequences, since his father's death.

Behind his responses to the war, the racial situation, and the structure of the university, he always gave the impression that he didn't have much to lose.

I think of myself as black, he'd written on one postcard; *I've got everything to gain and nothing to lose. The bastards will kill me one way or another, so why not fight back?*

I dropped some acid and took a ride after a rally at three in the morning on I-90. It was like turning the wrong way on a carousel, he wrote in another letter.

It was hard to know what was exploratory and what was self-dramatizing and self-destructive for him. Often in Buffalo, especially that spring when the campus was cresting for an explosion, I thought of Richard, his father's failed career and sudden death, the earlier loss of his mother, and particularly his desire to write in a generation that didn't believe in writing.

By the time Richard followed me to Buffalo to begin graduate study in history, the campus had moved closer to a major confrontation. Demonstrations in France, Berkeley, and Morningside Heights haunted the imagination of most undergraduates I knew, and it wasn't possible that the Buffalo students would let themselves be outflanked. They prided themselves on being a vanguard campus.

It didn't take Richard long to establish his credentials as a leader of the campus Left. Although we didn't talk to one another too much, I would see him in the Union at the "correct" tables. Sometimes I sat down. More often than not, I stayed away from his turf. The lines between liberals and radicals were becoming visible and taut.

While the sides were shaping up, I was trying to help an experimental, communitarian college get organized, but instead of teaching, I was beseiged with other urgencies: Could students live in the house we had managed to secure for meetings? Could drifters, crashers, bummers, and speeders spend a night at the house? Did we *have* to have a curriculum? Couldn't we cook macrobiotic rice together instead? Could the basement be used for a radical media group? We were interested in film, weren't we? We were interested in communications, weren't we? We *were,* and we allowed the group to take over the basement.

There were few days during those times when emotions were unmixed. The meaning of education was up for grabs—one fellow teacher passed on a scenario for class he thought would interest me.

The class assembles in the room expecting the usual lecture on Coleridge based on the day's reading assignment, "Kubla Khan." The bell beginning the hour sounds, but the teacher does not appear; instead, a stranger dressed in the garb of the Orient appears and announces an incantation will be held in order to make contact with the Spirit of Coleridge. With the assistance of a dancing girl clad in a veil, the traveler places a cloth on the desk top, lights candles, passes out incense and turns out the lights. To a drum beat, live or taped, the teacher enters wearing whatever bits of exotica he can create. He salaams to the students. A flute is played in a quasi-oriental fashion. The teacher begins a slow dream recitation of the poem, pausing occasionally to watch the "Abyssinian maid" dance or the traveler sing some verses of Hare Krishna.

Was this meant to be a parody? I couldn't tell and that troubled me. I dropped him a note saying that "salaaming" was bound to be "offed" by the students—it was too slavish. He didn't send me any more scenarios. There wasn't much humor anywhere in those days, especially between Richard and me.

Although he didn't trust me politically, Richard would come to my office for intimate, familial chats, as he did at the end of a day in mid-November.

We talk about the pressures building up on campus and the endless war. I point out a line in Hemingway: "In the fall the war was always there. . . ."

"Do you think Hemingway needed war?" Richard asks.

"Probably. At least the threat of physical violence."

"It's hard to avoid," Richard says, "even if you want to get rid of violence. That's part of our problem. Sometimes killing is necessary."

"Don't be so prematurely heroic," I say. "You're not in the Vietcong yet."

We don't talk for a few minutes. The view outside my office window is pleasant; a few pine cones are on the ground at that time of year, and a few students are out with their friends playing frisbee. Even the advertised revolution hasn't put an end to frisbee.

I want to go outside and back in time, to a moment when war and killing were in the realm of make-believe for me. I wish I could take Richard and my other students back to that other time between World War II and Korea when commando techniques were applied in the schoolyard against anti-Semites and neighborhood bullies.

But this is another war, and we are their protectors; they ask us to write letters supporting their conscientious objections, to trust them even as they distrust us for having served during the cold war years.

No matter how friendly we are to students, or what stand we take toward the war or the university, we are suspect because most of us have been in the army. It takes a lot of backpedaling to convince students that the peacetime army had little, if anything, to do with

Vietnam.

"How far are you willing to go?" I ask Richard, not sure I want to hear the answer. He sidesteps the hook.

"I don't know; it's a question we discuss all the time. But there are more immediate issues now. That's why I came in. Buffalo's become an important crash spot, you know. Kids coming out of the Midwest are heading for Buffalo. *We* need some help with them."

"Who's we?"

"No one you need to know about. That's not important. We've got these two kids, no more than fifteen years old. She's pregnant. The parents have the cops after them. We need some money for her to have an abortion and get them on their way to Canada, if possible."

"Why are they important to you, Richard? How will helping them end the war?"

"It's all part of the same problem, the same system."

"That's ridiculous, getting them to Canada isn't going to help anyone, certainly not the Vietnamese."

"We're not talking about Vietnam now. We're talking about the system."

"How much do you want me to give?"

"Whatever you think is right."

I look out the window. There is no way for me to decide what is right. The teenagers from Cleveland or Sandusky need understanding and help. So do ten million other people. But I know that Richard isn't just asking me to give some money. He wants me to commit myself. He's got me over a barrel and is rolling it.

"Am I giving for them, or are they a symbol?"

"Does it really matter?"

"This whole country is papered with symbols. What am I supposed to do about it?"

"Everything. It's your problem. We've all got problems."

Richard is asking me to buy his trust. I'm willing to pay something for it, but how much? I can pay him enough and settle the score between us with bad faith, or I can give something that might have some practical value for the young people from Cleveland.

I write a check for fifty dollars. I expect him to react immediately and positively when I take out my checkbook, but he's impassive. It's as if my capacity to write a check puts me on the other side. He respects me enough to ask me for money but despises me for having some money to give away.

I hand him the check. "This is a lot of money for me. You know that, I think."

"Most people I know could live on the taxes you pay."

"What do you want me to do?"

"Give me a hundred, five hundred, show that you really care."

"I've shown that I care. Find someone else down the hall to give another fifty."

"I don't know anyone else in this department."

"Too bad."

"I would've expected as much from a honky pig."

"Then give the money back, Richard."

I reach to take the check back.

He holds onto it. "I'll take it as it is."

As he goes out the office door, he half smiles and makes a peace sign. I smile with equal irony and raise a semiclenched fist.

It was the last time I saw Richard for a while. The school year managed to come to an end, and I spent the summer in Oregon, working on a project with a friend.

The pastoral interlude, with all its ironic implications, did wonders to relieve the tensions of a politicized Buffalo winter. When I came back from Oregon, I wanted to talk with Richard. I felt too privileged to bear a grudge, too fond of our relationship to remember only our last encounter.

When I call, he seems pleased to hear from me, and when I ask if I can stop by he says, *of course, but can I come between three-thirty and five?* It will be better if no one else is there.

After our most recent meeting, I'm not at ease in the midst of his symbols: a poster of Mao; a Venceremos banner; a number of Black Panther buttons attached to burlap curtains; the stale, sweet muskiness of grass and incense; a Dylan poster, of course. Richard points me to the sofa. "Too many people have crashed on it, but it's comfortable."

He takes a record out of the pile ledged against the couch. It is a Leonard Cohen album. He is sparing me hard rock, acid rock; we are off to a good start. He knows I would prefer a ballad, something folksy, or jazz: Pete Seeger, Louis Armstrong, Charlie Parker.

It feels good listening to the music. I find that I like Cohen's lyrics. "Just flow with it," Richard says. "Just let what's inside you *happen.*"

My usual annoyance at his language rises, and then, under the spell of the music, I relax.

"What are you feeling?" I ask.

"I'll show you."

Richard walks upstairs slowly, twisting his neck tortuously from side to side. An old football injury hasn't let up. I follow him.

"Let me show you something."

I watch Richard as he walks to the back of the bed, an old brass one, and points to the red curtain hanging evenly behind it. I am reminded of the synagogue, the red velvet curtain concealing the Torah. I'm surprised that Richard has such a luxurious and resplendent curtain in his room; it is out of place. I can't imagine what he'll show me.

With ceremony, he draws the curtain back: a shotgun, oiled, slick, shiny, hangs on the wall by its buckle strap.

"What's that for, Richard?" I haven't seen a rifle close up since peacetime basic training a decade before. It looks more lethal now— especially enshrined as it is—because of its glorification and the possibility of Richard's using it. "What in God's name is that for?"

"In case we need it."

"Need it for what?"

"For the strike. We're not going to lose our pride. They can take away everything else, but they can't have that."

"If the police ever come here, Richard, you'll be slaughtered. So long as you've got that thing, you'll be killed."

"We're not going to give up our pride. We'll defend ourselves."

"Get rid of the gun, Richard. Promise me you'll get rid of the gun."

"Why?"

"I don't want you to get killed. It's as simple as that. Enough people are getting killed. And Bunny needs you. Don't be a god-damned fool and get killed for a symbol. If there's a revolution, go out in the street and get killed, if you want, but not for a symbol."

He looks at me with softness in his eyes, "They've taken so much from us. Where will it stop? Tell me and I'll get rid of the gun."

"Promise me you'll give it up for six months," I say. "If the war hasn't stopped, we'll go over it then, okay? Promise me."

He shakes my hand, and I can feel his relief. I am enough on the other side to make an impression, but in the last analysis, he can trust me.

I didn't call to find out if Richard had given up the gun. I really didn't want to know what he, or his collective, was up to. It was best to stay away until I heard from him, or until the climate on campus had changed.

When I heard next from Richard, it was to testify in his behalf at a trial on campus. He had already been acquitted in city court on arson charges (he hadn't wanted to drag me into that), but *could I come on campus and be a witness?* Reluctantly, I said I would. I trusted him not to put me in a position where I might have to lie. People I knew lied only to themselves, if they could get away with it, not to others.

The chief witness at the trial, a liberal historian, claimed to have seen Richard near the building where the arson had taken place. The fact that he had been harassed by Richard and some of his friends at a faculty meeting over ROTC came out under cross-examination.

Perhaps the historian was not going out of his way to implicate Richard, but I knew his testimony would not damage his long-range ambition to become a college president. It wasn't so unusual for administrators to walk over the rubble and through the teargas to a better job.

Then it was my turn. No one asked if I had seen Richard or this, or that, or if I knew whom he lived with. I would have said nothing about the shotgun anyway, I'm sure of that. Could I imagine him committing an act of arson? *I could not imagine him involved in a random firebombing,* I said. I wanted to believe that; I never asked Richard if he was.

Richard was acquitted and allowed to stay in school, but I knew that he wasn't likely to stick around much longer. He had merely wanted to defend himself against false charges, to insist on his rights. A month after the trial, he decided to leave school and go west.

Succumbing to a need to mark his passage, I plan a small farewell party for Richard. It's a quiet evening as he and I sit on my porch, waiting for the group of friends to arrive, listening to old records: Judy Collins, the Beatles, early Dylan. We talk about what people will do in the summer. For months the Buffalo campus had been bitterly entangled. Cambodia and Kent State put an abrupt and seeming end to student protest. If this was ever fun on California campuses, it isn't in Buffalo where the winters are hard and long.

I can't believe, standing on the porch with the oak trees full in June and a cool breeze coming over Lake Erie, that a month or so before we had all felt near the edge of catastrophe. I'm relieved, but feel empty, incomplete. I need a greater sense of resolution. Where is everyone? Why is the campus empty now? Why doesn't anyone call me at three in the morning asking for course credit to go west? What happened to the lost soul who called himself The Young Stalinist for the Apocalypse? As the porch fills with guests I sit in a circle with them, observe, listen, try to figure out how we've gotten here.

Richard leans against Janet, leader of the Women's Coalition.

"How's the Perle Mesta of the Left?" he asks.

"What will you do this summer?" Janet asks.

"The question is not what will I do this summer, but how I can support myself till September."

"What happens then?" David asks, still wearing a red and black CP [Communist Party] pin on the lapel of the one Brooks Brothers Harris tweed jacket he has worn all through his post-Ivy League Vietnam years. He has come with Janet in tow. For all his ideology of sharing, he's somewhat ill at ease with Richard playing up to Janet.

"I guess I'll go west," Richard says, "like a stoned Horace Greeley."

"I've always wanted to go west," Janet says. "My real mother lives somewhere out there, I know, and my stepmother had all her advanced Girl Scout training in Yosemite. She says it's beautiful."

"It sounds absurd," Richard says. "Anyway, I'm not sure I believe you. The history we wanted to make may be on the run, but we don't have to turn it all into parody tonight."

"Hey, stay cool," Fred says, putting *Sergeant Pepper* on the phonograph. "There's still mystery and magic left; they can't take that away from us." No one says anything. He passes a large joint around. Fred has been stoned for three years.

David laughs, "Do you want to put us in orbit?"

"We've got the rest of our lives to be mellow," Fred says.

He passes the joint around, but no one is too interested in getting high. I pretend to inhale.

"I've gotten a job," he says, "I've found a way to escape the family business. I'm not going to let my father and brother cut off my balls with their petty capitalist schemes. I'm going to carry a line for a chain of head shops up and down the Eastern Seaboard. You should see the trunk of my car. It's filled with Zig-Zag paper, incense, one deflated water bed, and some beautiful photographs of breast feeding and natural childbirth scenes."

Fred looks hurt when we laugh slightly at what he is saying.

"It's a good job," he says. "People out there need these things."

"Too many people like you thought we could forget the war with dope," David says.

"Hey, folks, this is a farewell party for Richard, remember?" Fred says.

"Right on," Janet says, "right on to California."

"Thanks," Richard says. He goes on in earnest. "Since this party is in my honor, and I'm just a little stoned, I'd like to ask one thing. I'd like us to hold hands and sing, 'We Shall Overcome.' "

It's an impossible request, and Richard is probably the only one who could make it and pull it off. We humor him, joining hands, and begin to murmur the words. I discover that I am, after a few suppressed parodies, singing the song with everyone else.

When it ends, Richard raises a clenched fist. He is poised between sincerity and theatricality. Neither he nor I can resolve the contradiction, so when he moves to the top of the stairway, I embrace him and send him on his way.

The Self: After Vietnam

Education and Community **12**

Here on the Maine coast, I can imagine, for the first time since Kent State, an education for the future. The cycles of nature are forcibly present, and traditional patterns of village life are ongoing. At this distance, even our most recent severe fractures seem capable of healing. For a brief moment, I have the familiar American impulse to name and catalogue the world in its concreteness and specificity; to draw order from the bedrock of natural phenomena. I stand at the edge, as I see it, of learning, of a need to express and pattern unyielding experience through language.

The transformation of nature into culture seems understandable on this unprotected shore. The task of shaping images of what we have been and might be (and of handing down this portraiture through time) becomes comprehensible where life is still lived on a human scale. The malaise of postnineteenth century culture and the remedies proposed to deal with it do not apply here. Stripped bare and laid open to the bone, this village can represent the best of the past and a possible model of the future, if only as an object of meditation.

Away from the urban tangle and multiversity, I can still believe

---

This essay is reprinted with permission from *Sphinx*, Winter 1976.

in a group having knowledge of one another; of experiencing together and holding in common shared responses to symbolic performances that might be as binding as ritual. In short, this small coastal town, despite its puritanism, has the potentialities of a civilizing model. The outlines of a human community and polis are visible, so I would like to think.

But it becomes clear, when summer is over, that our community life—the moral crucible of any culture—has been severely damaged.

When I return to teaching English at the end of summer, it is hard to believe that a literary culture could, really, correct this common failure in any way. But I cannot accept alternate propositions that advance, say, mathematics and music as the foundations of a new literacy; though, clearly, a firm sense of the history of science and music, their methods of validation and internationalism, should be part of modern man's syntax.

We have heard about the death of the word, the disappearance of art, the failure of sequential patterns of reasoning.

> An advance in art is considered to take place to the degree that art divests itself of the characteristics of art. Whatever mode comes closest to a score of zero for the art object is assigned the foreground position.[1]

Critics have submitted too easily, though, to the assertion of post-culture. Language is central to our image of man. Calling it into question calls for an end to this humanness. Still, it is true that many American students have been uncomfortable with language and literature as primary modes of expression. The reasons for this are elusive, but there are some dominant tendencies:

• For most contemporary students, the terms of pre-1945 literature do not represent the symbolic and semiotic field through which they move and have moved. The idea of a close relationship between literature and community is itself now a literary construct. Literature and community are not corollary notions for our students. Concrete examples of shared literary experience, of a resonating literary community, are simply absent. The writer is seen, at best, as someone who works in private and makes money in public.

Shakespeare's London, Gertrude Stein's Paris, and even E. B. White's New York are the stuff of biography and memoirs. If there is a cult of the poet on many campuses, this should not be taken as a sign of community. The poet has become, in many ways, a sacred *celebrity* for our time. In America, we characteristically put someone at the head of the group and say: Perform for us, tell us who we are. Our poets are on tour, they read to us, but are they part of us?

• Except for a few advocates of popular mythology, most literary critics and scholars take as subject matter icons and emblems that are sealed off in history, that do not constitute our everyday field of perception. There is a dramatic failure of correspondence between the visual anthropology, so to speak, of TV, current film, photojournalism, and the symbolic design of our established texts and critical models.

• Writing and moral survival are not coordinate terms for the contemporary student: there is no longer the confluence of historical mission and literacy that was keenly felt from Marx to Orwell and Camus. Even as late as the 1950s, writing took its place in the undergraduate community as a mode of sanity in a culture manipulated by advertising language, in a culture given over to mass forms of expression.

For the student of the fifties, writing and integrity were adjunct functions. There has been in America in the 1960s a turning away from privacy as a means of survival. Group action and gesture have challenged privacy, and the word has not remained dominant in this shift. The new Left did generate articulate spokesmen and a new generation of historians, but they were not, finally, the voices who were heard by a generation.

The literate vanguard were too academic all along for those who wanted to surf, or trip, into the future. When Vietnam "ended," those

who had been articulate critics of the society found that only aca-
demics (word-men) were left to listen, and so many protesters went,
alas, to graduate schools. After Vietnam, language surrendered even
more to rock, and then there was silence.

  • Privacy has not merely been pushed to the margin of importance. From a variety of perspectives, it is seen as a causal element in
the fragmentary quality of Western life. Most important in the assault
upon privacy has been the influence, if not the exact text, of Marshall
McLuhan. For McLuhan, the transition from aural and tribal culture
through the Renaissance ideal of individual man to the radical Protes-
tant insistence upon the literalness of the word points to the origins
of alienated and dissociated modern man.

  For youth after McLuhan, verbal facility and egocentrism are
often coordinate terms, and even when language moves beyond
privacy in the service of social issues, it is soon indicted as rhetoric. A
distinguishing feature of the sixties was the number of literate books
—composed in privacy—signalling the end of privacy.

  • Visual and mixed media have become the new literacies. The
great American movie equals, if not replaces, the great American
novel as the *literate* undergraduate dream. If delayed gratification has
been an unacceptable psychological concept for this generation, so
has *suspended* narrative judgment and action.

  Temporal orderings of events have been significantly replaced, as
preferred orders, by the desire for simultaneous, spatial renderings.
In practical terms, this means that a group of students, given a chance
to say what it wants and values, would rather talk about their lives
than read the lives of the poets; would rather become a self-analytic
group than read Freud; would rather see a video replay of their
group interaction than study the translation of a novel into film.

  • In this sense, the classic modern moment is passing, is perhaps
over. The world of Picasso, Eliot, Stravinsky, and Joyce has given
way to a new constellation. This shift from the modern to the postmodern represents a turn from the last effort to work with established

patterns of congruence and symmetry to a period of openness and randomness.

Relativism has replaced moral irony as a technique of aesthetic organization. There are no rigid fields in the old sense: literature has become visual; environments are seized as aesthetic spaces; and aesthetic spaces have become political settings.

George Steiner locates the shift from modern to postmodern tendencies in broad outline, as clearly, I think, as any recent commentator:

> They include the ideology of the "happening" and of autodestructive artifacts, with their emphasis on the immediacy, unrepeatability, and ephemeral medium of the work. Aleatory music is a striking case of the diminution of creative authority in favor of collaborative, spontaneous shadow-play (Werner Henze has declared that there is exploitation and the menace of arbitrary power in the very function of the composer). More and more literary texts and works of art now offer themselves as collective and/or anonymous. The poetics of ecstasy and of group feeling regard the imprint of a single "great name" on the process of creation as archaic vanity. The audience is no longer an informed echo to the artist's talent, a respondent to and transmitter of his singular enterprise; it is joint creator in a conglomerate of freewheeling, participatory impulse. Away with the presumptions of performance in a classic *oeuvre*, away with masters.[2]

It hardly makes sense to lament old classificatory and Aristotelian approaches to knowledge in this atmosphere. We must, instead, struggle for new syntheses of tradition and emergent sensibilities. Yesterday's wind has eased up, and there is quiet activity on the mudflats. It seems fitting again to be writing here about an education for the future. Only a few miles away, one of the New World's early land deeds was granted by the Indians. A promise of newness lingers.

• We start, then, with the initial premise that community life is in a shambles, that we are perceived by our neighbors as having a small degree of selfsameness. For most of us, each day is a struggle to

impress ourselves upon an unanswering environment. It is in many ways a fictive enterprise because we achieve selfsameness not in isolation but through continuous interactions with a fairly stable community. The situation in our universities is a mirror image of the larger social situation. Our schools are no better or worse than our society demands them to be. Each semester is a failed possibility. An emergent community within a class surfaces at the end of a semester, one or two students leave as friends, perhaps hand in hand, and only the idea of a course remains.

This has always been the experience of university: to carve an enclave out of the larger, imperfect whole. But it will not do at our advanced moment of disrepair. The problem of literature and community is only an instance of the larger problem. The question is, then, what can we do to create a symbolically coherent community in a society that is neither symbolic nor communal in any integrative sense. We cannot expect to remake the university or the society, but we can try to articulate and enact paradigms of community behavior, so that the context in which knowledge is gained may be as compelling as the knowledge itself. Modes of insight and response, styles of inquiry and discourse endure long after any item of information is forgotten.

It would follow that an intensive experience of community life both within and outside of the university should be encouraged. So long as the boundaries and scale of the experience are observable and limited (a city neighborhood, a cooperative living project, a foreign village, etc.), a person might be in a position to make comparative judgments about the quality of life and the institutions which support each. There is now sufficient and exciting bibliography in the areas of local history, American Studies, and sociology to prepare the student for this living investigative venture: e.g., Robert Coles's *Children of Crisis,* Lewis's *Children of Sanchez,* and Bettleheim's *Children of the Dream.* Instead of "going west" or "east," a typical undergraduate formulation (a picaresque journey fashioned, perhaps, more after literature than life, a journey lacking moral exactness), the kind of experience I am suggesting would keep personal goals and cultural needs in mind.

Any group of people who gather together with some frequency—for whatever purpose—constitutes a kind of community whose potential, even reality, often goes unexplored. For teachers, this community is the classroom. It would seem worthwhile for students to have some experience of group awareness. Contemporary theatre and dance offer opportunities for achieving greater degrees of freedom through discipline; of training one's total system in order to gain access to enlarged areas of sensory awareness.

In our age of systems analysis, of ecosystems and environmental aesthetics, it is historically regressive to isolate one sensorial function or mental faculty from another, to isolate the individual from group dynamics. We need now to look for synergistic models. If we look at the best examples of contemporary theatre and dance, we find a classic sense of discipline. New theatre and dance (Twyla Tharp) do not renounce rigor; rather, they apply rigor to different ends, allowing the performer to realize himself and the director's or choreographer's concept at one and the same time. Because of the increased reciprocity between idea and enactor of idea, a margin of spontaneity and uncertainty can be left unresolved.

Theatre and dance offer special possibilities for general education because they approach the rhythms and actualities of everyday life: through dance and theatre training, we can hope that the student will respond to art and ideas with increased sensory awareness which would also mean increased attentiveness to others. The function of this training would be not only to provide self-awareness but, just as important, to demonstrate that one's actions and potential actions are shaped by and shape the living context in which one moves.

Dance and theatre training would be valuable experience in themselves. They would also provide a groundwork for verbal interactions of various kinds. If one has achieved a measure of body freedom and relatedness, then a measure of verbal freedom should follow. If one's expressive play gestures can be accepted, and if one's *body self*—our most basic formulation of ourselves—can be accepted, then more sophisticated areas of self should gain articulation with greater ease and grace.

Certain moves in this direction were made during the sixties, of course, both within and without the university, but in my model it makes little sense to strive for verbal interaction and body freedom simultaneously. There is, to be sure, a regressive element in my program, and it is precisely for this reason that a separate context should be preserved for this kind of probing.

My assumption here is threefold: that heightened body awareness will, in time, prepare the way for modes of cognition; that given the freedom to express oneself in nonverbal terms, one will naturally want to move towards abstract formulations; that there is a need and a tendency, as Stuart Hampshire notes, for the "unsocialized levels of the mind" to be "made accessible to intelligence."[3] We need to pay attention to separate faculties in the early stages of an integrative approach to education and not rush headlong into easy synthetic formulations.

• Some study of Western symbology would seem to be in order, especially those approaches to symbol that can, without difficulty, bridge the gap between high and low culture, methods that get at underlying structures and patterns. Northrop Frye's *Anatomy of Criticism* is an exemplary "structural" work in this mode.

It is not possible to imagine that the ordinary field of American symbolic life will change very much in the years to come. Instead of being merely contemptuous of popular culture, we should prepare students to locate the deep and abiding mythic patterns embedded in popular culture. We might even argue that popular culture contains, in a limited sense, the "truths" of our social life—the ongoing wishes and expectations of a social group; that serious literature reflects the great constructive and innovative visions. It does not seem crucial to me whether this task is done by Jungians, Freudians, or structural anthropologists. What matters is that undergraduates have the experience of connecting serious disciplines with the ingredients of everyday life.

• Liberal educators do not, in the main, associate an education in the humanities with a sense of task or project, with discovering how what they teach can be applied specifically to individual students. But there must surely be ways of connecting the concrete aims of individual students and the needs of society with the broad aims of general education. If we cannot find ways of making these connections, we will continue to *produce* students who regard their education only as a maze from which they have escaped.

Robert Frost once suggested that students should not enter college until they could say what they wanted to know. Perhaps this is not possible, but I would think the first step toward solving this problem would be to recognize it as a problem. Specifically, we should consider the first year of university life as a crucial year and study (see the Electronic College of the First Year) intensively how, in that year, students might begin to conceptualize what their education could be.

In one way or other, students and an informed teacher must come together to effect some synthesis between task and field. Perhaps a seminar on goals and their ramifications could take place in this first year. Part of this first year reform should be a conference on the future. Very often the problem for an undergraduate is that he cannot see the unfolding meaning of what he is doing; this is especially important because there is not a stable community against which a sense of growth and the complications of that growth can be weighed and evaluated.

• Style, as we understood it in the fifties, pointed to the particular and unique act of voicing that a writer was able to impress upon the text. Because the text was taken to be an autonomous structure, it followed naturally that the writer's voice (his persona) was a disembodied creation. For the student of literature, the cultivation of style was equivalent to making a self in words, a self-as-subject to be placed in a text as world-in-itself.

This critical emphasis on "voicing" and "artifact" encouraged us, then undergraduates, to become ventriloquists of sorts. In an attempt to create our voices, we often ended up "throwing them." So that, perhaps without intention, we found ourselves alienated from ourselves in the act of creating ourselves. From the perspective of the created self, it was a short step to an exalted sense of privacy and pride in becoming something like a living hieroglyph.

There is, no doubt, some connection between the aesthetic preference for the great modernist hieroglyphs (Joyce, Eliot, and Pound) in the fifties and the stylistic effort to achieve individual voicing. In this sense, it was as if we were writing to please ourselves as critics, or putting it another way, as if we were writing to satisfy the critical standards of the moment. How can selfhood and style be brought into meaningful relation? How can stylistic sophistication be applied in the service of self-realization? Most important in all of this is the recognition that human identity, though capable of variation, cannot be willed anew, cannot be willed into being as a supreme fiction. If we create a self, it is in the sense that we edit and select the most relevant and indicative details to reveal the self in clearest outline and find through analogy and metaphor previously undiscovered dimensions of selfhood.

If we keep this clearly in mind, we will not so much think of voice as creating a self as giving a tonality to a form of emotion and cognition already present and imminent in the self. At best we imprint ourselves upon our code; at worst we use the code without self-consciousness. Every utterance suggests a possible future and echoes a past. We ought to be aware of this.

• In many ways, the notion of categories has given way to the open field; this can be seen clearly in the turn towards mysticism, new awareness and use of media, and in skepticism toward curricular structure. The essential problem, as I see it, is the misconception, from the outset, that there are inflexibly defined fields; that there exist orderings of experience separate from the human standpoint of the individual observer. Students have, in this sense, rebelled against a devaluation of their role as knowers. If each discipline were to emphasize its constructive biases, were to dramatize the role of style and intuition in the development of that discipline, students would not want to separate totally objective and subjective artistic and scientific formulations. If we could dismantle myths of severe objectivity, then we could oppose unexamined subjectivity. Texts are available on this issue: Thomas S. Kuhn, *The Structure of Scientific Revolutions;* Peter L. Berger and Thomas Luckman, *The Social Construction of Reality;* Michael Polyani, *Personal Knowledge.*

• The structure of the university—with its too numerous departments, majors, centers, research groups—testifies to the "progressive" fragmentation of modern man. We have for some time been losing our common sense, our commonality. What an education of the future must do is stress the whole organism in relationship to a knowable community. A healthy nationalism and internationalism should be biomorphic, taking growth and interaction as its cues at every turn. When we let part of ourselves get objectified as a separate function, when we surrender our communities to abstract national goals, when our cultures do not symbolize what we are becoming, then the way has been cleared for ideological intrusions which serve as false orderings of human affairs. We know all too well from twentieth century history that men will destroy to preserve a myth of order.

Our image of order should be organic, with body and mind evolving as a system; our image of community (including education) should be bionomic, favoring those symbolic forms which look back to or re-create *harmony* between man and his environment at all levels.[4]

In most aspects of artistic, cultural, and scientific awareness from the end of the nineteenth century to the present—from relativity theory and cubism to Living Theatre and the new fiction of self-consciousness—the relationship between the observer and the observed has become confused and, in some radical instances, fused.

An extreme metaphor for this situation would be an astrophysicist looking into galactic space and seeing his eye looking into deep space. Contemporary experimenters in both art and science have become aware of personal and cultural *style* as paradigms and variables of inquiry.[1] No longer can we as teachers—any more or less than sculptors or historians—make fixed claims about objective consciousness.[2]

As teachers, we participate actively in knowing what we claim to know, but as teachers, we have not, in the main, kept up with the advanced epistemological concepts of our time and admitted this participation. We have yet to recognize the shape of selfhood as a parameter of knowledge—our chief glory and limitation.

For these reasons, I am going to speak personally here. I come to this relationship between knowledge and autobiography in the broad-

---

This essay is reprinted with permission from *New Directions in Teaching,* Fall 1972.

est sense with a special urging, because in many ways I feel that my own education pushed me in another direction. Perhaps it would be more just to say that the cultural moment of my undergraduate years (1954 to 1959) meshed with the intellectual predisposition of my college during those years to make me feel that there was in the life of the mind no place for *selfhood,* as I now begin to understand it in the context of humanistic psychology.

We were encouraged, especially in our freshman English course, to examine the way in which language shaped our experience. We were, I now know, put onto some of the more vexing implications of Benjamin Lee Whorf and Ludwig Wittgenstein without being told about it, but we were not asked to see the connection between our language and our *basic needs*—if I may use a phrase that will call up, as I mean it to do, intimations of Freud, Karen Horney, Erik Erikson, Alfred Adler, and Abraham Maslow. We were asked to express our language, but not *ourselves* in and through language.

Because language was seen *as self* and not as the expression of an *emergent self* that constantly eludes definition and becomes somewhat obsolete as one pushes deeper through materials inside and outside the self, certain assumptions were made in our course of study, assumptions I internalized and now resist.

Some of the favored academic writers of that moment were Jane Austen and Henry James, to name two novelists, and T. S. Eliot and Donne, to name two poets. Drama didn't count for much in those conflictless, somnambulant Eisenhower years. In all cases, these writers were extolled for their *conscious* control of experience, their awareness of form (literary, not evolutionary or teleological), and for their impersonality; ironically, theories of *persona,* mask, negative capability, antiself and *self as speaker* haunted my terribly personal late-adolescent dreams.

Unexpressed were denials of sexuality, politics, and revelation; denials of any struggle for self-realization that called for the renunciation of language in action or the falling away from language into the enfolding silence of selfhood.

But I was eager to make it, and I learned quickly how to write finished, if not superior, New Critical papers. When my freshman English instructor, the son of a famous poet of the twenties, told me that my passion for Thomas Wolfe was somewhat embarrassing, I believed him. And when a brilliant, intellectually nihilistic professor told me in my senior year that spring was a literary convention, not a groundswell breaking the mind's freeze, I almost believed him. A residual New York schoolyard skepticism made me think him somewhat lunatic, however, and I couldn't really believe, after hooksliding on a concrete schoolyard for so many years, that the lilacs pressing off the trellis into my room were a mere convention.

Still, I didn't reject him outright, as Frost might have said, and I wonder even now, in dark moments, if the sense of "moral evolution" I now embrace isn't another fiction, another literary mode.[3]

So when I first set out to teach in 1962, I carried the *word* forth and believed I could save provincial souls from confusion and embarrassment by making them see that *they were what they wrote.* A comma set here, a parallel construction shaped up there, a margin full of mandates to *expand, modify,* and *revise*—all these injunctions seemed salvationary and terribly important as they still do, and I could hear—in my inner ear—the approving voices of former professors, especially the one who had so dispatched Thomas Wolfe (he's entered a religious order recently, I hear).

After a few years, I realized that it wouldn't be enough for me to teach freshman composition as I understood the task. I had been accustomed for four years to lead from ideas and the enthusiasm generated by them to writing, but my students did not respond to this approach. They were afraid to participate, and I knew intuitively that their fears were related to the class as a group. I knew also that my role as an imported "authority" from Ann Arbor supported their fears.

In a moment of creative desperation, I left the room one day—a moment I have reported—and asked the class to break up into small groups to discuss a question I had put to them and to assign a spokesman for the group. As soon as I left the room, I heard the hum of voices and felt, in a way unclear to me then, that I was setting out on a new path in education for myself. I later wrote about that experience and others, and I want here to summarize some of my recent feelings and thoughts.[4]

Many American students fear self-exposure and the rejection of their feelings by peers and teachers. The classroom becomes for many students a context in which they experience again—for the thousandth time—uncomfortable silence and loneliness.[5] There are many ways, however, in which this situation can be faced; many ways in which human growth can be facilitated.

Most of these methods call upon the teacher to establish an atmosphere of trust in which the group can share feelings and validate each other's experience, but all too often the teacher leaves out of these sharing experiences his own gift—even if it is the gift of his loneliness and isolation.

What I am suggesting here is that we, along with our students, might become in class—at crucial moments—*autobiographers of the now:* that we share with our students what we are thinking and feeling in the *act* of teaching and demonstrate that many of their expectations and fears are common to us; that we differ more in the roles we play than in our common humanity.

If we can let our humanity break through our roles in this way, we will find that our students may follow suit.[6] Students will not encounter one another or us until an atmosphere of trust has been established, and trust will not be established until someone, perhaps the teacher, will say implicitly, "This is how I feel now; I know you will accept and respect me, if not my point of view."

The kind of teaching I am advancing calls for great tact, subtlety and skill. Two passages from Katherine Anne Porter's masterful short story "Holiday" will help to make my point. The narrator, who has moved from a position of exile to one of community, by participating in the life of an inbred German-American Texas family, says after the death of the matriarch of the community:

> They wept away the hard core of secret trouble that is in the heart of each separate man, secure in a communal grief; in sharing it, they consoled each other.[7]

What Katherine Anne Porter dramatizes for us is the way we only can be authentically alone, as opposed to lonely, when we are "secure in a communal" awareness—be it grief or joy.

I believe in the fervid attempt to express oneself through language. It is only through language, or other symbolic and semiotic gestures, that one has a chance *to relate oneself to the world knowingly.* Still, language is not the *self.* But in a paradoxical sense we can teach ourselves and our students who we are both by pressing language to a limit and by recognizing that there is a voice beneath the *I* that narrates, a private voice that is as valid as the crafted public voice to which we give utterance.

As teachers, we can sanction both voices and hope for integration. If we don't, our students are likely to remain lonely because they will feel an unacknowledged tension between the private and public spheres of selfhood, and they will not try to close this distance unless the integrity of the silent self, as well as the difficulty of giving it words, is spoken for. Too often in our teaching, we mistake emergence for stammering.

At another point in "Holiday," the narrator says:

> I loved that silence which means freedom from the constant pressure of other minds and other opinions and other feelings, that freedom to fold up in quiet and go back to my own center, to find out again, for it is always a rediscovery, what kind of creature it is that rules me finally, makes all the decisions no matter who thinks they make them, even I; who little by little takes everything away except the one thing I cannot

live without, and who will one day say, "Now I am all you have left—take me."[8]

In an atmosphere of trust—an atmosphere free from the pressure of other minds and opinions—we can encourage in ourselves and in our students the possibility of rediscovering our centers and letting those centers emerge in writing. We can also, through recognizing the integrity of this center, allow our students to "fold up" without making them bear the burden of failure; without making them feel that they must use words, at any cost, to express themselves.

By sanctioning "that freedom to fold up in quiet," we can, in a curious way, make speech possible because, as I have suggested, the fear of not expressing oneself *wholly* in words has been removed. By recognizing the center of being, the self that encompasses the linguistic "I," those of us who have attempted various modes of encounter techniques in our classes can avoid an assault upon the other in the name of openness, an assault that can be as devastating as domination of the other through authoritarianism.

If our project is the writing of autobiography by students in the hope that self-reference is an important activity in a mass computerized society, we should not put our students in a position where we seem to be saying *that self and language are equivalent.* It is too severe a claim, and even a mind as finely wrought as Henry James moved balletically around his unspoken center. Moreover, the demand for instant openness will close doors we meant to open.

By relaxing our expectations, recognizing emergent selfhood, we can, perhaps, establish a mutuality between self and other, between "I" and self that is probably the most any of us can achieve.[9]

As I reflect upon what I have said, it occurs to me that my concern for conservation of selfhood falls into place with the general concern for ecological harmony that we are seeking in the society as a whole. Karen Horney brings this to mind when she comments about the withdrawal of love:

All these withdrawals entail a considerable *waste* [italics mine] of energy and often much misery. But the most ruinous aspect of them is that we lose interest in our real self because we are not proud of it.[10]

Self-realization and an authentic aloneness of self-centeredness are not exclusive terms, though they tend to be in our thinking about such matters; true aloneness does not preclude interaction and (*Gemeinschaftgefuhl*) social interest. Indeed, the more we accept ourselves, the less narcissistic we may become and the more capable of sharing with others.

If we want to avoid psychological and spiritual waste and at the same time to encourage introspection, we must honor the voice that says: "Now I am all you have left—take me." If we do not honor that voice, aloneness may turn into the waste of loneliness, and the center will neither unfold, nor fold up, in creative quietness.

On 13 January 1970, *Look* forecast an onrushing future of New Sex, New Politics, New Schools, and the Human Revolution. In this "special issue about the seventies," George B. Leonard, John Holt, and Gloria Steinem, to name a few of the contributors, recorded their seismographic response to the new vibrations pulsating across the land.

After five years dominated by dissent on campuses and in the streets and a decade of apocalyptic thinking—by Norman O. Brown, Herbert Marcuse, R. D. Laing, Paul Goodman, Buckminster Fuller, and Marshall McLuhan, among others—there seemed nothing "special about these prophecies of a liberated, self-centered, decentralized, and bio-oriented America—unless it was the familiarity of these millennial claims.

Yet less than two years later, the *New York Times* pronounced on its front page: "Youth Rebellion of Sixties Waning" (24 October 1971), and not long afterward (30 January 1972), "Metamorphosis of the Campus Radical," an essay in the *New York Times Magazine,* reported a new era of quietude and responsible radicalism.

I did not agree wholly with this unveiling of a generation's tombstone; there were and are still, after all, signs of innovation and redirected energies on campus and in the society, but it was self-evident to close observers of American society, especially those on campus and in the classroom (an accurate theatre of evolving and shifting consciousness), that these elegiac forecasts were *essentially* correct. This does not mean that there will be no more struggle in America, that the radical impulse is dead. But it does mean that tactics will be less incendiary, expectations scaled down, and mass support diminished.

Conflict will persist against a tide of nostalgia (*Summer of '42, The Last Picture Show,* Humphrey Bogart and James Dean festivals), but those riding the wave of the future, whether they have a media vision of an *expanded cinema* or one of political ecstasy, should know that the promised land continues to elude us.

Where two and three years ago, for instance, my students demanded and responded to self-actualizing classroom experiences, Esalen enactments, educational analogues of encounter groups and sensitivity training, they now are beginning to ask for structured courses and "new" old curricula that will *ensure* a coherent understanding of American and English literature; that will make possible getting into a "good" graduate school and, later, landing a job.

Where even last spring (1971), only one year after Kent State, Cambodia, and a bitter strike on our campus, my students preferred to write and share their own poems rather than read established poets like Yeats and T. S. Eliot (only Allen Ginsberg and Gary Snyder seemed at that time to be exempt from trials of relevance and obsolescence), my students this semester would rather, in a course on the modern short story, explicate D. H. Lawrence, Eudora Welty, William Faulkner, J. F. Powers, and Edith Wharton than write their own stories or use the stories we are reading for introspective ends.

Last semester (fall 1971) when a graduate student of small group dynamics (following the model of Slater in *Microcosm*), who had been observing my class, announced to the group before Christmas that I had been too permissive and friendly to allow the class *to murder me symbolically,* she was met with laughter and derision. Two years ago, under the sway of tribal and ritualistic pressures, it might have all seemed plausible as well as serious.

Most teachers walk a tight-rope and try to respond to the needs of students without compromising their own integrity and sense of social and individual relevance and function. This is especially true for teachers of literature and the humanities whose disciplines and objects of engagement dramatize the encounter of individual and historical consciousness (in this case, my ongoing, though restrained, interest in developmental learning set against opposing tendencies in many of my students); whose disciplines dramatize the importance of literature in making this encounter explicable and affective.[1]

Even writers we might regard as hermetic and autotelic, from Joyce to Borges, reflect in the structure and content of their "fabulous" fictions the felt needs of the community. All writing and teaching is anthropological. There is no getting around that, nor should we want to. In the dialog between self and society and in the internalized drama of self-other-world lies our individual humanity and his torical validation. However protean and pseudopodic one may take himself to be as a teacher and intellectual, however capable of positing new worlds, he will, only at his peril, lose touch with reality.[2]

So the question has become for me and some of my students: how can the significant gains of the sixties—personal, social, and political liberation, the careful nurturing of individual and social energy—how can these introspective, ecological, and participatory gains be preserved without giving way to what has come to be felt as an overreaching of boundaries, an excessive and, in many cases, irreparable testing of social and perceptual limits?[3]

And, conversely, how can we *not* give way, *not* let go, without becoming inertial, entropic drop-ins, without *regressing in the service of the fifties*? Especially at a time when even Nixon has met Mao and Chou En-lai, has crossed the Great Ocean to signal the end of the fifties.

This question is a difficult one for me, one that I am in the process of working out and which I find distressing because I, too, feel a pull towards structure at the same time that I regard the best of my own experiments in education and intellectual transformation during the middle-to-late sixties as valuable. For the moment, I have fixed my mind on a possible resolution of this conflict: a new and redefined sense of style.

In the fifties, to the second generation of New Critics entrenched in the university (to those teachers who had been shaped by the seminal works of Eliot, Pound, Brooks, Tate, Ransom, Empson, I. A. Richards), literary style meant those aspects of the literary text that gave it organic and intrinsic wholeness; those formal qualities of tone, image, voice, diction, persona, tenor, paradox, and ambiguity that seemed to make the work autonomous and self-referential, a *world* unto itself.[4]

This point of view and the vocabulary informing it were quite useful and teachable in their way. A good teacher could, within a month or two, put his students in a position to read a text closely, to make connections that felt almost technological in their exactness. By the time one was a senior, the tools had been interiorized and the student felt like an insider, a *critic* (the word had been sacralized) who could put Whitman in his place and stand against commerical and *kitsch* culture.

But this method made no distinction between self and style, between the narrative and syntactic "I" and the self. Biography and autobiography were ruled out because they implicated the life of the author and violated the text. Implied authors, value-systems, and historical contexts were declared out-of-bounds and alien to the text, and, xenophobically, one didn't read works in translation because only the original language could carry the meaning. Tolstoy gave way to Jane Austen, Proust to E. M. Forster: the McCarren Act found its mirror image in the literary establishment.

Because no distinction was made between self and language, a policy of containment, finding its equivalent in our foreign policy, prevailed. A set of tools was developed to decipher difficult texts, the early modern hieroglyphs ("The Waste Land," *Ulysses*). Invariably, these works gave way to analysis and yielded up their formal symmetry. In an age of secrecy and cold war intrigue, hermeneutics flourished.

For all its usefulness and refinement of consciousness, this method, put simply, failed to pay attention to history and the less accessible reaches of the self. It failed to see the literary text as a mediating process of symbolization between self and world.[5]

It was as if one were to try to understand a child's language without reference to internal stimuli and the significant persons in the child's environment (*Umwelt*); as if one were to fail to see the child's emergent language in the context of a play space in which relationships between inner and outer reality are constantly being tested, just as later the creative adult tests new possibilities of inner and outer transactions through symbol and metaphor, new possibilities of transforming fantasy objects and relationships into social and cultural alternates.[6]

It is at this point that I can begin to imagine a way of moving backward and forward at the same time: towards the text *and* the self. This could be accomplished in a number of related ways. Instead of emphasizing style as a discrete phenomenon, literary style can be viewed as a version of an *identity theme,* an imprinting of identity that takes place within the society of infant and mother and is later capable of transformation and adaptive permutations.

I believe the proposition that man is distinct from the animals in not having an innate identity can avoid many pseudo controversies, and widen the scope of psychoanalytic understanding. But if the proposition that man has no innate identity is taken seriously, we must demonstrate how the human infant acquires an identity. I see the answer to this question in the "imprinting" of an identity on the human child by the mother. The mother does not convey a sense of identity to the infant but an identity: the child is the organ, the instrument for the fulfillment of the mother's unconscious needs. Out of the infinite potentialities within the human infant, the specific stimulus combination emanating from the individual mother "releases" one, and only one, concrete way of being this organ, this instrument. This "released" identity will be irreversible, and thus it will compel the child to find ways and means to realize this specific identity which the mother has imprinted upon it. The Innate Releaser Mechanism (124, 125) has, then, an analogy in the human infant insofar as there is an innately determined readiness in the human infant to react to the maternal stimulations with a "somatic obedience" experience. This "obedience" represents, however, fulfillment of the child's own needs: in being the instrument, the organ for the satisfaction of the maternal Otherness, the full symbiotic interaction of the two partners is realized for both of them. It would, however, be a mistake to see this "organ" or "instrumental" identity as too narrowly defined. The mother imprints upon the infant not an identity, but an "identity theme." This theme is irreversible, but it is capable of variations, variations that spell the difference between human creativity and "a destiny neurosis."[7]

We could, for example, in studying Lawrence or James, pay attention to the text, biography, letters, supporting documents, locate an essential "identity theme" (the "attached child," the "abandoned child") and see which transformations of, if not escape from, this theme make the work viable as a model of developmental necessity and metaphoric freedom.

We could also regard student writing *about* these texts *as texts themselves displaying the same governing principles:* the persistence of an identity theme and the possibility of transformation. A teacher would not only comment on a paper's "objective" value; he would also *make explicit* controlling metaphor, intractable points of view, recurrent habits of diction, and insistent thematic preoccupations.

This could be done as decorously with a student's paper as with a text and need not entail any psychoanalytic interpretation. It could remain descriptive and give the task of naming an identity theme to the student himself and let the student suggest desired transformations. Each paper, like a poem in the body of an author's poetry, could represent a partial statement of an identity theme and a partial attempt at adaptive and creative transformation.

James, for example, remained an "exile" to the end, but the extensions of this "theme" touch upon American history, Anglo-American relationships, familial configurations, aesthetic "distance," and self-definition. Lawrence's inability to demythologize the power of woman to create and destroy leads his characters to passionate unions and savage attacks; variations of this theme implicate the class structure (usually embodied by an upper class woman) and sanctify nature through a journey to the innermost folding of a flower. This deep ambivalence towards "attachment" leads him, as well, to philosophic statements of aloneness (Birkin in *Women in Love*) and primordial acts of rescue and compassion ("The Horsedealer's Daughter").[8]

We would not, in this context, so much assign a theme as encourage students to discover their own themes as they emerge congruently and contrastively with and against a work of literary art. In this way, cognitive and aesthetic patterns could be set in a developmental context. *How* we see and *why* we see the way we do would be brought together through examining *what* we see, what we take ourselves to be. With the work of Piaget and Bruner in mind at one end of the scale and Freud and Erikson at the other, we can focus on what they have in common—patterns of thought and symbol formation.

To my mind, this approach to teaching literature would separate teaching and psychotherapy without relinquishing connections between *reader response* and *psychic structure*. This thematic and transformational approach could take us back to the text without giving up the gains of applied psychoanalysis and the best insights of the human potential movement.

Reestablishing the boundary between the explication of a text and self-revelation, between the naming of an identity theme and free association, would make it possible to remain literary without retreating from personal experience. This approach to style would draw together, at least for me, the best of the fifties and sixties in an act of historical synthesis which is the ongoing challenge of teaching.

What we are going through now in American culture and higher education is not so much a waning as a reclaiming and consolidation of gains *beyond old boundaries and within overextended ones*—very much as Shakespeare's pastoral plays (and staged pastorals within these plays) test and go beyond limits of social, political, and sexual order and return with a humanized, an energized sense of order.[9]

Such a consolidation can only take place within the self, and it is no wonder that biographical and autobiographical texts are so popular, and that media presentations of historical biography (*Elizabeth, the Queen; Nicholas and Alexandra; The Forsythe Saga,* for example) are now so visible.

What I am urging is a form of autobiographical performance on the part of students—one that neither gives up the self for the text nor one that seals off the self from the enlarging perspectives of aesthetic experience. It is very much a *via media,* an intermediate area between student and text, where the contours of the *me* and *not-me* can be rehearsed.[10]

It is a return to style in the service of the self and a return to the self in the enactment of culturally meaningful symbolic gestures. To bring one's identity theme into contact with an established literary identity theme seems both relevant and pious, personal and selfless.

For me, this drawing together of stylistic and developmental concerns defines a generational synthesis.

The Uses of Autobiography 15

To discuss the "uses of autobiography" is to address myself to nothing less than the uses—I hesitate to say the meaning—of a liberal education. When we take autobiography as our subject at this advanced moment in history, we expect nothing less than a discussion of the relationship between selfhood and knowledge. And by situating the self in our thoughts about curriculum, we define ourselves within a tradition of liberal skepticism. It is very much a modern impulse to take seriously or even to conceptualize the self as central to the idea of education.

Our interest in autobiography defines us as liberal in a more precise and complex way than I have suggested. Our interest suggests that we are aware of the role the self plays in shaping experience, that we are aware of the unavoidable interventions of our selves as the medium and conduit of our perceptions. This attitude of mind makes us skeptical about dogma in any form. This tentativeness is an important element of liberal thought. My first thought, then, in making use of autobiography—in a composition course or elsewhere—would be to demonstrate the participation of self in claims made about the

This essay was first presented at the Conference on College Composition, New Orleans, Louisiana, 5-7 April 1973; it is reprinted with permission from *New Directions in Teaching,* Spring 1979.

nature of the world.

This participation can be demonstrated quite easily, I think, though the level of discourse depends, as always, on particular students and teachers. We might begin with a text, an example of student writing, in which the task has been set to make an objective statement about a general issue or phenomenon, the kind of issue we can expect to engage the common reader. We could then ask the students in class to uncover the hidden agenda by asking questions like this: What kind of person asks this kind of question? What do you tell us about yourself when you make this kind of claim? What metaphors, with what associations, dominate the text? After a period of this kind of questioning, we could turn the tables around and ask students—for we are not interested in solipcism—to try to make "wholly" subjective statements about equally general issues. To give this side of the issue a clear and didactic intent, we should not be wary of encouraging day-dreams, free association, dream, reverie—these and any other data of modern consciousness. We could then ask students to excavate the public content in their private worlds. A group of young men and women will not take long to unearth the politics, sociology, and anthropology of interiority.

Once these two stages of inquiry have been enacted, we are then in a position to make two claims and to raise a question:

- What we commonly call objectivity inheres in subjectivity.
- Subjectivity inheres in objectivity.
- Are these terms applicable to intellectual life in general?

We ask these questions because we want at every point to underline the intellectual impact of our efforts and *to make it clear* that we are not merely asking students to be idiosyncratic. We want most of all to make it possible for our students to believe that they are capable of imaginative and intellectual activities consonant with work they study and admire. This is not exactly, on my part, a rage for relevance; it is a quest for something more profound—a sense of equivalency in method between the operations performed in the classroom and the operations of received intellectual history.

During the 1960s—does one now say *Goodbye to All That* or *Ah, Wilderness?*—many of us, including myself, often mistook content for method, believed that relevancy and radicalism resided in topicality alone and not approach. But in a calmer moment, we know that the object of study should go hand in hand with the study of objects—crystals and crises may equally illuminate. And we should not forget that our prophets often have had traditional beginnings: Buckminster Fuller as sailor-engineer; N. O. Brown as classicist, and Freud as neurologist.

We can now ask ourselves if these explorations are applicable to intellectual and imaginative life in general. Let's start at the literary end and consider F. Scott Fitzgerald, a writer who opens himself up for autobiographical and biographical investigation.

The Mizener and Turnbull biographies, along with Nancy Milford's *Zelda,* Fitzgerald's *Letters to His Daughter,* and the *Crack-Up,* to name a few documents, allow us to see a repetition of Fitzgerald's life in *The Great Gatsby:* the journey of the wide-eyed, midwestern, moral aesthete to the east—Gatsby's Oxford as a thin disguise in the novel for Fitzgerald's Princeton—and the unnerving, unalterable discoveries that define that journey. We do not have to dig too deeply into Fitzgerald's life to see how the boy from St. Paul—living at the edge of high society—told his story again in *The Great Gatsby:*

> Yet high over the city our line of yellow windows must have contributed their share of human secrecy to the casual watcher in the darkening streets, and I was him too, looking up and wondering. I was within and without, simultaneously enchanted and repelled by the inexhaustible variety of life.[1]

But what is important for our purposes is that Fitzgerald has also reconstructed his story and found in it two older stories: one dealing with the archetypal journey of the provincial who wanders to the city and charts a course from innocence to experience; the other dealing with the discovery and history of America, with the fate of our frontier pastoralism and all that it has implied for us as a nation. It is this process of repetition and reconstruction that interests me here. Cassirer has, as well as anyone, defined this process in his *An Essay on Man:*

> Symbolic memory is the process by which man not only repeats his past experience but also reconstructs this experience. Imagination becomes a necessary element of the true recollection. This man was the reason why Goethe entitled his autobiography *Poetry* and *Truth* (*Dichtun* and *Wahrheit*).[2]

I now turn to a harder case—to the subjective element located in the objective, to what George Steiner has called "subjective inter-ference" (though I prefer the word "participation"):

> This is so, to a lesser degree, of some part of the debate between Einstein, Bohr, Wolfgang Pauli, and Max Born—from each of whom we have letters of matchless honesty and personal commitment—on the issue of anarchic indeterminacy or subjective interference in quantum physics. Here are topics as crowded with felt life as any in the hu-manities.[3]

To make this difficult point—difficult because it reverses our ordinary conception of science—I rely heavily on the essay "On Trying to Understand Scientific Genius"[4] by physicist and generalist Gerald Holton. With an expert's knowledge of physics and the history of science in mind, Holton, working as a psychobiographer, gives us a humanized Einstein who sought the meeting ground between intuition and experience:

> To these elementary laws there leads no logical path, but only intuition, supported by being sympathetically in touch with experience [Einfuh-lung in die Erfahrunt].[5]

He portrays an Einstein who brought a child's response to discrete and shifting phenomena into focus with his love of rational and invariant theory (Einstein preferred the nomenclature "Invarianten Theorie" over "Relativity Theory"). In the crucible of his passions and preferences, he forged an invariant theory of variability. His love of "inherent symmetry" found a mirror image in the physical universe; or, as Holton says about the nature of Einstein's genius: "There is a mutual mapping of the mind and life-style of this scientist, and of the laws of nature."[6]

Holton suggests further that Einstein's experience in the Swiss Kanton Schule at Aarau—with its progressive tenets derived from the enlightenment educator Pestalozzi—enabled him to develop his style, a style encompassing both a passion for simplicity and a respect for variation: "Here, at last, he was in a place that did not squash, and may well have fostered, the particular style of thinking that was so congenial to him."[7] I can do no better than quote Einstein himself at this point:

> Man seeks to form for himself, in whatever manner is suitable for him, a simplified and lucid image of the world [Bild der Welt], and so to overcome the world of experience by striving to replace it to some extent by this image. This is what the painter does, and the poet, the speculative philosopher, the natural philosopher, each in his own way.[8]

So what we have been talking about is a style of cognition, a way of mapping one's subjectivity onto the objective world, or the other way around, of opening an autobiographical door that may lead others to the world. In practical terms, the teacher of literature may need the assistance of an historian of science (Holton), or a text (T. Kuhn's *The Structure of Scientific Revolutions*), but this should not discourage us from taking our own familiarity with style and grafting it onto the sense of autobiographical participation in science as well as art.

My intent in this short essay has been to place autobiography in the context of broad curricular issues, to move through autobiography as a genre to an understanding of self-portrayal in all kinds of knowing. Moreover, I have tried to steer a course between despairing early modern traditionalists, like T. S. Eliot and W. Lewis, who reject pluralistic interiority, and late modernists, such as Borges and Robb-Grillet, who endorse a move from self-creation to nothingness.[9] I have argued, in brief, for the interdependence of seer and seen, of dancer and dance.

I end, then, with a sense of world and mind as potentially homologous structures. Speaking only of literature, Virginia Woolf put it quite well some time ago: "For it is only by knowing how to write that you can make use in literature of your self; that self which, while it is essential to literature, is also its most dangerous antagonist."[10] This is the difficult balance: to humanize one's claim to knowledge while chastening the self at the same time. A paradigmatic example of this is Freud—who constantly monitored his "third ear" against the vocalities of his patients. In this sense, the autobiographer becomes the hidden biographer of his audience. He speaks for us. We put his self to use.

Toward Cultural Autobiography
(1950-1980)

Quietude, the Apocalypse, and Nostalgia   16

For years, it seemed that my contemporaries and I belonged to no specific generation, at least as I would have used the word to describe the "lost" generation or the thirties (the Great Depression) or the forties (the war years). Those of us in college during the 1950s were, of course, living through the Eisenhower years, the cold war at its chilliest, and the McCarthy era, but we did not feel connected to those forces and issues.

We were against Ike, saw McCarthy as a menace, and did not want to sell out to Madison Avenue. But our position was one of negativism. We lived with a sense of loss and absence, but when it came right down to it, we did not know what had been lost or was missing, because we had not been, nor did we stand *for,* anything.

Once my freshman roommate (the late Larry Goldstein, a promising TV writer and producer) and I walked across the town common on a soundless, crystalline winter night looking, like Antonioni characters, for a cause, but could not find one and had a pizza instead. And one spring, a well-heeled and multicolumned fraternity decided to give a lawn party for the poor kids in town, but they couldn't find

This essay is reprinted with permission from *The American Scholar,* Winter 1973-1974.

any, so they made martinis (very dry, of course), lobbed frisbees, and sported with tartan-clad girls.

We did not think of going to Paris to meet Sylvia Beach and write the great American novel; we had not been to the dust bowl or felt the betrayal of the Hitler-Stalin pact; we had not gone to Europe to fight fascism and then finish college on the GI Bill, although we took on some of the veterans' experienced looks and gestures and wore their gear.

The adults we knew had touched history somewhere—in the Lower East Side, at a café, at a rally in Union Square, through a Norden bombsight (a magical object to those of us reared on war movies), but we were just afloat and floating, just going to college, as we would have said to anyone who asked us what we did.

Rushing ahead somewhat in this microgenerational autobiography, it seems, in retrospect, that we were becoming experts in nostalgia, and it is no wonder, now that we have come of age, that our movies, I mean the ones created by my contemporaries—*The Last Picture Show; Play It Again, Sam; The Summer of '42; Love Story; Easy Rider; Five Easy Pieces*—are bathed in nostalgia.

Nor is it surprising to me that many of my friends are in film and media. Our experience has always been mediated at a remove from the real. Our war was the *The Purple Heart;* our suffering, *The Grapes of Wrath;* and our twenties (glamour), photographs of Zelda and Fitzgerald at Cap d'Antibes. I once saw a girl glide through the fountain at the Plaza Hotel in New York after a prom in 1954, and knew that she had read *Tender Is the Night.* We even exchanged Fitzgeraldian glances.

Given my sense of things, it is fitting that Sontag and Warhol, fifties people, should have advanced Camp and Pop, essentially aesthetics of nostalgia, into the American scene.

In place of authentic experience, we were, without knowing it, learning to reinvent the past and circumvent the present. Our fiction and that of a half generation before us would show that later: Richard

Brautigan, Ken Kesey, Leonard Cohen, Philip Roth, and John Updike. We would all become *The Boys of Summer* in time, in different ways.

But while we thought that we were idling, poised on the runway without a flight plan, and before we knew that we were becoming experts at filling in an apparent vacuum with nostalgia and a sense of the past, some of us were taking literature and a certain approach to it seriously—not as a counterenvironment, as I might see it now, but as a refinement of consciousness.

We used to joke and say that we lacked a direct object in our experience and speech, that we were only "aware of. . . ." But we did not doubt that *aware of* part. It seemed our destiny. Being a part of the fifties was to be *aware of awareness* and the writers who stood for well-wrought self-consciousness: Henry James, Jane Austen, E. M. Forster, T. S. Eliot, James Joyce, and the seventeenth-century poets.

Every person-hero we admired was turned inward, every concept and style folded into itself: James Dean, Marlon Brando, method acting, action painting—even the two-handed set-shot, which began decorously at the wrist, came up to the eye level (we wanted, like James, *to see*), and then snapped in a studied arc toward the hoop. We focused on the form of consciousness (awareness), not content. And the form was containment. Perhaps we were like Dulles's principle of foreign policy in the end.

But we would not know that for some time: not until the mid-sixties did we begin fo feel discomfiture with this point of view. Then, in the face of political and social pressures within and without the university (the most important, the war in Vietnam), and in the face of apocalyptic claims about inner realities set forth by humanistic educators (John Holt), psychologists (Fritz Perls), culture heroes (R. D. Laing) and visionary poets (Allen Ginsberg and Gary Snyder), we would have to ask ourselves: What can we do with our awareness, our sensibility, our sensitivity?

And in asking that question, I, for one, became aware that I was really asking: Can I contain experience through awareness by making it literary, and even if I can, will that be enough?

Again, am I flashing forward? Is that my subject? To dissolve my theme in attitude? It would not surprise me. It is a characteristic fifties gesture—like posturing in front of Starks on Broadway waiting for a Saturday night to pass (remember *Marty*?), or waiting for the Rosenbergs and Chessman to die, knowing the inevitability, but mustering attitudes anyway. As I have said, we were becoming experts in mulling over the past—even the present.

So when some of my friends and I set out to teach in the early sixties, we had one thing clearly in view: mind, awareness, a muted assault upon the limited and betraying consciousness of Madison Avenue.

It seemed to us that if we could not affect the national temper of life (we were already psychic minimalists), we could at least convert a student here and there to our way of privatism and personalism.

If it did not feel like a return to the values of Bloomsbury, it was because we lacked their genius, because the literary tools we had acquired to implement our awareness (the New Criticism) had been machine-tooled to precision and not handcrafted like the art criticism of Roger Fry. At the same time, it did not feel hermetic, because we felt that we were part of a community of other privatists with some shared assumptions.

Without hoping for too much or too little (my voice becomes increasingly Eliotic), we fanned out to spread the word with some modesty and a hidden, scaled-down evangelicalism. We knew that we were taking our place in society with everyone else (even those who had gone to the Harvard Business School), but we felt that our place was, although invisible, potentially influential. We could even imagine our awareness of taste and human distinctions (the values that were blurred on TV ads) reaching *someone* in power.

When JFK was elected and met Mailer and heard Casals, it seemed to us that he knew, magically, that we were "out there." His knowing made our mission public in some coded way, and attacks upon him validated our task and even made us feel self-righteous.

In some ways, it occurs to me now, he was a model Ivy League professor. Touch football and Cape Cod reminded us of summer vacations and brought back images and sounds of softball—for which all of my friends and some writers who grew up in the fifties have a special fondness. The quietude and pastoralism of the wide-ranging outfield spoke to us.

If John Kennedy had not been assassinated, we might have joined history, believing it possible that men and women of sensibility and awareness could, perhaps, enter the public arena without selling out, without compromising their sense of integrity.

Many of us believed that public speech itself was necessarily rhetoric, and rhetoric was a betrayal of consciousness. Although we would not have invoked Orwell then—he spoke out of a socialist context that was alien to us—there was a sense that all public utterances were a form of Newspeak. But Kennedy seemed able, somehow, to preserve *his* voice in the public sphere. His unwillingness to become entirely the occasion he moved in, his resistance to preset role-playing (filling in a pre-established political scenario) became a new kind of role: the Kennedy image.

If JFK had not been assassinated, we might have moved into history. It might even have happened later with Robert Kennedy, but we were two-time losers in our search for an affiliation with history.

Except for a brief period (from fall 1962 to fall 1963, my first year of teaching), it was hard to imagine a bridge between our job as teachers of literature and the world. It is at this point that the central paradox defines itself: How can I talk about missing history, a sense of absence, nostalgia, when in so many ways history was fought out during the sixties on college campuses by the students and professors who lent their weight to social issues: racism, the war, ecology, university reform, a new spiritualism?

Literature, as *we* had known it, was written off as irrelevant, and biological age, however prematurely invoked, became a decisive factor. Except for some teachers my age, who gave themselves over completely to protest, most who joined and marched did so with an uneasy sense that they were sympathetic to the moral and political content of the issues but were skeptical, even frightened about the style and tactics; or they experienced protest as an ecstasy of sorts and then, as they say, came down.

In the midst of confrontation, there was a McLuhanesque feeling that the message was right, but the medium out of hand. We had added content to our world view but had not relinquished form. As we moved closer to students on the strike issues, the sense of differences in *style*—the overreaching of boundaries, the failure of control, the use of explosives and drugs that were literally and figuratively "dynamite"—became more pronounced.

As teachers, we were in the curious position of being part of an establishment that was challenging the establishment. And if our students were in the same bind, they did not acknowledge it openly. It seemed inevitable that it was for us, "the elders," to justify and vindicate ourselves (aging took place quickly in the late sixties).

Most teachers made some effort to achieve some kind of rapprochement, although some, whom I cannot speak for, retrenched. As important, I think, as the public attempts to meet the generation of the sixties—attending meetings, signing petitions, giving bail money, writing letters on behalf of conscientious objectors, even going to jail (forty-five of my colleagues were arrested and finally acquitted on charges of entering a building in violation of an injunction while protesting the presence of four hundred city police on campus)—were the shifts in classroom attitude and method: the place where students and teachers really face one another.

In a way, the changes that took place in the culture at large were mirrored step by step in classrooms across the country, beginning, I would say, during 1966 and 1967, without teachers at that time being fully aware of the larger implications of what was taking place.

It was, for example, during that year after some tentative and unselfconscious efforts toward freeing the space in the classroom in the previous years (1962 to 1966), that I first thought of the class as a *group* holding the possibility of a shared attempt at trust and openness. It was during the summer of 1967 at a "be-in" (how remote that phrase seems now) in Ann Arbor, where I was completing my graduate study, that I realized how my efforts toward shared experience in the classroom reflected broader tribal tendencies in the culture.

But I still felt that these efforts were a reflection of, not an engagement with, the culture. I was not so much in history as running alongside it. At least that was the way it felt. No matter how much I extended my methods, the students reached further out, testing new, if tenuous, limits of behavior and perception. Every step I took toward the synthesis of literary study and modes of self-realization was left behind in the wake of experimental extensions of action and consciousness: drugs, communal living, nonverbal communication, self-purifying diets, meditation, alpha-wave feedback. Survival, sixties style, had become a fad.

From 1967 to 1970 I tried to keep up. During this time I moved from an awareness of group behavior to enactments of group process: to modes of classroom interaction derived from the humanistic theories of Carl Rogers and Abraham Maslow, and from the educational theory of A. S. Neill, Paul Goodman, Sylvia Ashton-Warner, Edgar Friedenberg, Jonathan Kozol, Herbert Kohl, Kenneth Koch, John Dewey, George B. Leonard, et al. I went as far as I would go in the fall and winter of 1969 to 1970. During that semester, I planned to teach a course on the literature and theory of mental crisis in which we were to read, for example, established texts such as Gogol's *Diary of a Madman,* Dostoevsky's *The Possessed,* and some of the basic works of Freud, Jung, and Laing.

In less than a month the students made it clear that they preferred to discuss and write about their own psychological autobiographies than to approach the subject at a distance. I had misgivings about this project, but swept up by the temper of the times, I went along for the swim and almost drowned.

We did learn a great deal about ourselves, the foundations of a learning experience, and the conflicts underlying the strike that would dominate our campus a few months later, and we did reach shore. But I half knew at the end of the semester that my age of pronounced experiment was over for a while. I could not, finally, as a teacher of literature accept the death of literary tradition, the sense of an ending that had become so popular beneath the standards of Marshall McLuhan, Norman O. Brown, Susan Sontag, and the survival culture.

I believed strongly, having read widely in analytic psychology, that our experience had become too therapeutic; that, even if the approach was valid, I was not properly trained to deal with it; that what I was advancing would mean the end of the university as I had known it. I found myself calling everything into question, but still acting as the questioner, the teacher. Did I want to give up that role?

I felt too that my students were being prepared only for an imaginary and theoretical future. What would happen if history turned on them, as it has, and they were not prepared to get on with the daily tasks of making history over an indefinite period of time? What if they were not even to have the experience of failed idealism through literature, were not even to rehearse the complexities of disappointment?

One colleague had for years been telling me that his own dark mission was to initiate his students into a tragic view of life, to make them aware of their own mortality and finitude. He would come to mind in the midst of my attempts at innovation.

In a certain way, the strike at the State University of New York at Buffalo, as much as I was caught up in it, gave me time to think about my future as a teacher, because there were few classes that spring and most of them were focused on strike issues and, after that, on Cambodia and Kent State.

What interests me now about those discussions, with respect to my own increasingly tempered attitudes toward education, is that they were articulate and often very intelligent. Where I had found students silent before literary texts, they became vocal and passionate (even rational) discussing ROTC, defense contracts, and tenure decisions, and they had read Marx, Marcuse, Paul Goodman, and others.

If their tastes were predictable, they were no more so than my own undergraduate reading: Empson, C. Wright Mills, Fromm, Reisman. But when it came to the implementaton of these ideas, all boundaries collapsed. Liberals became rightists; centrists, "pigs"; when there were meetings with administrators who, given the forces at work, were ready to make significant concessions, the ante went up and the game was lost. Once again for me, form and content were at odds. I respected the moral energy of the students, but I wanted it shaped, controlled. There were only half-awarenesses at the time.

When the summer of 1970 came, I went to the northwest to work on a book with a friend (few people I knew ever gave up their projects through these years) and to relax found myself reading books dealing with the great tradition: Kitto on the Greeks, Collingwood's *Autobiography,* A. C. Bradley on Shakespeare. Sitting on a headrock looking across the Juan de Fuca Straits at the Olympic mountain range rising straight from the sea, I wrote a letter to a friend and made an unexpected, Arnoldian case for the life of the mind, the criticism of life. He and I tend only to speak about softball, and I think that he is still bewildered about what I wrote to him that summer.

When I returned in the fall, our campus was especially quiet. It came as relief (one could actually imagine teaching for a whole semester!). It also came as a disappointment. A conservative engineer had been named president, and liberal faculty (*this time*) wanted opposition from the students. But there was to be no third wave after the strikes of 1970 and Kent State-Cambodia. The Revolutionary Theatre, as Robert Brustein has called it, had, it seemed, dropped its curtain and thrown away its scenario.

Every generation tests its limits and, willingly or unwillingly, steps away from the outer boundary to a position beyond the old boundary. But still I felt as if the counterculture could not be dead, and this provoked two contradictory impulses in me: not to get swept to the right by prevailing winds and so to continue my student-centered approach to education; at the same time, to reinstate a "course" orientation.

It seemed as if I would have to move forward and backward at the same time: to continue my explorations but to reclaim some lost intellectual ground, I had planned to teach a course on post-World War II American drama, putting emphasis on the structure of the family (it seemed the inescapable theme), and as things were unfolding, the subject fit the moment well. The backgrounds and experiences of the class led into the themes of the plays: *Long Day's Journey, Death of a Salesman, The Glass Menagerie,* and so on.

Too often in American education, texts are not thought of in terms of the specific phase of development that students are going through. In this case, the issues at stake for the students were in the plays: the positive and negative values of the nuclear family, generational conflict, the use and misuse of fantasy. Without getting away from the texts, it was possible to ask students to draw analogies between the texts and their experience. Because the plays described, in the main, middle-class family life, analogies came easily.

In the spring, in a course on modern American poetry, I tried again to achieve a balance between the personal and impersonal—but in a different way. Instead of asking students to personalize the "established" poems, or to impersonalize them, I gave every other class to student poems—and made it clear that my aim was not to decide which poems were best. Rather, I was interested in exploring the experience of each poem.

If a student poem could unfold a Richard Wilbur poem, or if Wallace Stevens shed light on us, so much the better. But the intention was not to opt for one against the other. Although I now have second thoughts about the obliteration of distinctions, the erasure of values, I wonder if that large class of forty students could, in any other way, have turned out as many satisfying poems.

My second thoughts touch, briefly, attitudes toward maintaining an aesthetic hierarchy: there is a natural, even reflexive, impulse to rank one's tastes and passions. They concern, as well, notions that through language good poetry provides models of the necessary struggle for discovery. Too often student poetry is facile and uninteresting —the severest judgment one can make about a young adult's experience—because the most available language is seized as an adequate expression of individual experience.

When a highly energized generational argot presents itself as a kind of linguistic ready-made (found object), and when there is a common fund of shared experience (both conditions were operative in the mid-to-late sixties), the difficulty of writing poetry is seemingly reduced. If anything, though, it becomes more difficult, because socially compelling language must be re-created and reimagined before it takes on the life of an individual voice.

But in the midst of strong communal impulses and vanguard tendencies toward anonymity (John Cage) and self-effacement (Living Theatre), it was not always entirely clear where I wanted to make a case for individual expression. In the last class, one of the students who had been writing songs played and sang them on his guitar. In their openness and directness, they seemed in retrospect to sum up the spirit of that particular moment in American educational cultural history.

This past year has been a time of reflection for me, a time to reconsider my explorations in education over a decade of teaching. It now seems to me possible, in ways that require subtle and careful articulation, to teach a person-centered class without relinquishing commitments to education and to literary study as a rational criticism of life.

It is possible to move toward freedom within the closed frame of the classroom, but it was important for me to discover at what point the frame begins to tremble; to discover, that is, how humanly nuanced a discussion can be without becoming psychotherapeutic and anti-intellectual in tenor.

There are times, of course, when I think of the high points of campus energy and its risk-taking sense of promise. A few weeks ago, two of my former students were hitching on Main Street, geared with backpacks and orange nylon Alpine ski parkas. I stopped and asked them where they (Bob and Ray, seriously!) were going.

"West," they answered in unison.

"For the Primal Scream?"

"It's one of the things we want to get into," Bob said.

I wished them well and drove them two miles west. When they got out, I felt a sense of loss, for their presence, for a generation, for a part of myself. They looked for all the world like an animated Joseph Cornell assemblage called *Possibility: the 1960s*; their leaving flooded me with nostalgia.

A few days later I had lunch with another former student, someone I had known for seven years, beginning with his first year at the University of Michigan. An all-state wrestler and debater, he had moved from civil rights to SDS, to Weatherman politics, to drugs and meditation. Now he had given up almost everything, including hope, except caring for the child of the woman he lived with as a friend. All through our conversation, I felt the tenuous and inappropriate basis of my nostalgia.

It was impossible for me not to be aware of his sadness and the severe risks he had run. Once again, I was aware of history, off to the side. When we parted, he asked me where I was going *for the summer*. And I asked him how he was going *to live*. These seemed to be the questions defining and separating our lives. The irony of all this is that I will probably spend most of my academic life encouraging students to achieve a measure of the freedom I could not accept in its apocalyptic fullness.

If it is difficult to let go of a child, it is almost unimaginable to let go of a generation. What began in the fifties as a sense of personalism and quietude has been transformed by the sixties into historical abandonment.

Perhaps someday my contemporaries will discover history. I doubt it. We are destined, I think, to become biographers and auto-biographers. At least, though, we will have learned that self and history are bound together, that solipsism is a grand illusion.

We will, I trust, never confuse isolation with self-created, autono-mous worlds again. We will not mistake a displacement of self as an aesthetic or political triumph. We can, at least, tell our history of history as truthfully as possible. I tried a little later in *Forgive the Father: A Memoir of Changing Generations* (New Republic Books, 1978).

From Frisco to Disco (1960-1980): The Cultural Legacy of Protest 17

There wasn't much oo-ing and ah-ing last New Year's Eve among my friends when the illuminated crystal ball began its countdown at the top of the Times Building to welcome 1979. No one wistfully sang "Auld Lang Syne" or lifted a glass of *Extra Dry Great Western* (who could afford imports?) to toast the departed spirit of Guy Lombardo. We didn't catalogue the disasters of 1978 or invoke the possible blessings of 1979 ("the dollar will hold against the yen"; "Mexican oil will keep OPEC at bay"). As TV cameras in Times Square panned the mostly adolescent faces, eager to be seen coast-to-coast, we looked at each other with a sense of absence.

Where had the 1960s gone? Had we missed a decade? Was it true that the sixties *weren't* coming back? We seemed to be on the verge of the reluctant admission that, like it or not, we had shared apparently little with each other for a decade. Was it possible that we had been living outside of history? We challenged one another, after a few rounds of the *Great Western,* to see what we could make of the 1970s in the year left to us to make anything of it at all.

I'd been a decade-watcher for some time and was pleased to see my puzzlement mirrored in the group. I'd been trying since the shoot-

This essay is reprinted with permission from *Journal of Thought,* Winter 1980.

ings at Kent State in the spring of 1970 to figure out what America might become after almost a decade of heightened activism and the quest for self-realization.

I'd tried to get a handle on the emergent decade but hadn't been successful. Still, I believed that there was a shape to the generation of the seventies. There had to be. We were a country in which decades counted. They had a texture and lineament: the Gaslight Era, the Jazz Age, the Depression, the War Years, the Cold War and Silent Generation, the Vietnam Era.

I'd tried to come up with a name for the seventies, failing so far, but I didn't believe, finally, that the seventies would turn out to be different from other decades. We were a country of shifting identity, but we always laid claim to meaning somewhere. I had this faith in an emergent identity because I had been part of the Silent Generation, a generation whose identity, though muted, had survived its silence to find a language for pockets of private experience sequestered from the corporate ethic and the Madison Avenue hype of those days.

Our books and films had shown eventually the yield of this privacy and suppression. The anguish of our interior lives, lived under the weight of conformist and institutional pressure, had shaped a voice of tremulous, poignant, and sometimes romantic (even nihilistic) rebellion: *Catcher in the Rye; On the Waterfront; On the Road; Goodbye, Columbus.* If my generation, with its apparent anonymity, had surfaced to have an enduring identity, the seventies would emerge, too.

My New Year's resolve was, then, to try to make sense of the decade whose terminal year we were going into with such little enthusiasm and sense of purpose. I'd had some luck at the culture-watch before and thought I might again, and I have to admit I'd been gathering evidence in search of a generational revelation for some time.

Maybe it would be easy enough to call the seventies the Calvin Klein years and let it go at that: the years of cranberry and pale plum, of wine and mauve loose-fitting linen blouses and painter's pants. I could do a "reading" of popular taste and fashion and have done with it; but I knew that these ripe fruit colors pointed to deeper versions of the life impulse that had piqued the public's imagination a decade before. I'd sensed this when I saw the first stirrings of fashion begin to replace factions. I'd wondered what the patches on star jeans might mean after the show of ideological emblems in the sixties, but I hadn't been able to come up with a comprehensive idea.

I was almost glad to be a provincial going into this search for generational meaning. Walking back from the party in the light, sifting snow, I felt as if I might have a chance to take the measure of the culture's style.

Here on the Niagara Frontier, away from the cultural fadism and trendiness of Los Angeles and New York City, places I'd been before, I might have a chance to see what America was like after the years of Vietnam and protest. These had been, after all, the two great facts of our national life from 1963 to 1973.

I might have a chance here on Soldiers Place—where the echoes of vanished Union battalions can almost be heard marching in the cool summer dawn—to weigh the values and shape of America in the late twentieth century against the lingering provincial days of heaven and common sense that were so much—we would like to think—a virtue in the nineteenth century.

There was something to be said for the long, white winters; for the deep freeze; for the sunless, almost arctic light. One could do worse than look out upon the country from Soldiers Place. One could do worse than judge national extremities from the locale of the heart or what was left of it.

What *had* happened to America in the wake of the longest war in our history? What were the ratios of life and death? How had America responded at remote levels of feeling in relation to the photo seen around the world?: the Associated Press photo of National Police Chief Nguyen Ngoc Loan killing in cold blood a Vietcong lieutenant in 1968?

That photograph, in its chilling horror, in its expression of a war without justice and without the pretense of due process and international ethics, furnished an icon of outrage for a generation and became, I think, something like a gloss of *The Deer Hunter*. This picture gave the generation of the sixties an image as compelling as the Warsaw ghetto photograph of the small boy with arms raised, standing between watchful mothers and Nazi troops, had given my generation.

What then had this terrible war wrought? There had been, to begin with, two sides to the sixties: cultural and political—sometimes separate, sometimes merged, sometimes present in different ratios of imbalance. One side, the cultural and psychological side, tried through groups, therapies, and shared consciousness (if only for a weekend at Esalen) to achieve transcendence and inner peace, oneness within and without. This side of the revolution tried to go beyond inner ego-trips and guilt trips and hang ups and uptightness to freer and more trusting interpersonal relationships. Some people used the word *polymorphous*.

Because of its overly romantic view of human possibilities, because of the obstinacy of the American war policy, because of the misuse of drugs and music in the service of narcissistic and sexual adventurism, this side of the sixties worked against itself. Because of the accrued historical rage against puritanism and its remnants, this side of the sixties often led to self-parody, moral confusion, and neurological chaos. Most teachers who then lived at the center of energy saw some of this risky experimentation.

It was hard for me, for instance, to know what was exploratory and what was self-destructive in Buffalo, especially in the spring of 1969, when our State University of New York campus was cresting for an explosion, though it didn't actually come for about a year. There seemed to be a moral and manic testing of limits that thrilled, became destructive, even grotesque, and failed in the end.

I saw this testing of limits when I went to the gym for a spectacular in the spring of 1969: Allen Ginsberg, on the college circuit, sang Blake songs; Lucas Foss—avant-gardist, Hebraist, and then conductor of the Buffalo Philharmonic—accompanied him on accordian; Archie Shepp, trumpeter and composer, "rapped" about jazz; a rock group played; a gifted, half-mad, ex-addict, and flamboyant poet, John Wieners, talked about heroin; the Mother-Fuckers, a roving commune from New York City, were there to superintend.

Another commune, the Hog Farm (where do they root up now?), turned up the amplifiers. The sound blasted through and caromed around the gym. All around me students gasped, leaped, and shouted, "Om," and tried to pull me into it. I always thought, but never said, "Om, om on the range." We were living in difficult times, but I couldn't suppress my one-liners and bad jokes, at least to myself.

They held hands and formed a circle, the object of which was to lift a dwarf, whose cultural attitudes were radical, above our heads. I ducked and crawled to the side of the gym. I didn't see how this rite or performance could save anyone.

My tropism towards irony and my skepticism about salvation were attitudes typical of the fifties, my generation. In the post-World War II period we had been made suspicious of big talk and big ideas by the cold war, by the claims for and against America, by the claims for and against Soviet communism. The spectre of the A-bomb hovering above these ideological struggles had made us wary of rhetoric.

Students in the 1960s, however, felt that growing up in the suburbs, that growing up with "Beaver" and Johnny Carson had sedated their basic energies and instincts—both sexual and social—so, they had railed against the coma of the middle class. From the emergence of rock and roll to the Beatles they turned up the amps and asked America to wake up. I heard something like this aural history in the gym.

This cultural side of the sixties largely receded from public view when the Vietnam war ended, though it left behind countercultural enclaves in Vermont, Colorado, New Mexico, and, of course, California. It took to the hills with its alternative life-style and pretty much faded away, leaving an archeological trail of food co-ops, transcendental meditation centers, and deflated water bed outlets.

The other side of the sixties, the political and activist side, is better understood and less confusing on the face of it than the cultural upheaval. The war in Vietnam seemed to young Americans clearly to be so unjust and racist in its objectives, so opposed to our historical commitment to self-determinism among nations, that it may be difficult now to understand why these objections to the war weren't understood by the American public and a series of presidential administrations, or how it might have been understood and underestimated.

This failure to understand the youth of the sixties would be hard to comprehend if the only issue to understand had been the war itself. But there were other issues and aspects of protest. The youth of the sixties were protesting the patriarchal and socioeconomic basis of Western culture itself. They were protesting the accrued abuses of technology in the West. The indictment reached back to the beginning of the scientific revolution in the seventeenth century and stretched forward to the university's contribution to the military (ROTC) and Pentagon (defense contracts) establishments.

This critique of Western technology and postindustrial society seems somewhat hard to fathom, now that we're in a period of constriction and youth is clambering up the steps of schools of management and engineering. But a decade ago, the history of mechanization was taken to be a burden that had to be thrown off by a generation that saw helicopters whirl both Americans and Vietnamese to terrible deaths.

Without being strictly Marxist, the youth of the sixties were rebelling against the dominant class and the institutions that define it: the family, the school, and organized religion. The Vietnam protest baffled mid-America because good people in the heartlands couldn't understand that patriarchy itself, in its several male-dominated guises, as it might have been put, had become unacceptable. The war-makers

were seen as bad fathers, and no one over thirty (remember?) was to
be trusted. The students identified with all the people they perceived
as victims of perverse male authority: Third World people, children,
the insane, Native Americans, Chicanos.

I saw the remnant of this rage against authority when I went to
Berkeley in 1973. Political graffiti defined the reach of white fantasy
there: *Power to the People; Tanya, We Love You; Off Hate.* On television, I saw the Symbionese Liberation Army (SLA) get burned in
Los Angeles. I heard Manson declare, "There is no such thing as
death."

Even mortality had lost its authority.

I thought there of Billy Pipps, a nonideological black, who was
drawn into the student movement at Buffalo and had overdosed
mysteriously during our strike of 1970. He had been convinced by
some young Stalinists (a two-man operation, Young Stalinists for the
Apocalypse, working out of a liberated broom closet in the student
union) that he would play a heroic role in a new society without
masters or landlords.

I once heard Billy tell Jerry Rubin at a drug and politics conference: "Put your pants on, man, it isn't decent." Billy was aware
that there is room for decorum and civil restraint, even in a revolution, perhaps *especially* in a revolution. He was more civilized in
attitude than a somewhat distinguished American critic and dramatist, a fierce anti-Stalinist, who argued, despite his invocations of
Aristotle, that the leaders of the student movement at Columbia in
1968 should be shot.

Billy was buried without fanfare next to Millard Fillmore, Buffalo's forgotten president. The honor was meant to forestall an investigation. It pleased me that Billy was given some dignity in death,
however much he might have wondered about going into eternity at
the side of a local (national) official. He hadn't even been able to get
along with the cops, to say nothing of a president.

The sixties can be defined, I think, through the experiences of the
cultural celebration in the gym *and* the political deaths of the SLA

members and Billy Pipps. Those years must be grasped as much for their texture and sensory qualities as for the issues and ideologies. What enraged mid-America about the generation of protest was, more often than not, the style, rather than the content, of protest, and the next generation, the generation of the seventies, achieved its identity by transforming the symbols and ceremonies of the sixties, not by continuing its ideological struggles.

The seventies have been hard to understand because no great historical event with a dramatic shape, like the outbreak of hostilities between nations or public demonstrations, has captured the imagination of this generation. The seventies have been hard to understand because styles, ceremonies, and symbols related to the sixties, *but detached from actual social history,* have defined them.

American culture, especially American youth culture, was left, after Vietnam, *with a set of gestures and attitudes cut off from a program of action.* The next generation—the disco generation—had to make use of these gestures as best it could in relation to social and economic reality often at odds with the gestural legacy of the sixties.

This disjunction itself is a defining characteristic of the seventies. But for the youth of the seventies, no *one* emergent reality—recession, toxic environmentalism (Love Canal), antinukes (Harrisburg), OPEC, even Watergate—has been able fully to displace the elemental bravura of the sixties and give the next generation a set of symbols truly its own, a set of symbols expressing its own identity. For the youth of the seventies, "retro"-history and second-hand symbolism have been the only game in town.

From Salvation to Self-Celebration (Cultural)

The specifics of the events in the gym point the way to understanding the origin of the cultural side of the seventies. It is only through understanding how the forms of cultural aspiration in the sixties became forms of cultural accommodation in the seventies that I can begin to understand, so to speak, "where America went." By focusing on the transformations of salvation into self-celebration, I can perhaps fulfill my New Year's resolve to discover and name the seventies.

Language and Parody. No one present at the spectacular in the gym really believed that the audience was a community that would endure beyond the last vibration of the MC5, though people acted as if they belonged to an ongoing Dionysian cult. The speakers themselves knew that their language was as much self-deceptive as it was a "put-on" for the audience. Everyone understood that the language used was aimed as much *against* a "repressive" society as it was *for* the people in the gym. The actual community in the gym served as platform for speaking to society at large. The culture of salvation was implicitly a culture of symbolic outrage. Yet there were those, the very young, counterculturally devout, who took the message of "rock redemption" literally.

Even as people let the Mothers maintain order, they were interested primarily in seeing at what point the Mothers would create disorder or invite police intervention because of their language. The celebration in the gym in 1969, like the Living Theatre's *Dionysus in '69*, was a testing of limits that parodied implicitly the idea of liberation in its utterances. The intent of the liberation was to define the repressive edge of the power structure. The denial of freedom thrilled as much as did the promise of fulfillment.

Hyperbole was required to acknowledge and ensure a disparity between symbolic performance and any possible social enactment. Students were tired of getting clubbed and maced. Parodic verbal performances were strategies of enraging authority while concealing at the same time the serious degree of felt hostility. A comedy of salvationary manners was implicit in the culture of the sixties.

The self-centered decade of the seventies was preceded by a decade of deeper self-relation, by a generation that manipulated language at its will to invoke personal and cultural transformation.

Before Werner Gerhart's *est*—a parody at every point of the human potential movement—the students of the sixties, the students in the gym, were beguiling themselves with language.

If utopian and pansexual language was the finger and bodypaint of a generation in the first instance, the failure of language to ennoble and sustain psychedelic reality laid up nonetheless a treasure horde of parodic elements for the next decade in *The Serial, Psycho-Babble,* the routines of George Carlin, the conservative skits of "Saturday Night Live."

The satire of "Saturday Night Live" and its movie spin-offs (*Animal House, Meatballs*) allows a new generation, the readers of *National Lampoon,* to set liberation aside even as they excite teenagers and college students with their sixties-inherited, x-rated language. The self-serving symbolism of the sixties (remember *The Greening of America?*) became rhetorical excess, a generation's attempt to convince itself that its language was essentially symbolic and self-protective, and then turned into parody in the seventies.

It is often difficult now to define the tone of self-presentation in those sectors of the society where the legacy of the sixties is strongest. The recent *Autoperformance Issue* of *The Drama Review* takes self-celebration at least to the edge of absurdity. Deborah Hay says in one of her calmer and least self-serving statements:

> The same material I use dancing are [sic] used in my life. The same rules apply to dancing that apply to my life. Everything said about dancing is a reflection of myself. The dance is any moment when I am clearly in the act of doing just what I am doing.[1]

Tribal Form. The event in the gym prefigures the seventies in its group aspect and in its self-conscious celebration of a shared social style. The youth of the sixties and those adults who wanted to reject the dominant values of an advanced technological civilization turned to tribal and communal forms of organization—often drawn from the culture (real and imagined) of the American Indian—both as a symbolic way of making reparations for the devastations of Manifest Destiny and as a way of rejecting modern culture in its militaristic and thermonuclear aspects.

The students who circled in the gym, who danced a tribal dance and shouted "Om" (Far Eastern modes of transcendence grafted onto American Indian lore), were expressing a distaste for individual action, for separate existence, the fear of aloneness that Thoreau saw so early as an American characteristic.

In surprising ways that seem on the face of it to deny the terms of the sixties, disco culture sustains, in a transformed way, many of the stylistic preferences of that decade. If it wasn't clear in the middle sixties, it certainly was clear just a year or two later that the liberationist program of the antiwar movement (both from the culturally beatific and activist sides) became a pretext and ruse of middle-class enlightenment.

The middle class in America, always looking for a way to assert its "freedom" without giving up its capital or property, grafted itself onto the human potential movement in the sixties. Esalen became a household word, at least in Scarsdale, before it was bumped by a spinach diet and then joined the disco craze.

We went from apocalypse to the apotheosis of Bloomingdale's.

The disco phenomenon also has provided popular culture with a glamourous, superficial, and cosmetic approach to group pleasure with a measure of transcendence and salvation suggested by decor: lights, lasers, mirrored floors and ceilings.

Illumination and light shows in the seventies replace the claims for the inner light in the sixties.

Where identities once merged on the protest march or in a love ritual, or often irreversibly on an acid trip, American culture now had come up with a form of social merging that gave youth a chance to sustain its illusion, as always, of being *out* while reaping the economic benefits of being *in*.

> Long-awaited beautiful people make beautiful entrances, consenting with cool noblesse oblige to be glanced at as they settle onto the dance floor and then lose themselves in that mass of desiring, forgetful impulse, of cultivated personalities and uncertain sexual identities.[2]

The disco craze—just another American craze to be sure, but one for our time, and as good an index of social life as any—puts Hollywood and Broadway and upper-middle class glamour, high fashion, cosmetics, and styled hair back in the driver's seat while pretending that the liberationist program of the sixties in its political and cultural aspects is being preserved; while pretending that the liberationist program is even being extended along the lines of sexual liberation, i.e., homosexuality, bisexuality, transvestism:

> And as the record blasts "Le freak c'est chic," they open their arms and join the dance of brotherhood. The music pulses around them, the black leather jockstraps swinging above their heads, poppers heighten the smell of grass. Nirvana looms.[3]

The life impulses of the sixties, the affirmation of Eros, for all its egregious manifestations, gives way in the seventies to tasteful shades of red and pink and cranberry. The rejuvenating impulses of the sixties have been transformed into colors and hues of floral growth and freshness, of flesh tones and slit skirts. The generation that thought it could make America into still another flower garden of the human spirit sees its legacy preserved in the palette of contemporary fashion. The upper middle class, the private school and LaCoste alligator set has turned for its version of life to Larzard and lime green (money turned verdant).

Use of Horror. When the students lifted a dwarf above their heads in celebration that spring night in 1969, they couldn't have known that they were showing the next generation how to use symbols to skirt action, that scapegoats would in a few years replace underdogs. They couldn't have known that they were making as much of a point about the violation of decorum as they were about their beliefs.

The violation of decorum seemed to have a point in the sixties to the extent that the official culture itself was violating the sanctities here and in Vietnam. In holding the dwarf above their heads, the students were expressing their solidarity with an oppressed brother; they were acting in a compassionate and festive way towards one of their generation whose physical stunting stood metaphorically for what the whole generation faced in accepting the burden of racism at home and willed destruction in Vietnam. The dwarf did not seem grotesque in that moment. His deviation from the norm expressed a general desire to deviate from an unacceptable standard.

Life in America has changed since that evening, and the grotesque as a cultural style has been detached from any system of belief that could redeem it. The use of a dwarf to express the human solidarity of the wounded hero has given way to the grotesque itself as a version of deformed discontent.[4]

The meaningful use of the grotesque as an outcry against the misuses of authority has become a debased vehicle for adolescent rebellion in *The Rocky Horror Picture Show,* in *Pink Flamingos,* and as a form of mass madness in the Jonestown, Guyana, jungle death scene where belief had to be tested to the point of self-destruction, paranoia, and suicide-murder before it could be trusted.

The culture of the sixties, taken at its best, provided a context of shared belief that made symbolic action possible. In the seventies, the will to believe goes on in some quarters, the habits of sacred communion linger, but there is no real belief, just the wish for redemption. *Sacrifice, detached from coherence, becomes horror.*

The Merry Pranksters and Jim Jones's People's Temple both quaffed acid-laden Kool-Aid (the All-American drink) in an attempt to escape the limits of repression in America. The Merry Pranksters had the saving grace, at least, of comedy.

From Violence to Horror (Political)

Just as the evening in the gym serves as a paradigm for cultural values that were transformed in the seventies, so the experience of the SLA serves to explicate the political pathway of transformation.

Media. The kidnapping of Patty Hearst and its aftermath were essentially media events, almost completely so in a technical sense because the historical actors were unseen. They were, literally, hidden. What the public knew, it knew through tape recordings, still photographs, a film of the Hibernia bank robbery, and, finally most horribly, the burning out of the SLA on television. It was a media event from start to its recent finish—the marriage of Patty Hearst to her bodyguard—acted out upon an heiress of one of California's important media corporations: the San Francisco *Examiner*.

The kidnapping of Patty Hearst as a media event and as an occasion for graffiti that appeared all around Berkeley and San Francisco stands squarely between the sixties as a rhetorical and self-parodic decade and the seventies as an era of nostalgia; an era in which history and its re-presentation in language (*"Tanya, We Love You"*) were taken over by Hollywood and television as packaged nostalgia.

History got off the streets and went into the screen (silver and small) where it could be controlled and monitored without calling the cops. Real history went underground and appeared as docudrama: "Roots," "Holocaust." "Masterpiece Theatre" rushed in where angels feared to tread.

If the students of the sixties tried to live a new history in the present, the youth of the seventies were content, after 591 days of Patty Hearst's televised anguish and the SLA's filmed deaths, to relive earlier history: *Grease, American Graffiti.* The fifties were back and so was a thirties union feeling in *Norma Rae.* There was even in 1975 a made-for-TV movie, *Attack on Terror: The FBI vs. the Ku Klux Klan,* about the murders of Goodman, Chaney, and Schwerner in Mississippi.

History and entertainment had common ends, it seemed, especially when the history was brutal and almost unimaginable. And for those who couldn't forget the Vietnam War, it could be relived, too: *Coming Home, The Deer Hunter, Who'll Stop the Rain,* and *Apocalypse Now.*

Escapism. Escapism is to the political side of the seventies what glamour and disco are to the cultural side: a movement from depth to surface, a movement from content to style. Much of this escapism was inherent in the SLA episode. It was, in literal ways, an attempt to escape from society; an attempt to get money and food from the establishment and then to survive somehow, in the hills somewhere (didn't they rob a camping store in L.A.?).

The members of the SLA thought there was an imaginary space to step into. So did Billy Pipps. But it must be said that these cultural warriors, however misguided, paid a savage price for their desire to escape and find new worlds. In the seventies, it has been largely a matter of turning on TV and escaping there. As the creator of the "Galactica" series said:

> We want to make the midwest comfortable with space. That's why we have Lorne Greene. . . . It's people on the move. It doesn't matter where they're going; it's what happens on the way.[5]

After the SLA, after a decade of napalm and immolations, America chose to seek adventure beyond the fringe of known space. We turned from moral emptiness and darkness to mystery of the Black Hole "out there."

Terror. The use of force in the sixties, even the displays of violence, were focused. The encounters and confrontations that led to violence—like the murder of the freedom riders in Alabama, like Kent State, even the killing of the SLA members—had a tragic shape to them. Forces of irreconcilable opposition came into ultimate conflict. Even the assassinations of the Kennedys and Martin Luther King, Jr., become tragically comprehensible if viewed as the threatened fate of idealism and advanced liberalism in a culture resistant in its darkest corners to a message of love and enlightenment.

The use and myth of force in the seventies is more diffuse and metaphoric. It is difficult to know the origins and to gauge the impact of punk, neo-Nazism, the Jonestown mass killings, and the murder of Harvey Milk.

The murder of San Francisco's gay supervisor, Harvey Milk, by ex-Vietnam paratrooper Dan White turns around the political values of the sixties as much as the Jonestown suicide-murder orgy reverses the terms of salvation. In San Francisco, a "deviant" normal type vengefully protested his displacement by killing a "normal" deviant. In the seventies *force, detached from meaning, produces terror*.

And what social forces underlie Elvis Costello?

> Two little Hitlers will fight it
> Out until
> One little Hitler does the other
> One's will.

What misreading of history, what vague sense of destiny, leads a California Surf Nazi to be unconflicted by his use of dreaded symbolism?

The swastika just symbolizes radicalness—total surfing.[6] What fugitive impulse leads the *lumpen*-punk crowd to impale itself with pins and moves Sid Vicious to shoot heroin with a pen?[7] What massive failure of social coherence, of the possibility for reform, has led a population to seek phantom solutions to what I imagine are feelings of helplessness and powerlessness?

Just as symbols became detached from actual social history on the cultural side at the end of the sixties, so the use of force became detached from positive goals and values on the political side. Tribal love without humanity gives way to horror, and meaningful resistance gives way to terror in the movement from the sixties to seventies.

The *lumpen*-punk side of the seventies, as well as the economic constriction that produces it, and the life signs of glamour are seemingly antithetical in nature. They represent a curious transformation of the forces of love and death as they have been at work in the heart and psyche of the culture over the past fifteen years. The forces of love and death—which had an intelligible, if intolerable, shape in the sixties—have become detached from meaningful sources and objects.

The opposition of the "love and flower" culture to the war, the opposition of youth to the corporate establishment—these coherent oppositions became diffusely antagonistic in the seventies.

If history and nature condemn us to a struggle of the life impulses against aggressive and thanatotic forces (or any other terminological setting of the opposition), then we must assume the burden of attempting to keep these great forces in check and balance.

The youth of the sixties, wayward in some ways, proposed nonetheless real and symbolic alternatives to the war in Indochina and the conflicts at home. The forces of life gained momentum in largely uncatastrophic ways (despite clubbings and gassings, despite even the awful shootings at Kent State) and helped bring the war to an end.

The youth of the sixties took up the historic challenge of bringing some kind of moral counterweight into play against the misuses of power and authority. Sometimes the weights of their own bodies, like Billy Pipps's, were put on the scale; sometimes grams of destructive drugs were added to the scale as well. These are lamentable facts and ironies of a serious moral, cultural, and political struggle that was waged.

The youth of the seventies, acting out a scenario of which they may well be unaware, can't easily be ranged onto sides of love and aggression. Is punk in the service of life? Is multisexuality a celebration of life? Is disco an affirmation or denial of authority? Is the new ethnicity a celebration of cultural identity or a disguised denial of racial equality?[8]

The forces of life and death stalk the land in almost comic and trivial guises, but we know that cultural style is never trivial. The young girl with make-up and earphones who roller-skates around Soldiers Place is saying something about life, and the citizen who burned a cross on his black neighbor's lawn near here in a culturally recidivist act is saying something about death. But the use of new symbols and the retreading of old ones (KKK) call upon the deepest powers of interpretation.

It will be fascinating to see how the opposing tendencies within the common culture of the seventies will work themselves out in the eighties. It is easier, finally, to look into the past than the future, and New Year's Eve, 1989, will doubtless find me walking around my lamp-lit circle looking for the meaning of the eighties, for the meaning of the past whose uncertain future now eludes me.

The Professor and the Laundromat: A Cycle of American Life   **18**

I have mainly trace memories about doing laundry before my daughter came to live with me soon after the Great Buffalo Blizzard of '77. Before then, laundry just seemed to get done.

During childhood, shirts came geometrically ironed and wrapped in brown paper from the Chinese laundry; sometimes they were brought up from the basement, folded, and stacked on my bed in our spacious apartment overlooking the Hudson River by the maid (as domestic workers were called then); or sometimes they were hand-washed, hung out, and tucked into shape by my mother.

Between going away to college and coming to teach in Buffalo, I must have left laundry off at a trail of cleaners, but I don't remember doing this chore. Everything was more important than doing laundry during those years: domestic life, romantic life, professional life, moral and political life (especially during the Vietnam period).

All this changed, though, when my daughter came to live with me after the Great Blizzard. America had moved quickly by then from the dreamy utopianism and Marcusan surplus-thinking of the sixties to our new depression and it wasn't possible for me to afford

This essay is reprinted with permission from *Moment*, March 1983.

even small luxuries any more—like sending laundry *out.*

Laundry fell into the center of my life, so to speak, when my newly turned teen-age daughter came to live with me just at this socioeconomic turn, but there was still an interlude of happy memory and association about doing the wash. From 1977 to 1978, I had access to a laundry in the basement; from 1978 to 1981, I had only to walk across a courtyard to a basement. I had to descend, but not socioeconomically . . . yet.

During those years (1978 to 1981), I lived in an old apartment house—a pastiche of Gothic and Romanesque elements—that had been built at the time of the Pan-American Exposition (1901). This triangular-shaped building, facing both a wide tree-lined avenue and a large circle, defined Buffalo's industrial heydey as a point of transit between East and still emerging West.

Old high school friends sometimes called and asked: "Where is Buffalo?" "Why are you there?" Or they told me to come home. But I chided them, told them about my twenty-two windows, the vista, the gently sloping string of street lamps along Chapin and Lincoln Parkways, which at night easily brought to mind an image of the young F. Scott Fitzgerald, who lived in Buffalo for about five years in his childhood.

I told them that I was in a good place, that I possessed something out of their reach, that I belonged to America in a way they couldn't understand because they lived in the fragmented, anonymous, and violent city: New York. I especially felt this when I carried laundry on certain winter nights across the courtyard. On those nights, chill, pin-pointed with stars, I felt as if I had found a safe niche for myself during increasingly hard times.

I took pride on those nights that I had come out of a midwestern graduate school to SUNY-Buffalo as an assistant professor in a hot department when the university was at the height of its experimental ascent and expansion, that I had risen with the university, that I had made my way from the valley floor of graduate school to the high peak of Professor in about a decade, heeding, more or less, my literary and intellectual conscience as I had gone along. I had put myself in a position to take care of my daughter by taking care of myself. I had taken care of business, as my father might have said.

I had responded, in part, to the challenge of the sixties. I had marched a bit, signed some petitions, stayed up some nights helping some students head west and cross the border to Canada, but I also had conducted a career as usual—writing, publishing, going to a few conferences, cultivating friendships with most of my colleagues, getting to know a few administrators, spending summers near the right beaches, walking the right mountain paths—and had emerged through the bureaucracy and academic pipeline as a Professor by the end of the seventies at a time when a promotion to "full" wasn't a snap, when a few friends got stuck or crushed on someone's desk.

No matter how much I might have insisted to myself that I was a loser, I now had to admit that I had "moved the goods" (my father again). The little girl sleeping in the next room could rest easily; her father had arrived, taken his place in America. I had to admit that I hadn't died at the stretch. I had completed a cycle. Even I couldn't deny that, at the moment when Ronald Reagan made and won his bid for the presidency at the end of the liberal experiment, I had arrived within the American scheme of things.

So the Great American Experiment seemed still to be working: dispossession, emigration, hardship, work, education (and/or enterprise), upward mobility (success/wealth/fame). My grandfather, persecuted and threatened with military service under the czar, came at the beginning of the century to New York City where he struggled as a pushcart merchant; my father had gone uptown at age fifteen to work in the garment industry (manufacturing and then selling ladies coats and suits) and had worked hard for fifty years so he wouldn't have to go back to poverty, so his children could be educated. His children had gone away to college and university so that they could become professionals, make a contribution, leave behind the great

American struggle.

Between 1905 and 1978, three-quarters of a century, my brother and I had come full cycle from pushcart to professor and lawyer; from suffering to sinecure; from toil to tenure. In less than a century, a family that spoke no English, as it touched these shores and moved through Ellis Island, had turned out children who preserved the language and interpreted the laws. And within the larger pattern, I had enacted a smaller version of it.

It had taken our family two or three centuries to work itself out of the pale and medieval legacy of Eastern European peasantry, about a century to work itself up in America, and less than a third of that time for me to hum and whir through the stages of an academic career. Who could predict the new generation's Buffalos and Ellis Islands: The moon? Outer space? Atari hook-ups to alternate states of mind? New intellectual vistas through the combining of video and computer?

I felt on those cold winter nights, in the year or so after I had climbed to the Adirondacks of academe, that I had spun around and through the third circle of history: each narrowing, each accelerating, each refining the human instrument for . . . for . . . for what? I'm not sure I would have asked "for what?" if my landlord hadn't summarily and arbitrarily terminated my tenancy in the spring of 1981.

As it turned out, though, he owed someone something at my expense. I found a place after a few weeks with some added and attractive elements (a separate, renovated carriage house with rose bushes and a patio, to say nothing of dishwasher and automatic garbage disposal), but I had to give up ease of parking and, to my chagrin, *access to a laundry*.

I had to accept the fact that for two years, at least, the two years when my daughter would still be with me before going away to college, I'd have to go out to do the laundry—in all seasons, including Buffalo's legendary winters—to do the wash. Gathering up the laundry and going out with it seemed almost comical for the first month or so, an opportunity for wisecracks and anecdotes, a chance to show friends, if they needed to be convinced, that I was a dutiful parent to the nth degree. But most people knew this about me anyway and weren't interested in my adventures with the laundry. They even may have been a bit embarrassed that someone they knew had to go out to do the wash at mid-life. It didn't make sense to them that a Professor of English, a plinth, if not a pillar, of the community had to go *out* to do the laundry.

But there was some mirth for a while: until the first chill of winter began to make itself felt around Thanksgiving, until the severity of the Reaganomic recession declared itself. With the oncoming cold and assault upon the dollar, every carload of wash and every quarter in the slot took on added significance.

I was amused at first by the people I met in the laundromat and in the coffee shop (one of a chain) next to it—Your Host—where I waited, reading a newspaper, while the laundry was in the machine. I was amused at first by these people and by what they were saying.

Marie, the woman who manages the laundromat on Saturday mornings, my time, was talking with Sarah, a university student, who works as a night-clerk at one of the older hotels which (a3 become, in effect, a residence for wealthy and displaced elderly citizens.

Marie is overweight, her hair is gray; she almost never smiles, except when she seems to be smiling at something foolish you've done, something unintelligent, though she can't multiply and refuses, despite my urging, to get a pocket calculator.

Marie looks at Sarah as if Sarah has done something stupid. "When's Old Man Brown going to pick up his shirts? We don't have a layaway plan, you know. This isn't Sears."

Sarah doesn't get angry. "He died last week. His children came, but I guess they forgot to ask about laundry."

"Why didn't you remind them?"

"I wasn't on duty."

"If you wasn't on duty, why didn't you leave a note?"

"I suppose I was upset. I get attached to some of the older people."

"Well, I don't get attached to these shirts. They don't mean nothing to me. They just take up room."

"I'll try to remember," Sarah says; "I'll leave notes in the future if I can remember."

"You better remember," Marie says, "or there won't be room for other shirts. Lots of old people will have to keep dirty shirts in their rooms."

"I see what you mean," Sarah says, as she smiles at me. She's seen me around the university and now at the laundromat.

I wait a few minutes, so Marie won't think that I'm second-guessing her on the question of the shirts (I know she doesn't like to be talked about), but when Sarah goes to the detergent dispenser a few minutes later, I ask her what Marie will do with the shirts.

"She'll wait thirty days and give them to the Salvation Army or Goodwill. The clothes get cycled down."

"From the horsey set to welfare. Someone in here will probably end up wearing Old Man Brown's shirt. What will happen to their shirts?" I ask.

"I don't know. Most of the people who come in here don't send out shirts. I suppose they stay in the family and end up in a yard sale. I don't know, I haven't worked in the hotel that long; I haven't been coming here that long. I don't know too much about dead people's clothing."

I go out of the laundromat to Your Host to wait for the machine to go through its cycle. I usually have enough time to go through a few sections of the Saturday paper. I'm beginning to recognize some of the regulars (maybe becoming one), to get a sense of the atmosphere.

Four men sit at the front curve of the counter, aware but inattentive to the others, and stare out the window at a good, but used Cadillac. Each looks past the other and tries to make eye contact with the owner—one of them, but luckier, or more crooked. It's not clear to me who these people are, where they live, how they make a living, if they work at all.

The owner of the Cadillac, who wears Dingo boots, Jordache blue jeans, a suede jacket, Swank jewelry, who actually twirls a key-chain, leans against the side of the Caddy, near his monogram: "BL." I want to ask the waitress, a kindly looking, rotund black woman, who these men are, who "BL" is, but I've been in the new neighbor-hood long enough to know that some of these men are horse players and touts, bookies, runners, strong-arm men, and maybe even killers.

I don't want to ask any question which might lead any of these men to think that I'm snooping or that the waitress is helping me out. They have enough reason already to think that I—with my tweed jacket and blue Oxford button-down—am a government agent. So I sit, half reading the paper and looking at "BL."

One of the men at the counter turns to me.

"I saw you looking curious. We're curious too. We want to know too how Big Louie gets his bread, but we don't ask any questions. He worked construction like us, got laid off like us, but he drives a Caddy. But we don't ask any questions. He says he hit it with the horses. Louie says he hit it big all summer at Fort Erie and Wood-binc. Maybe he knows something we don't know. We go to the track too, we put money on the ham-and-eggers too, but even when we win, we end up giving it back. You can't beat the horses, but maybe the big shot knows something we don't know. What do you think? Do you play the horses? You don't look like a horse man."

"I go to Fort Erie a few times each summer," I say; "I let my daughter bet a few bucks on a couple of races."

"That's nice. Not me, since I was laid off. I know I'm not young, but I can still work; I'd give anything to be back on the fork-lift. I'm as strong as an ox, but they don't want old guys anymore. I even dyed my hair, but they laid me off. I tried to give someone a C-note, but he nixed it, said 'Wait, the heat's on,' but that was an excuse; he nixed it himself. I'd give anything if I could work. My name's Tie. What's yours? You new around here?"

"I moved this summer; my landlord gave me the heave-ho. You probably know him; Mr. X, his father used to own Club ———."

"I wouldn't mess with him," Tie says; "he's got important friends. You didn't try to use any muscle, did you?"

"Do I look like a muscleman?" I ask.

"No, I guess you're a college man; I can tell. That's no long shot."

"You're right. What kind of name is Tie?"

"I used to wear good ties, hand-paints, when times were good, when we built the P-38s, P-40s. Those days are gone forever. I don't buy any new hand-paints, and I'm not going to wear the old ones, but they still call me Tie. Where do you work?"

People I know ask, "What do you *do*?" Tie wants to know where I *work*? This is a harder question to answer, especially when work is hard to get, and people who get paid ought to work from Tie's point of view.

"I teach, Tie; I teach at the university."

"Elmwood Avenue or Main Street?"

As far as Tie is concerned, there are two universities whose one difference is where they are, how far they are from where he is or isn't working. So far as Tie can tell, all college people are different from him.

"It's good work, if you can get it," he says. "When I was coming up in the depression, you went into the plants if you could or into construction if you were lucky. Then you went into the army, and if you didn't get your butt shot off in Europe, you were lucky to come back to seniority. You're lucky. I bet you get to make your own hours. I bet it's easy to make overtime, time-and-a-half."

"Yeah," I say, "I take the money and run."

"That's a good one," he says.

"I've got to go back to Marie's," I say; "my wash is probably done. I've got to throw the stuff into the dryer. See you."

"Yeah, I'll see you. Who knows?"

I thought about finding a new laundromat or going more deeply into debt to get an apartment size washer-dryer. I wasn't sure if it made sense or was even safe to get thicker with the crowd at Marie's or Your Host.

These people lived at the edge of society and might pull me over with them. Many of them were impoverished, lived on food stamps, welfare, and owed money to the mobsters they called Shylocks (this was the only piece of folk anti-Semitism I came across).

Who knew what they might do? Because the neighborhood was near a major hospital, a famous cancer research institute, and a spate of halfway houses connected with the Buffalo Psychiatric Hospital (a state facility), many of the people at Your Host and Marie's were capable of . . . who knows what?

Many prostitutes, alcoholics, and dead-enders—who lived in the city's few furnished apartment houses in the adjacent bohemian and gay part of town (Allentown: Buffalo's Greenwich Village)—walked in front of Your Host, stopped for coffee, and did their laundry at Marie's.

I thought it might be wise to move the laundry closer to my old established and socially enclosed neighborhood: near the quaint pastry shop (purveyor of croissants for the mostly Ivy League, station-wagon set), the take-out quiche place (fast food for squash players), and the quilt boutique. I thought it might be best to prevent a potential slide down the . . . into . . . who knows what?

I wasn't sure exactly what posed such threats (I hadn't seen anyone mugged, beaten, or abused), but I felt as I walked from Your Host to Marie's that there were dangers and risks: that the toothless vagrant, the faceless man who drank coffee through bandages, the dystrophic woman who painstakingly and sorrowfully folded her laundry—I felt that these people, *they*, the others—the ones who hadn't known James's "the lucid air of the American night," possession, belonging, the people without a future—might do something to me. But what?

I had to admit at the same time though that I was getting used to the new neighborhood, to the feel of Marie's. I knew how to work it physically now, to make the most efficient use of time. I was beginning to feel less self-conscious when I went in. I noticed that some of the nurses and nurse's aides, even Marie, called me "dear" or "honey" when they wanted something: "Is that dryer free, dear? Or you got more?"

I had loved the walks across the courtyard on Soldiers Place, carrying the whitened load under the silhouette of the bare catawba branches set against the winter sky. I had cherished the silence there too, but it was quickly beginning to seem like part of a different social era.

I go back to Marie's and am eager to be finished with this Saturday's load. The "boys"—the Saturday Afternoon Discussion Group—are waiting for me at the museum. As much as I'm getting caught up with the life in the laundromat, I don't want to admit that I have been displaced too; that I'm one of the people who have to go out to do the laundry. I don't want to admit that I'm not as interested in our legendary colloquies (the waitresses are disappointed if we talk for less than two hours; our abstractions amuse them) as I was before my encounter with the laundry began.

But I recall going to a lecture a year ago on the most recent fashionable subject in the literary corner of the academy—"On Deconstruction: Images and Afterimages, Traces and Erasure"—and weighing, as I drove down Main Street, the lack of subject matter against the *actual* image of Chevy mechanics warming their hands over a trash can rigged as a stove, as they milled in a circle, carrying placards.

I go back and Michael, whose growth is stunted, tells me that it's his thirteenth birthday; that his father, a GI stationed in Hawaii, hasn't sent anything. He tells me that he and his mother were so upset that they stayed up all night watching TV. He wants to know if I want to hear about the movies. I tell him no.

I want him to read books and will give him a nickel for every book he can tell me about whenever I see him. I don't think he believes me, so I give him thirteen cents for his birthday; it's not much, of course, but he now believes—I can see it in his eyes—that I will give him a nickel for every book. He's already thinking of short books.

"Do you know what?" he asks.

"Not about TV, I hope," I say.

"No, not that. You know, I'm not going to get married even if there's a nonsmoking section."

"I know what you mean," I say, "but keep an open mind."

It's clear that Michael is intelligent. He has spoken with surrealist and unconscious logic about his situation. I'll go for twenty or thirty nickels if it will help him get out of the laundromat, but I doubt if he'll make it.

You can tell at Marie's how people live by the quality, kind, and variety of laundry. Joe X, a strongly built black man, for instance, has mainly white tee shirts, blue jeans, and threadbare workshirts, as well as a few fancy silk shirts. It's easy to see that he works hard all week and then goes out on the town now and then, probably Saturday night.

He folds his laundry carefully, squaring the sleeves of the tee shirts (something for which I don't have the patience). It's obvious that he's in control of his life, has a few bucks in the bank, and knows how to survive in America. He's probably got a union job which is secure even in these times.

Joe X is about my age, about my size, though more muscular. It occurs to me that he could use another workshirt, something less faded than the ones he's folding today, and it dawns on me that there's a flannel shirt—a relic from an old romance—that I would just as soon get rid of. It happens to be in my pile today. I offer it to him with the flimsy excuse, "It's too big for me; it's never fit."

Joe has seen me around ten or so times and isn't wary of me as a person, but he doesn't understand why anyone would give him a shirt off his back.

"How much?" he asks. He figures *I* need some help.

"Nothing," I say, "I just can't use it."

"Okay, all right," he says. "Sure, though? Want something?"

"Nothing. I'm sure; I'll take it off my income tax."

"That's it," he says; "screw the IRS whenever you can."

I like thinking that Joe will be wearing my shirt to work. I want the shirt to work for someone who's working now. I no longer give discards to the Ivy set for charitable auction.

I wanted to enter the halls and club rooms of Ivy in the silent (but upwardly mobile) fifties and worked hard in high school so that I could go to one of the better colleges where army pants, button-downs, and sneakers (with Wigwam sweat socks) were *de rigeur,* but the years have dulled the sheen on the Ivy. The privileges seem few for the exclusions they entail.

I gather up the whites and sigh with relief because I won't have to come back for a week, though the weather is likely to be a little worse when I do.

I then drive a few blocks to my new rented house, wedged between an alley and a narrow side street, where from our second floor you can see the top of Edwardian turrets and the rough facade of an old horse and carriage livery, now a garage run by an eighty-one-year-old wit. "I came from Russia when I was five. I'm still rushin'. I rush to work in the morning. I rush home for lunch."

When I turn the corner onto the side street, I hear a crash and a siren. I pull over. Two police cars surround a twisted Corvette. An early middle-aged man, suave and well-groomed, lies spread-eagled over the hood. Four cops have guns drawn. It's probably a drug bust. A lot of drugs go back and forth over the nearby Peace Bridge between Buffalo and Fort Erie.

One of the cops searches the man, and when he decides that he's clean, the others lower their weapons and begin to take notes. A crowd has gathered and begins to calm down when the guns are put away. Someone begins to play the guitar on a nearby stoop. A few children join the guitar player and begin to hum.

Other people come out of doors. My neighbors, I suppose. The tall and elegant lady, who lives next to me, walks with difficulty. A former school teacher, she has informed me already that, though a bit infirm, she "remains interested in life." An older, middle-aged woman comes from across the alley; she usually wears black and tends her yard. I see her go off to church every Sunday.

We all stand around while the police take notes and talk into their squawk box. We look at each other with pride for not being in trouble, for being on the right side of the law, for defending our neighborhood by showing our approval of the police as they perform their dangerous job.

It's a crisp fall day, a good day for burning leaves or going to a football game; it's also a good day for standing in the street with these new neighbors. I see, in my mind's eye, my father's old neighborhood on the Lower East Side, life in the shadow of the Brooklyn Bridge, just after the turn of the century. I see fire hydrants . . . spraying water . . . kids running around . . . sparkling arc. . . .

F. Scott Fitzgerald and
the Conflict of Generations **19**

If an "advanced" colleague had asked me why I was going to the Twin Cities to attend the F. Scott Fitzgerald Native Son Conference and I had replied, "to pay homage to Scott Fitzgerald, to acknowledge an appreciation of influence," I'm not sure our hallway conversation would have had much of a future.

My "theoretical" colleague would have gone about his business for a number of reasons that touch upon the present state of American literary and academic culture.

Every literary subject and approach expresses some professional self-interest, some cultural commitment, some claim, finally, about the nature of reality. The traditional terms of homage and appreciation are not in line with the vested interests of contemporary criticism and so provoke mild suspicion or silence.

Understanding this skepticism and silence may be the best revenge for those who believe that the terms of historical connection and continuity can be severed only at a price too great for any individual or country to pay. If we deny homage and appreciation to the writers who have created our literature, shaped our perception of

This essay was first presented at the University of Minnesota Conference on F. Scott Fitzgerald, St. Paul's Native Son and Distinguished American Writer, 29-31 October 1982.

our own destiny, and given us part of our language, then we invite something like the destruction of our culture through the dual (and only seemingly opposed) annihilation of the past *and* the vengeful return of it.

What commitments and silent assumptions of American history and culture in our present state have made it difficult for us to pay homage and to express an appreciation of influence? When I say "the present state of American literary and academic culture," I am referring to American culture since 1960, a period I would then divide into two segments: (1) the death of John F. Kennedy and the subsequent expansion of the war in Vietnam; and (2) the decline of activism after Kent State (May 1970) and the turn to mock protest, caricatures of militancy, the grotesque, horror, and punk, on the one hand, and simulations of oneness (disco), commercial hallucinations (laser and light shows), TV self-realization (Donahue), intergalactic escapism (*E.T.*), and video as well as other *games,* on the other hand.[1]

The terms of homage and appreciation towards literary elders, including the Lost Generation, were not in fashion during the first phase of post-1960s culture along several lines of disaffection. Unlike the student-GIs who came home after the Second World War with a feeling for European culture and a zest to live again, who were looking for the origins of the culture they had been shipped out of, students of the sixties were disenchanted with the past: with their immediate familial past (the nuclear family); with the past, near and far, of America as a country ("don't trust anyone over thirty"); and with the history of Western civilization (Mao replaced Aristotle as a figure of veneration).

The students during the first phase of the sixties were more interested in undoing traditions, even the concept of tradition itself (unless, oddly, those traditions were non-Western), than they were in establishing links with the past, especially a past as seemingly luxurious, affluent, and charming as the twenties; especially with a writer as seemingly interested in the manners, morals, rituals, and summer places of the rich as F. Scott Fitzgerald.

I remember trying to teach *The Great Gatsby* during the period of Vietnam protest in a standard survey of American literature, trying to convey my own undergraduate enthusiasm for the novel and finding that my students were surprised by the claims that I was making for Fitzgerald, by the place I claimed he had in American literature, by my presumption even to ask them to consider Gatsby's fate at a time when the fate of American moral and political history hung in the balance in Southeast Asia.

I tried to get them to see past the first sweep of the "green light," to consider Fitzgerald's own ambivalence towards the dominant class, but they insisted on not looking past the great houses and landscapes of East Egg.[2]

They were convinced that Fitzgerald stood for the landowners, that he worshipped Wall Street, that he preferred the unfurling of a bright and particolored spinnaker to the unfolding of Hegelian truth. They were not open to an "appreciation" of influence unless these were non-Western and reached back through post-Civil War American literature to our romantic and transcendental period.

These students could read and respond to Emerson, Thoreau, and Whitman—*Walden, Leaves of Grass,* and "Nature" (especially the "transparent eye-ball") were something like sacred texts that were taken as seriously as *The Whole Earth Catalogue* and *One Flew Over the Cuckoo's Nest;* but students in the first phase of post-1960 American culture were not interested in American and literary culture of the industrial era (from the Robber Barons through "the Diamond as Big as the Ritz" to the social and economic chronicles of John Cheever).

These students and the culture for which they stood were not interested in seeing themselves as "sons," native or otherwise, of an American writer who seemed to sing the praises of the republic in its capitalist and imperialist phase. It wasn't possible to locate for them Fitzgerald's own ambivalence, to show his own roots in romanticism (the overriding sense of Emersonian "possibility"), to indicate his own passionately tender feelings for childhood ("Babylon Revisited"), his own reluctance to grow up.

For students who were on the barricades, who wished to go to the barricades, F. Scott Fitzgerald had become a national anathema. They couldn't forget, as it were, Hemingway's self-serving and mis-attributed joke in "The Snows of Kilimanjaro":

> He remembered poor Julian and his romantic awe of them and how he had started a story once that began, "The very rich are different from you and me." And how someone had said to Julian, "Yes, they have more money."[3]

The students of the sixties were convinced that Fitzgerald was a PR and advance man for the rich (hadn't he written "The Rich Boy"?), and they wouldn't have been interested, if it had been available, in Matthew Bruccoli's clarification of the misrepresentation:

> The best-known anecdote about Fitzgerald appears in Hemingway's 1936 story, "The Snows of Kilimanjaro": "He remembered poor Scott Fitzgerald and his romantic awe of them [the rich] and how he had started a story once about them that began 'The very rich are different from you and me.' And how someone had said to Scott, 'Yes, they have more money.' But that was not humorous to Scott. He thought they were a special glamorous race and when he found they weren't it wrecked him just as much as any other thing that wrecked him." The only true thing in the passage is the quotation from Fitzgerald's story "The Rich Boy"—which did not begin the story. The rest never happened—or, at least, it didn't happen that way. In 1936 Maxwell Perkins, the legendary editor of Fitzgerald and Hemingway at Charles Scribner's Sons, lunched with Hemingway and the critic Mary Colum. When Hemingway announced, "I am getting to know the rich," Mary Colum replied, "The only difference between the rich and other people is that the rich have more money." The mechanism of Hemingway's reaction seems appallingly clear: a standard way to get rid of embarrassment is to assign it to someone else. In this case "poor Scott," whose "Crack-Up" articles were appearing in Esquire, provided an easy target.[4]

The terms of homage and appreciation were out of favor, and students as well as intellectuals became more interested in discovering myth than locating themselves in history with its obscrvable connections, traditions, and associated textures.[5]

The thinking of the period favored an escape from history through two kinds of myths or fantasies. Radical youth looked either to the primacy of the self (to values of self-creation) or to the denial of the self through participation in a range of ceremonial or tribal behavior.

Whether radical youth claimed to be wholly original and autochthonous, or whether they choose to be wholly unoriginal (we might say, aboriginal) through transpersonal commitments, they embraced in common a rejection of lived and living history. The claims for the autonomous self and the superficially contradictory claims for the collective self concealed a deeper affinity: a rejection of a social self formed in relation to others through time and progressive events.

It's true, of course, that Jay Gatsby "sprang from his Platonic conception of himself," but we remember that he put that self-created identity in the service of a "vast, vulgar, and meretricious beauty." If F. Scott Fitzgerald wanted to forge a self and characters expressing that self, who could transcend time and history, he wanted equally to find a home in time, space, and history for that personality. He was on this issue, as always, divided. Or, we might say, insistent upon unity.

Whether students were leaving cities for the desert or mountains in quest of primitive ceremonies or self-contained meditations, or reading Harold Bloom's *The Anxiety of Influence,* they secretly shared a rejection of the history they associated with the trespasses of American domestic and foreign policy, i.e., racism and imperialistic aggression.

> That even the strongest poets are subject to influences not poetical is obvious even to me, but again my concern is only with the *poet in a poet,* or the aboriginal poetic self.[6]

Whether students and poets (Gary Snyder, Allen Ginsberg) were celebrating the *Infinite I AM* or the *Infinite I AM NOT,* they were
stepping aside from history. Whether intellectuals and critics were
celebrating the self (*Love's Body,* or its annihilation through transpersonal codes, *Writing Degree Zero),* they were stepping out of the
stream of time.

Neither of these tendencies—held individually, joined, or amal-
gamated—made F. Scott Fitzgerald a writer of that moment. F.
Scott Fitzgerald is as much as anything (I am tempted to say, *above
all things*) a poet of time. We can't read F. Scott Fitzgerald without
encountering time as a main character, time as an accomplice, time
as a confidant, and the culture of the sixties wanted to go beyond
time. Fitzgerald may have wanted to arrest time, but he understood
that at best the poet could create only Keatsian "slow time," that the
sylvan historian of time couldn't stay "forever young" or go beyond
and outside of "all breathing human passion."

The students and intellectuals in the first phase of postsixties
culture couldn't accept the double temporal implications of the end
of *The Great Gatsby:* "So we beat on, boats against the current,
borne back ceaselessly into the past." They wanted to step out of time
into myth and meditation.

If young radicals began the decade with a dedication to protest
against specific historical injustices, they appealed quickly, if not
always self-knowingly, to non- and antihistorical justification for their
actions. This turn away from history in the name of ultimate history
became clear in the seventies as the fate of fading radicals unfolded:
*diets and deities came to replace revolution and rebellion as terms of
self-definition.*

The second phase of American culture since 1960 made the terms
of homage and appreciation toward Fitzgerald difficult for another
set of reasons. If the students of the early sixties wanted to escape
history and time, the youth culture that emerged in the seventies
wanted to *erase* them, wanted to act as if there were no binding

contingencies (moral or political). They wanted to act as if social life and society itself were some kind of mirage. These students didn't so much go against history as deny its significance.

The tastes of the seventies were deflections and parodies of shared social life, if not an outright challenge to the notion of society. The significant events of that seventies were staged, not lived directly.

Political action and direct protest gave way to performances of rebellion. The actual stage of history, we might say, gave way almost to a set of visual phenomena and games—light shows, video games, illuminated disco platforms—that gave the illusion of involvement: a simulacrum of significance.

If the students of the early sixties opposed one set of liberationist terms against a set of repressive beliefs, the students of the seventies rejected the idea of belief itself. These students turned from commitments with often tragic implications—war protest, intentional violence, willed imprisonment—to filmic escapes (*Star Wars, Close Encounters*) and video diversions.

Significant commitments gave way to the manipulation of signs, and a feeling of failed meaning went along with the shift in emphasis. This shift in cultural emphasis from antagonism and a search for alternatives to the erasure of meaning and the manipulation of symbols went along with a corresponding interest on the part of the literary critics and intellectuals in semiotic signs, all those diacritical features of reading and writing that we associate with semiotics, structuralism, and poststructuralism.

The second phase of post-1960 culture challenged the set of codes and conventions through which we live and touch one another. If meaning was challenged without self-consciousness in bars and video parlors, high-powered critics like Roland Barthes and his epigones in America were putting up the intellectual scaffolding for what was going to be a public hanging of Meaning.

When Barthes says, for instance, that "discourse combines signs which have referents, of course, but these referents can be and are most often 'chimeras,' " we wouldn't have to struggle too hard to apply this kind of deconstructive idea to pop corners of the culture where one set of chimerical electronic impulses devours others.[7]

When Roland Barthes talks about photography's essence, "that-has-been," and says that what has been seen has been "absolutely, irrefutably present, and yet already deferred," we understand the direction and intent of his argument.[8] The French obsession, now shared in America, with the failure of meaning, the failure of the code, becomes all too clear.

F. Scott Fitzgerald doesn't fit this particular mood of failed significance. Although we associate Fitzgerald with the elusiveness of the past and the meaning associated with it, we know also that Fitzgerald never gave up trying to reinvent the past in the present, to project the past into the future. This is how we can read the end of *Gatsby*. This is how we can connect the future which was already "behind him" with the "orgiastic future" ahead. This is how we can understand the "green light" that "recedes before us."

This light is different from the beckoning lights of science fiction and space exploration films whose source is only before us, whose emanations don't include our origins.

Gatsby's light, Fitzgerald's sense of illumination, has more in common with Emerson and Henry James (the passion *to see* comprehendingly and comprehensively back through and beyond American history to a reimagined future) than it does with the contemporary electronic revolution in light.

To pay homage to Fitzgerald at this present state of the culture, to acknowledge appreciation for his kind of transforming imagination may date us somewhat, but it seems to me a necessary act of making new sense, just as Nick needs to step back at the opening of *Gatsby*. I see a new sensibility emerging in America, a sensibility that may put F. Scott Fitzgerald again more centrally in our literary pathway.

I would characterize this new sensibility as a *caring* and *tender* response to some of the obvious threats to life in our time. As students become more caring and tender in relation to these threats to life and reject inevitably the evasive denial of them, as they discover once again the need to preserve the best of the past and use it as a catalyst for the future, they will come back to F. Scott Fitzgerald with a renewed sense of connection.

They will then hear "a warmth and tenderness," a "tenderness toward human desire that modifies a true firmness of moral judgment," that Trilling heard so accurately.[9] They will hear his tenderness in relation to the reassertion of a quest for meaningful history, and then F. Scott Fitzgerald will be home again.

I meant to write an essay of appreciation showing how F. Scott Fitzgerald had influenced my work. I meant even to talk about the snow in Buffalo, "our snow," the snow of Fitzgerald's childhood, my adulthood. I meant to mention Point Abino, the alleged real "green light" that flickers across Lake Erie and beckons even now. Well, one fine morning. . . . Meanwhile, I know what to say next time I see that theoretical colleague.

Threat and Evasion in Contemporary Technology 20

Each American generation expresses a unique and divided identity. The sixties set passive love against militant activism; the seventies embraced and parodied the sixties; the eighties seem to stand for biomorality *and* technological escapism.

Young people looked for a cause in the seventies, with and without rebellion, but no set of issues added up to the galvanizing moral trespasses—racism and an unjust war—of the previous generation. The generation of the seventies turned then to reenactments of some of the activist and communal ceremonies associated with the Vietnam era, but these gestures and signs, however poignant at times, were usually at odds with the actual social history of the late Nixon-Ford-Carter years.

These imitative gestures led to parodies of protest (punk, streaking), simulations of communal oneness (disco), caricatures of militancy (the abduction of Patty Hearst and the immolation of the SLA), commercial hallucinations (laser and light shows), and self-realization on TV (Donahue).

The students of the eighties, however, are more like the students

This essay is reprinted with permission from *Reporter,* 16 September 1982; an abbreviated version also appeared as "Students of the Eighties: Survival and Escape," *The Christian Science Monitor,* 24 September 1982.

of the antiwar years than they are like the surf-Nazis and trekkies of the seventies. Today's undergraduates organize their responses increasingly around a set of unified issues, though these same students, divided in their commitments, flee in other ways from the implications of their own concern.

The articulate, often young, voices of the eighties are, whatever else is true, speaking out against what they take to be *threats to life.* These threats represent to them the actual and possible extinction of life (both moral and biological) as we have known it and arouse immediate passions on and off campus and cut across, as well as go beyond, traditional social and political lines of liberal, conservative, and radical.

A catalogue of felt threats to (or assaults upon, or outrages against) life might be listed as follows: the nuclear threat; the threat to human rights through political terror and torture; the ecological threat on land, air, and sea to most forms of life and the function impairment, to say nothing of extinction, of many species; organized and gratuitous violence; the creation and sanction of a permanently dispossessed and suffering class of people at the bottom in America as a result of Reaganomics and related forms of imbalanced human bookkeeping; and the threat to the embryo (Pro-Choice).

These threats assert themselves daily, constitute a single, nonparanoiac perception of danger and lead today's undergraduate to say with one of my students: "This is the eighties, folks, no nirvana, no utopia, just the struggle to survive in a world that seems inexorably approaching disintegration."

Although students now *do* recognize these threats to life, and a new era of protest *has* begun among undergraduates and in town meetings across the land, there's another side to the unfolding era. The antinuke and disarmament movement *is* growing, and Amnesty International grows in influence, but as much as these crusades meet issues head-on, there is an equal, perhaps larger, sense of *evasion* among youth culture, an evasion reflected in contemporary technology and the popular arts.

The evasive fads and fashions of contemporary youth culture deny the threats to life, and it is precisely this conflict between threat and evasion that contemporary educators must face and understand if they are to meet this generation directly.

What is the trajectory of this flight?

Fascination with computers. There is a society of hackers (computer fanatics) on most campuses, who flock to computer centers at night and computer courses in the day in the dual pursuit of escape and advancement. A kind of closed-circuit narcissism may become an occupational hazard. According to *Rolling Stone,* "Each (hacker) seems to be a self-sufficient system of man and machine."

The lure of the computer (the sanctification of the bit and the chip, the magic of miniaturization) soon may begin to serve as a form of social avoidance in which the traditional enlightenment guidance systems of reading and writing increasingly are left behind. Servan-Schreiber, who offers "panegyrics to the silicon chip," says favorably in his *The World Challenge,* "A person who cannot read and write can learn to operate a computer."

TV and Video Art. Just when trenchant criticism has been directed at the misuses of fantasy on TV ("Fantasy Island," "Love Boat," the ongoing pseudorealities), an implicit claim for evasion of social reality comes in the name of avant-garde video. When Nam June Paik surfaced as an aesthetic force, a *Saturday Review* critic wrote approvingly about his 1974 *TV Buddha:* "An eighteenth century Japanese statue of the Buddha sits gazing into a screen that beams the figure's own image back at him. This is the ultimate in closed-circuit television—an object and its image locked into an electronic eternity." With advances in cable, earphones, and superradios, who knows how self-wired America may become?

Fascination with Space and Space Exploration. Movies about people going into space or "aliens" visiting us have obvious box office appeal; somewhat less obvious, outside the theatre, is the desire actually to go into space.

Elisa Wynn, founder of a local chapter of a space colonization group, the Niagara Frontier L5 Society, says: "A lot of what we're talking about sounds like science fiction now. The best way to get moving on it is to get private enterprise to start making a profit up there." Many of my students would like to go for the ride; the M.B.A. students want the profits as well.

Video and Other Games. Video and the computer, in their *combined* capacities to process and display information, to put the chip to work for the screen and video disc, provide the most obsessive forms of escape today. Video parlors (electronic saloons?) turn out new retinal ailments and maladies every day, but the most enduring damage may be to the conscience of a generation.

If Pac-Man addicts come to believe that the threats to life, like the game, are "just circuitry," or that playing Space Invaders can deal with real missiles; if those who play Dungeons and Dragons renounce the rigors and anxieties of facing conflict for an escape into another life "where they have some control over their destiny," then a generation may find itself unable to deal with problems that aren't artificial (and should we now add *videoficial*?).

There is, doubtless, some poignancy in these modes of evasion—making use on a mock and miniature scale of technology and circuitry similar to the ones that actually threaten us, taking external threats symbolically into our own hands, displacing our fears; gobbling up the enemy—but we must face the true enemy: ourselves, our international counterparts.

There is, finally, no closed-circuit solution to the problem of survival.

The task of humanistic education over the next decade or two ought to be to unearth the serious content of games, to relate constantly the advancements in computer and video technology to the ongoing bodily, spiritual, and aesthetic needs of people here and abroad; to transmit and display human suffering and the threats to life on a worldwide basis; to insist on the application of information (food resources, population demographics) to what should be caring kinds of human encounters.

Literary and philosophic types will have to bone up on their software and hardware to become more effective; the programmers and their advocates may have to become somewhat less effective as mere shifters of signs, glyphs, and ciphers.

If this generation is divided between those who would *survive* and those who would *escape,* the academy is divided along parallel lines: between those who see the perilous writing on the wall and those who only would study its style and structure. We need to overcome this division at such a late day of the thermonuclear century.

Each generation reinvents a new style, a new technology for its version of the struggle between life and death. Teachers and educators must discover, decade after decade, a new edition of the human drama if their subjects and approaches are themselves to stay alive.

A Summing Up

Twenty-Five Years Later
(Amherst College Reunion Essay) 21

We entered history together twenty-five years ago and hold in common many articulated and hidden assumptions. We were put together for a common journey through time and history by the fact and circumstance that most of us entered high school at exactly mid-century (1950) and then came to Amherst College by some roll of familial or cultural dice in the fall of 1954 in the immediate *aftermath* of the Scottsboro Case (1931), the fading echoes of the Great Depression, the Second World War, the holocaust, Hiroshima, and the McCarthy period.

One of the first facts about us, then, is that we were born closer to the nineteenth century than to the twenty-first, closer to music of Brahms and Schubert than to the dissonance of Berg and the chance compositions of John Cage. Though we saw ourselves as part of a postwar generation and the inheritors of the modernist tradition in art and technology, our origins lay closer to the late Victorian era than to the onrushing, contemporary world of medical engineering and "interactive information retrieval systems." A number of our professors were, in fact, children of the nineteenth century.

This essay was delivered as part of the Amherst Class of 1958 Reunion Panel: *American Culture, Then, Now, and Tomorrow.* It also appeared, in a somewhat abbreviated form, as "An Appointment with History," *Reporter,* 4 August 1983.

Many of us were born into families whose grandparents remembered the western frontier as a still vital, though fading, force in American life, and some of us were born into families who still spoke one or another non-English language, even if this later quality was something of a taboo subject in the assimilative togetherness of the 1950s.

Despite being hell-bent on social integration and making hay while the sun shone on the postwar boom, many of us would hear later (might always hear) echoes of an earlier era when the corn was sweeter, the air cleaner, and the city streets filled with the energetic cries of vendors and new Americans—not the cries of the newly dispossessed and the screams of urban violence and terror.

My mother, a child of Russian and Austrian immigrants (the Pale and Leipzig), remembers, despite near childhood poverty, a flourishing garden in Pembroke, Ontario, where three thousand French-Canadians and twelve Jewish families formed a community, as she remembers the near wild Stevensian landscape of Western Pennsylvania (Altoona and Williamsburg), where verdant hills beckoned to the imagination of an eager, but lonely, first-born American child.

My father, a son of Russians only, remembers the surging vitality of the Lower East Side of New York not so long after the turn of the century when a kid might run through the spray of a hydrant all the way "uptown" (that charged word) and become George Gershwin or, not quite so far uptown, Union Square, and become, God forbid, a Socialist.

We may feel pulled back for some of these reasons, to a real or imagined America that we find simpler and more acceptable. Some of us—I hope not too many—may base an ardent neoconservatism on these feelings. I suspect that many of us have felt the tug of Fitzgerald's by now all too famous "boats against the current, borne back ceaselessly into the past" and that we long for an America fraught with more imagined possibilities for self-fulfillment.

We're probably eager to get away from many of the negative uses of advanced technology by corporate interests: fast foods, anonymous subdivisions, and the menacing discoveries of high energy physics: the terrors of infinitely small matter and infinitely large releases of energy.

Most of us probably would want as much an America of restored nineteenth century urban design and architecture (like historic Charleston) and pristine ecology (Thoreau's Massachusetts) as we would a world of video-text, TV talkback, and Qube systems. Or perhaps we would want—and might even be able to influence—the synthesis of both worlds: pastoral and electronically futuristic.

So, we were a generation born closer to the nineteenth than the twenty-first century that came of age in the aftermath of terrible history, and it's one of the mysteries of this generation (the silent generation, remember?), however, that we spoke so little about these catastrophic events (the severity of the depression, racism, the holocaust), if we spoke about them at all.

We were led to believe that the memory of recent history would foul up our postwar boom, corporate and Madison Avenue hype, and our possible place in it. Our parents and teachers had seen too much of history for a while, it seems, and they preferred a kind of personal and cultural amnesia in exchange for emotional and sometimes political safety (HUAC [House Un-American Activities Committee]). Instead of facing holocaust victims and McCarthy's prosecutors, they preferred silence, and we guiltily felt that we had survived and outlived other people's suffering. We chose, without feeling it as choice, *not* to remind ourselves of what we had missed.

We doubtless felt also that our own history would be diminished inevitably by a comparison with the previous period. What could *we* ever do to match the defeat of the Nazis by the Allied war effort, the heroism of the Flying Tigers? We even may have sensed that it would be healthier for our generational integrity and identity to act as if the history of the previous generation didn't exist, or, more problematically, *that history itself* (that invisible, impersonal, shifting, and binding idea that shapes our lives) *wasn't important.*

This illusory belief in the escape from history may have worked for us for about a decade, if that long, but by the time the Vietnam War had reached a peak in the late sixties and the antiwar movement had reached an equal gathering of momentum, it wasn't possible for most of us to act as if history had not impinged, or called upon us in some important ways.

Many of us knew as we watched antiwar protests and other "countercultural" events on television (the medium that radically separates us from our grandparents), or even marched in some of those events, that we could not treat history as if it were a wave we chose not to ride to shore.

We knew increasingly from the Free Speech Movement at Berkeley in 1964 to the sit-ins at Columbia in 1968 that we were somehow in the current of history and had to respond to it one way or another. We couldn't step out of the water. I think it's fair to say that we knew—by the time of Kent State in the spring of 1970—that we paid a heavy price if we thought we could treat history as if we were innocent bystanders. We knew then that it would act upon us, our friends, our companions, our wives, and our children if we didn't act upon it.

We knew we couldn't live outside of history so long as the Vietnam War led to brutal arrests at home and bodycounts in Southeast Asia, but if you were at all like me, you were somewhat bewildered about the terms in which we could enter history.

Too old to fight, if we were patriots; too settled to resist, if we were antiwar, many of us wrestled on a day-to-day basis with our consciences and checkbooks and did the best we thought we could as discomfited middlemen to express a moral response to a moment of terrible history that *had* reached us.

I can see, in retrospect, that I tried to understand how the war in Vietnam affected American domestic and university life *through experimental teaching and writing*: typical, if not dishonorable, act of a fifties middleman; it's even possible that my writing, as an act among millions of related acts, contributed in some oblique and Tolstoyan way to the "climate of opinion" (famous phrase of our generation) that put an end, finally, to the war in Vietnam, though its Missing in Action (MIA) and Amerasian legacy continues to haunt us.

If few of us became "activists," it may be equally true that few of us became "ex-activists," who then turned against the sense of history we had just discovered. If we were not on the barricades in the sixties, we didn't have to give up history like the Paris Communards on the slopes of Belleville on 28 May 1971.

Without initial belief, we didn't became apostates.

Our generation (in Ortega's terms: *our life problem,* the spirit of our times, the environment of our collective life), which refused history in the fifties, which approached it ambivalently in the sixties, may turn out to have a more enduring sense of its force and power than those who came after us and were in it, or those who came before us and lost faith in the radical ideas and ideals of the thirties. In some paradoxical sense (one of our favored terms), we may have found history by missing it when we were young; we may have a more enduring appointment with history because of our missed connections long ago.

As we come together after a quarter of a century, we can say that we've discovered history in our own way, from our point of view; that we've established our own context, and this discovery comes none too early. We, our children, and soon, if not already, their children will face increasingly the darkest threats to the earth that mankind has known.

We lived in the shadow of Hiroshima and its horror (the fundamental breach of the rights of noncombatants secured by the Geneva Convention) and naively knew the meaning of detente as mock-terror in the guise of "take-over" (a frightening, if finally absurd, drill); we now face, with our children, the actual nuclear pollution and the felt dread of the possible extinction of the earth, the obliteration of man and the idea of man (the humanist legacy), of what we have been and might be.

If we once thought that we could escape history, we now have discovered it only to face the possibility of the End of History, not in the Judeo-Christian and Marxist-humanist sense of the end of injustice and labor, but as the negation of human story. We face a dark wood "in the middle of the journey of our life" and must act upon our experience and hard-earned knowledge: that we cannot escape history, but can choose only to act effectually or ineffectually in it.

There is no one clear path of action. Action remains open as always in the best traditions of liberal democracy (our Emersonian and republican traditions as sons and daughters of Amherst, town and college), a matter of debate and rational disagreement; we must, however, face the fact of the dark wood and insist on finding light, of saying, with Goethe, at his death, "mehr licht."

If we began our journey in silence and inwardness—the muted drama of the psyche in the fifties, the cult of Freud, the inarticulate murmurings of Brando and the Actors' Studio—we come to maturity face to face with the spectral future of the earth and globe as our responsibility. We began our journey by taking the circumference of the inner life as our world and boundary; we now see that the palpable earth, the latitudes and longitudes of the once good earth, are our deeper legacy.

I remember lovingly drawing maps of the world in grade school—lavender for Peru, canary yellow for El Salvador—and then losing that ecstasy of the world's diversity through self-consciousness and the anxiety of "making it" in the postwar period. Maybe you shared that sense of the world as a radiant morsel with me; maybe we have a second chance, as did America in relation to Eden once, to get back to the palette of the earth's wonder.

It's possible that our essential closeness to the nineteenth century, not noticed at first or taken as a liability, may turn out to be a moral asset (a reminder and model of a less endangered world) and give us some of the terms of wholeness to make such a struggle for wonder possible again. Where there might be ash and cinder, let us paint robin's egg and Delft blue.

These seem to me to be the pressing, if not the only differentiating, elements of our generation, but I have left out so many significant changes in the movement from the modern to the postmodern era that I must, in homage, list them and leave you with a chart (at the end of this chapter):

• the shift from a culture of narrative and myth, with its preference for coherence, to one of information and feed-back, with its penchant for process (computer programs);

• the transition from a culture of print and reverence for the word (with all that this implied about a stable, canonical literature and tradition) to a society of interactive electronic texts with obsessive emphasis on visual phenomena and the displacement of original experience by photosensitive images;

• the movement from the two-handed set-shot and the cult of Jackie Robinson's heroism to the high-priced glitzy slam-dunk;

• the expansion of life-expectancy from sixty-five to seventy-five to eighty, augmented each day by breakthroughs in medical engineering;

• the shift from the idolatry of the stable Victorian family to one-parent families, to say nothing of serial and open marriages;

• the destruction of nature's bountiful plant and animal life and the emergence of hunger, malnutrition, and endangered species as global features;

• the changes in modes and speed of transportation with accompanying shifts in perception of time and space: from sitting in railway cars to floating in space shuttles.

I could extend this list—it's open, after all, to the historical imagination—but I want to end this series with what may be the most obvious but least observed distinction between our generation and the present: the shift from a man's world—defined at an all-male

Shift of Cultural Values

Dominant Values	1950s	1980s
Time	Nineteenth century legacy	Twenty-first century
Music	Harmony	Dissonance
Body	Mortality	Biomedical longevity
Space	Linearity	Circularity (interactive)
History: A	Aftermath	Future
History: B	Escape	Disappearance
Media	Print and aural	TV and video
Psychic point of view	Inner	Outer (global)
Story	Narrative, myth, and coherence	Information, feedback, and process (computer programs)
Sports	Heroism	Money, glamour
Longevity	Sixty-five	Seventy-five to eighty
Family	Victorian stability	Open
Nature	Bountiful	Endangered
Transportation	One-directional (classical)	Spatial-temporal (postmodern)
Gender	Male dominant	Egalitarian
World	Detente	Thermonuclear terror

college by young men, many of whom had gone to all-male high and prep schools—to a society happily humanized by the presence of women as equals, partners, and co-workers.

For our daughters' sake, and even for our sons', we should be especially grateful to the pressures of history for beginning to unseat male authority, for making the world a slightly more egalitarian place.

This seems like a good place to come to rest for a while. We can come back to some of these issues when we celebrate our fiftieth as an Old Guard in 2008, though we will have changed by then, which, as Amherst relativists of the fifties, we should know, and the issues will look different.

Still, you and I had better continue to face a threatened future with moral resources drawn from the past, the country's, our own. Our task over the next decade or two ought to be to make serious use of the information revolution, to respond quickly to the spiritual and aesthetic needs of people here and abroad; to make known human suffering and the threats to life on a worldwide basis; to insist on the application of information (food resources, population demographics) to what should be caring kinds of human encounters. Let's put the electron to work in an America and world once likened to Eden.

Let's join Eden (the nineteenth) and Electron (the twenty-first), the best of two centuries. That's it, as Robert Frost might have said long ago on a snowy night in Amherst town.

Our Place in Time
(Horace Mann Reunion Essay) 22

We entered high school—or should I still say Third *Form* (it sounds a bit outdated now)?—at precisely the midpoint of the twentieth century (1950). I don't remember any of us talking, though, about our falling so symbolically between the nineteenth and twenty-first centuries, or about Horace Mann being an embodiment of older, nineteenth century values, even though the main stone building, to say nothing about the terraced grounds, declared itself as somewhat Victorian in its scale, wooden smell, and wax polish.

In retrospect, it seems odd that we didn't see the intriguing balance of our position—of our place in time—but I suppose we thought we were living outside time (a common enough failing of youth). Only our futures mattered to us. We were a "goal-oriented" generation, to use an idiom of our era. We believed that our intelligence and socioeconomic position—most of us came from affluent families—would protect us from time and what were for us its only legendary ravages.

So far as we were concerned, only our parents and grandparents were retrospective and looked backwards to the depression and one or another form of exodus from Europe at the turn of the century, if

This essay is reprinted with permission from *Spectrum,* 1984.

not earlier. We looked to the future, to the promise of the post-Second World War economic boom and our rightful, inevitable place in it. We thought of ourselves as modern, postatomic, cybernetic. Born before TV and the ballpoint, we were, nonetheless, in the fast lane of the twentieth century.

We felt we were entitled to all the perks the future could offer. We had staked our claim by becoming Horace Mann students, by singing Ivy League fight songs in assembly, and by cheering for the maroon and white. We felt that our matriculation at the Horace Mann School *For Boys* (another Victorianism) confirmed our essential excellence. We believed we were destined to take our places in, or to move into, the upper reaches of American society just because we were H.M.'ers. We were headed, after all, for an Ivy League school and, afterward, an equivalent graduate or professional school: those guarantors, we thought, of success in America.

We listened, a bit bemused, to the stories our parents and grandparents told about suffering, displacement, and political terror. These stories seemed to us, however, to be only disquieting footnotes to the larger American story of success and achievement in which we would play a role, make a contribution, and, doubtless, take a profit.

One classmate's father knew Alexander Karensky during his years of exile from postrevolutionary Russia when he worked as a printer in the Bronx; another classmate's father had known the Greenwich Village poet Maxwell Bodenheim in his late and tragic phase; another classmate's father had been denied a high post at Columbia's Medical School because he was a Jew; and my own father had left Seward Park High School at age fifteen in 1924 because more food had to be put on his family's Chrystie Street tenement table.

We knew these stories, or ones like them, but they were irrelevant to us, distracting at best, and in any case our fathers (mothers still weren't too important professionally for most of us) had "made it" by the time we entered Horace Mann at midcentury. So it didn't make much sense to give too much credence to these plaintive narratives.

Besides, too many differentiating experiences lay between many of us and most of our fathers: summer camps in the Adirondacks and Maine; European travel (teen tours); dancing school; braces for everyone who needed them; proms and even debutante parties *cum* cumberbunds for those of us who could bear to wear yet another Lester Lanin beanie.

With these buffers, why think about pogroms, Ellis Island isolation, childhood diseases, dangerous working conditions (Triangle fire), child labor, or lack of education—all of which had been familiar experiences to many of our grandparents, if not parents? One close friend's father had emigrated from Russia in the twenties and worked on the docks as a "steve" before "making it" as a food wholesaler. He never got over immigrant humiliation, a "greenhorn" accent.

It was hard for us to keep these historical realities in mind, after all, when many of us lived in apartments on Central Park West and Park Avenue with real or replicated Louis XVIth, if not XIVth, mirrors, inlaid escritoires, and Portuguese tile bathrooms with pseudo-Baroque wainscotting.

Even if we didn't actually live in these apartments (though some of us did), we all pretty much had gone to parties in which such decor and artifacts were common enough. Even if we lived in Brooklyn (where?) or Queens (huh?), we could imagine living in, even owning (we were on to co-ops and condos early) these apartments with these acquisitions *because we were going to H.M.* The world was our oyster, even if we hadn't yet eaten one, even if it wasn't kosher.

We had an appointment with success and privilege—not Samarra —and if meeting it weren't quite as simple as meeting someone under the clock at the now-razed Biltmore (still a fad in the fifties), we expected, nonetheless, to be *there,* wherever *there* was, on time when the time came, dressed for the occasion: grey flannel slacks, blue blazer, cordovans, Oxford button-down shirt, J. Press silk rep-tie, our generational uniform.

We weren't looking back very much to the world of our grandfathers, and we weren't looking much beyond our immediate futures, much beyond the golden Fitzgerald years after graduate and professional school when we would enter the ranks of the educated elite who would make big bucks on the greatest island in the world ("I'll Take Manhattan . . ."), while perhaps making a social contribution, like cole slaw, on the side. This was still the big-money era—King Farouk, Aga Khan.

We weren't thinking, for these reasons, about the significance of our perfectly equidistant position between two centuries—and what it might signify: falling between ethics and the electron. All we had to do, we figured, was do well in our studies at H.M., add some sports or extracurricular activities, and, if possible, score high on the SATs—all leading towards admission into a good college. Not all of these tasks were easy, and some even had beneficial implications that we couldn't see at the time, but for us the course seemed easy enough to follow. There was no need to look too far back or ahead.

And then there was the fact that we had come of age just *after* the depression, Hiroshima, and the Second World War. Because we came so closely upon the heels of so much oppressing history, we had paradoxically a diminished sense of history with its chastising realities. It was as if we suffered from a form of cultural amnesia or hypnosis in which only positive and optimistic thoughts were allowed access to consciousness.

The McCarthy period aided this process of suppression or repression of history and politics. As our parents' generation was called to task (and before committees) more and more for its commitments in the thirties, they wanted to remember less and less, and we followed suit.

Some of us tried to stay alive to history—one idealistic classmate used to comb Yorktown to monitor neo-Nazi movements—but most of us were willing to try to forget history. We responded to the witty promise of Adlai Stevenson's bid for the presidency and his unmasking of the leisure of the theory class, but we were willing to accept the benefits and dividends of the Eisenhower years and the economic boom that Madison Avenue and TV packaged for our actual and conceptual consumption.

This period of grace lasted for about a decade, by which time most of us had finished the core of our graduate or professional training or had established ourselves one way or another in banking, commerce, stocks and bonds, etc. We lived in this state of relative innocence about American experience until 1963 and the assassination of John F. Kennedy.

That intrusion of violence and disruption, followed by the assassinations of Robert Kennedy and Martin Luther King, Jr. set us back and made us question the unqualified terms of success and advancement to which we had hitched our wagons. If so much potential violence lay beneath the surface of everyday American life, what could we make of our unexamined commitment to the status quo? Could we assume that America would stay stable through our careers? Were we part of the problem or the solution? It wouldn't be quite so easy, after these events, to embrace "success" as an unexamined term. The shadow of modern terror, hysteria, and irrationality had crossed our path. The world of our fathers and grandfathers looked a little less remote to us.

Then came the Vietnam War, a national crisis of conscience that would leave none of us unaffected. We could no longer pretend that we could exist *beyond* politics and live *outside* history—that twin myth of the immediate postwar period which claimed that we came "*after* the last generation" and "at the end of ideology."

We were thrust *into* history one way or the other: through our students, children; through our revived sense of identity as active and critical Americans who had to put their shoulder to the wheel of history. Some of us even marched, got arrested, or defended legally those who had opposed the government's war policy.

We may not have looked back in our race towards advancement and success, but some of the usable and enduring terms of a nine-

teenth century education had been instilled in us through our traditional and substantive courses in literature and history at H.M. There
was nothing trendy or "relevant" about our education.

Our headmasters and teachers—more or less classical, more or
less humanistic—had insisted, through their labors to make us studi-
ous, that we face some of the tests of time as they had been recorded
by historians and authors. We were encouraged, in this fairly *un*progressive context, to face historical struggles beyond ourselves. How
many of our contemporaries studied ancient history, world history,
nineteenth century history, and American history at so young an age?

We were asked to face some great issues and conflicts and to
register a considered response in serious *Quarterly Themes*. These
themes—in the hands of bright and imaginative students, especially
eager and lively students mainly from the City—led generally, even
inevitably, to ethical conclusions.

H.M. asked us to put our adolescent idealism into words, to
articulate and to describe our dawning awareness of the human predicament. Some of what we said went against what would be for a
while our often more superficial commitment to making it. We contained within ourselves a version of nineteenth century doubleness: a
commitment to material progress and social conscience, without
appreciating the ambivalence at the time. We had stored up a better
self for the future, put a humanistic conscience in the memory, if not
savings, bank.

I like to think that our H.M. education was there for us when we
needed it after the bubble of optimism burst in 1963 and continued to
explode until the midseventies through a war and a recession replete
with energy depletion. I like to think that we were able to face
historical difficulty and the necessity for moral response because we
had been schooled in forms of criticism and evaluation that went
beyond or below mere socioeconomic success.

The H.M.'ers I've known over the years convince me that what
I'm saying is true. Avoiding extremes, we try to find, like classic

nineteenth century liberals (e.g., J. S. Mill), general solutions to common problems. We work for the public weal between the extremes of Left and Right. We have tried to imagine and build a world free of the spectre of worldwide totalitarianism, contempt for life, and abridgements of the Constitution in the U.S.

We turn out to be middle-of-the-road, but decent, I think. This is part of our midcentury perspective. We may have to admit that we're the best of the "middle class"—that term of opprobrium for the middle class. A close friend's analyst told him to put a sign—neon, if possible—above his desk saying *MIDDLE CLASS*. The good doctor thought this would clarify my friend's anxieties. My friend exchanged this sensible doctor for one who talked more "meaningfully" about Oedipal conflicts. I think my friend should have stuck with the first physician of his social mind.

The years 1963 to 1975—from the assassination of an inspirited national leader through the Vietnam War, Watergate, and economic pressure—tested, then, our educational resources and revealed the dual nature of our connection to the nineteenth century: social ethics as well as material progress. If this seems a surprising or antique association, just think: Most of our parents were born between 1900 and 1915, and some of our teachers were older than the century itself.

We now can see, however, our origins in the nineteenth century even as we face the onrushing end of the twentieth century with all of its technological possibilities. We are aware of this double destiny every day through two aspects of contemporary consciousness and technology: space exploration and the thermonuclear "balance" of terror. Our task is to recover some of the nineteenth century legacy and to join it to the humanistic uses of advanced technology.

These two great issues point the way towards the creative and destructive possibilities of our century. We can see the year 2000 in somewhat millennial terms as a symbolic terminus—a time when the global family will decide to end the human story—*or* as a continuation of man's quest to make his narrative the most human of all stories.

Our class and generation have a special feeling for this doubleness of the future because our parents began the century and our children will live their productive years near its end. For their sake (2000) and because we are heirs to our parents' immigrant beginnings in America (1900); because we possess or comprehend this century from our mid-point of consciousness (1950); because we contain the *entire* century, we will do our best in the coming years to preserve man's moral destiny. To betray this destiny would be a form of self-injury.

New Start in Changing Times

Faculty will soon have an opportunity to make a contribution to a "developing undergraduate college" (*Reporter,* 13 February 1986). This comes as welcome news. Many complex elements go into the making of a college, especially a new college, but none is more important than the quality, perspective, and commitment of faculty. As Secretary of Education William Bennett said not too long ago:

> A college is many things. It is a collection of dormitories, libraries, social clubs, incorrigibly terrible cafeterias. But, above all, it is a faculty. It used to be said, when this country was much younger, that a log lying on the side of the road with a student sitting on one end and a professor on the other was a university (*The Buffalo News,* 24 November 1985).

One doesn't have to agree with all of the secretary's Victorian assumptions to see the wisdom of his point.

At the same time, one-to-one dia-*logs* are expensive; no one professor can comprehend the whole intellectual universe (as still might have been possible in the 1840s and 1850s when Charles Darwin could look closely and base a revision of the existing world view on observation and reflection), and the scientific-technological break-

---

This essay is reprinted with permission from *Reporter,* 6 March 1986.

throughs of the past few decades—in data processing, subatomic physics, and space exploration, to name just three—call the log-sitting metaphor into question.

As cozy as the secretary's image may be, our faculty cannot build a new college of much use for our future out of yesterday's felled timber. We must ask current and real questions, the answers to which will address our actual situation: a large, diverse multiversity where students and faculty often don't see one another again after a course has ended and where many faculty are too preoccupied with their own writing and research—to put the best face on this issue—to meet one-to-one with any or many students, with or without logs.

We must ask, in this context, how can a relatively small faculty deal efficiently and creatively with so large a student body as ours? How can so many students get a feel for world culture—"visit" its icons, emblems, artifacts; "see" its geography, ecology, food resources —at relatively low cost? How can we best make use of our physical facilities so that education can take place conveniently? What assumptions can a faculty member make about the common intellectual background and preparation of the students? What knowledge do faculty share among themselves when specialization and field-consciousness have been so dominant since the end of the Second World War?

Is it possible for a large research university—with emphases on preprofessional and professional training, with embedded historical commitments to the apparently inescapable divisions of formal thought (humanities, social sciences, and natural sciences)—to find an original and sufficiently varied set of terms to meet the challenges of the future? Can our university find the techniques and resources to address, say, our new awareness of the profound connections between technology and culture? Can we find new ways to put our students in a position to shape and create knowledge instead of just storing it?

It won't be enough to give our students new information, new courses, if that's the way people are likely to think about a new college. The form in which knowledge might be imparted should be of equal concern with content. Attention should be paid to *how* students learn, as well as to *what* they learn, although faculty are better equipped, historically, to deal with the latter issue.

I don't pretend to have answers to these questions, but it occurs to me that a tentative reply lies close at hand through the range of knowledge available to the general culture through media. I'm thinking about the general education, as it were, that the Public Broadcasting System (PBS) and the British Broadcasting System (BBC) have offered to the public over the past few decades and the audio-visual archives that have developed along with, and in response to, these programs. I'm thinking, as well, about the printed materials that have been put out to accompany these series, such as Jonathan Weiner's *Planet Earth* and Abba Eban's *Civilization and the Jews.*

Might we not imagine something like an Electronic College of the First Year—as a first and inaugural step in the shaping of a new college—in which undergraduates and faculty both share response to, and dialog about, some of the fundamental ideas and events that have given form and substance to, as well as threatened, our civilization?

This Electronic College of the First Year might serve as a bridge between high school and the college's more advanced curriculum, whatever it might be. Although the issue of "remedialism" might be raised here, the focus should be one of creating a common fund of information, images, and resources, not of overcoming deficiencies. At another level, it would give faculty an opportunity to cross over from one discipline to another, from one language-system to another.

Kenneth Clark's "Civilization," the recent "Voyage of Charles Darwin," Carl Sagan's exuberant "Cosmos," "Masterpiece Theatre," "American Playhouse," "Nova," and the "Treasure Houses of Britain" —these series and others, as well as innumerable special programs, provide a wealth of material for elaboration, criticism, supplementary lectures, and symposia, to say nothing about ease of instruction, the possibility of seeing and reading a "document" more than once, and new modes of note-taking (recording) in this era of miniaturization.

In addition to the materials that have been prepared for Public Television, there is an impressive array of independent research materials. The Corporation for Entertainment and Learning, Inc., has developed a Video Encyclopedia of the twentieth century with seventy-five one-hour video cassettes that cover major events from 1893 to 1985. This pictorial history comes with a five-volume master index that allows teacher and student to select and "compose" history, so to speak, for viewing and discussion. The complete set, according to the *New York Times* (14 January 1986), sells for $8,500.

This example could be multiplied many times. The John and Mary R. Markle Foundation of New York has developed Kidsnet, a computerized catalogue of audio-visual instructional materials with two hundred titles in history.

> "The idea is to make history come alive to children in a way they can identify with," said Leo Eaton, who produced the six programs, each covering a different century, beginning with the eleventh. "We are a television community. We see the wars, the statesmen on the evening news. Why not history?" (*New York Times,* 16 January 1986).

One can well imagine students and teachers, interested in primary and secondary education, studying these materials both for what they may teach about history and to examine their very assumptions about "making" history for a young audience.

I'm not suggesting that these materials should be used uncritically. I envision, in fact, the use and criticism of these shared audio-visual archives (commerical and educational) as a first step, a beginning, towards a new and integrated curriculum. The Electronic College of the First Year would be one component of a new college.

I can imagine professors as tutors and discussion leaders in a transformed role. They would be in a position to know quickly what their students know in terms of cultural literacy (in relation to complicated areas of art, science, and technology) and would then be in a position to direct related readings and discussion in a way that fits their specific interests and the needs of their students.

The teacher could also guide the student and himself instantaneously through the world of available knowledge and information by including the use of information systems and their display. Although making use of audio-visual archives, newsreels, televised congressional hearings, data bases, film and record libraries (the accrued wealth of material that is relatively easy to distribute through time and space in flexible patterns), as well as information retrieval, the instructor could still make the most exacting bibliographic demands and the most traditional gestures. Tutorials could become global in and through many senses.

Looking back, we can see that American colleges and universities moved too quickly and destructively to dismantle curricula during the sixties as a response to student unrest, but given that disquieting history, we now have an opportunity to create an education for the future that is, in an Emersonian way, relatively unencumbered with past assumptions.

We are entering a new age, and our students should be there to meet it. Just as a new, very large array of twenty-seven dish antennas placed around an ancient New Mexico lake bed may soon be linked with installations from Hawaii and Puerto Rico to make the earth itself into a huge antenna, so we should think of our university as a source and resource of new connections—the data bases of which exist, in different forms, and remain to be put to use in a sensible fashion.

The State University of New York at Buffalo need become neither the University at Oz nor a Spaced-out Center to step towards the future even as it makes dramatic and living use of the past.

Bread, Freedom, and Prose   **24**

My contemporaries in education now must know, if they didn't before, that history has many cunning passages. Entering college in the
middle of Eisenhower's first administration, we rode the wave of
postwar middle-class aspiration into the swelling ranks of graduate
school and found ourselves gasping for breath on the shore after
Vietnam.

We thought Sputnik would launch us into a new era of expanded
possibilities for education, and we thought, as it seemed almost impossible not to during the sixties, that we were entering what Marcuse
and his followers called the postindustrial era; we found ourselves
instead stranded in ecological pastures that weren't very green.

The eighties turned out to be a period of "stagflation," energy
depletion, political conservatism, out-and-out panic-selling on the
world gold markets, and retrenchment in education:

> Americans who plan their careers, home buying, and otherwise structure
> their lives on the assumption that America has entered the "postindus-
> trial era" better take another hard look at what is happening.[1]

This essay appeared as "Non-Fiction in the Marketplace," *Buffalo Arts Review*,
Summer 1985.

My generation, which looked *first* to the corporations and Madison Avenue for expanding possibilities (1945 to 1960) and *then* to the human potential movement for augmented self-realization (1960 to 1970) has registered one shock after another over the past decade. We've heard the culture's message—The Age of Possibility is Over—from Kent State to Three Mile Island through Jonestown and then to Mt. St. Helens whose eruption seemed to mark the end of a pastoral dream, a fantasy which comes back every half century or so to capture the American imagination.

Teachers of literature and the humanities face a special version of this cultural redefinition and shift in national priorities. Most teachers of literature hold positions, if they're employed at all, in departments that have stopped hiring because of administrative freezes. These teachers belong to departments with false bottoms. There is no trap door leading to a new generation. A few colleagues have lost jobs, some face retrenchment, and many fear that their day will come.

Where loss of job hasn't been an issue, there has been pressure from within and without the university to get departments of literature and languages back to the basics so that they will serve the institution better, so they will reflect, as administrators are fond of saying, the real world.

This pressure has led to streamlined courses, remedial courses, "bone-head" composition curricula, and many species of business English and word-processor composition curricula that have been punched up across the country. This mobilized response to the budgetary, demographic, and cultural crisis in higher education seems to be working, or at least holding the line. Enrollments are up this year in the freshman class at my university.

But this victory is a mixed blessing. We may have numbers, and we may have bought or engineered a place in the future, but we also have cut a deal about what is *basic* education. Many people—including administrators, legislators, HEW (the Department of Health, Education and Welfare), and job-oriented parents and students—interpret "basic" too narrowly as education for the marketplace.

We are on board for what one institution in Western New York calls "learning for earning." The founding fathers of this business and secretarial school speak loudly and clearly to the fears and hopes of many young Americans in the new era of industrial computerization.

This is part of the context in which many of us are teaching and will teach English or, as they now say, language skills. One can rail against the economic gods, but this is the gaffe. Is there then a way, a set of strategies, that might allow us to serve the needs of man as well as the needs of the marketplace in our nonfiction writing courses?

I think we can develop what George Orwell calls the "power of facing unpleasant facts."[2] We can stress in this renewed age of fact (the return of *Hard Times,* the difficulties of gaining knowledge at even the most material level). We can raise questions about the description and evaluation of fact and phenomena that will push the student to the frontier where what is *actual* and what is *imaginative* touch.

Instructors could take the notion of "facing" seriously, not as a page-turning exercise, or a matter of looking up facts, as one uses a telephone book or dictionary; they might, instead, approach the task of "facing" as an authentic relationship between writing and experience.

For some, it will be existential; for some, psychotherapeutic; for others, Marxist, autobiographical, or theological. We can make use of the new circumstances of the new materialistic era to encourage our students to examine through writing the deepest penetration of fact in their lives.

We can help along the task of "facing unpleasant facts" through the art of choosing "the best word in common use." Hazlitt's dictum of 1821 rescues for us the job of prose instruction from the burden of *mere* composition just as it also pulls us back from the shimmering grate of contemporary literary theory:

It is not easy to write a familiar style. Many people mistake a familiar for a vulgar style, and suppose that to write without affectation is to write at random. On the contrary, there is nothing that requires more precision, and, if I may so say, purity of expression, than the style I am speaking of. It utterly rejects not only all unmeaning pomp, but all low, cant phrases, and loose, unconnected, *slipshod* allusions. It is not to take the first word that offers, but the best word in common use; it is not to throw words together in any combinations we please, but to follow and avail ourselves of the true idiom of the language. To write a genuine familiar or truly English style, is to write as any one would speak in common conversation, who had a thorough command and choice of words, or who could discourse with ease, force, and perspicuity, setting aside all pedantic and oratorical flourishes.[3]

Few words are less well understood than "common," and no word could better join the issues of aesthetics and utilitarianism for us.

The shift to basic education and a curriculum of necessity, if we must call it that, can lead us to another form of non-fiction that begins with a brutal encounter with reality and leads inevitably to the imaginative. I'm thinking of the documentary, or documented, approach to history. I'm thinking about the history of slavery and racism in the United States, the holocaust, and the gulag. (I'm not thinking of the television versions of these enormities in "Roots" or "Holocaust.") I'm thinking of written documentations in Dubois's *The Souls of Black Folk,* Terrence Des Pres's *The Survivor,* and Shostakovich's *Testimony.*

By directing our students to documentary and documented forms *against* the versions of the media, we can instruct our students and ourselves in the imaginative and moral uses of non-fiction. We can ask our students, for instance, *if it is possible to document the holocaust, or any event of historic horror, without becoming a moralist, without making our investigation a form of judgment.* We can ask students if it is possible to understand the nazi mentality *without imagining the unimaginable?*

As we ask students to face unpleasant facts, to use common words, and to deal with the question of the documentary—all in the service of clear writing—we might find a new humanism, a new basis for self-expression, arising over the next decade or two out of the ashes of investigation and facticity.

The students who would come out of this curriculum might discover, might feel the need to discover, the grounds for a new self, a self appropriate to the last part of the twentieth century. It will not be the discovery of the Freudian self that held sway from about 1885 to 1950 (from Freud's *Studies in Hysteria* to the cold war); nor will it be the potential self of the period 1950 to 1980, the self that took wing during the baby boom of the postwar period and flew upward with Tom Wolfe during the psychedelic sixties and his narcissistic seventies.

I think another kind of imagined self could push through the uses of the *factual, common, and documentary.* It might be a refashioned version of Dubois's jubilee self, a joyous self based on the sorrow songs of oppression, a self that will proclaim and defend the case for the human and the moral through documentation of the factual and common trials of this century.

The documented case for humanity—and the self that this documentation might shape—could serve to defend the cause of freedom and humanity in the next century. We only have to listen to the tempered voice of Frederick Douglass if we doubt that literacy, tested through the factual and common and documented, can forge a case for freedom:

These dear souls came not to Sabbath school because it was popular to do so, nor did I teach them because it was reputable to be thus engaged. Every moment they spent in that school, they were liable to be taken up, and given thirty-nine lashes. They came because they wished to learn. Their minds had been starved by their cruel masters. They had been shut up in mental darkness. I taught them, because it was the delight of my soul to be doing something that looked like bettering the condition of my race. I kept up my school nearly the whole year I lived with Mr. Freeland; and, beside my Sabbath school, I devoted three evenings in the week, during the winter, to teaching the slaves at home. And I have the happiness to know, that several of those who came to Sabbath school learned how to read; and that one, at least, is now free through my agency.[4]

One curriculum can begin to serve the ends of bread and freedom:

> The interests of the very few people in the world who care for the values of freedom must be identified with those of the many who need bread, or freedom will be lost.[5]

We must be able to imagine suffering and injustice as well as to report the facts of the desperate matter if we are to dispel the "smoke-screen" of "inhumanity."[6] We need to feel the reality of the suffering subject as well as to know the objective truth.

Because teachers in universities in America will be compelled and impelled to make use of advanced technology in the coming decades, they must be on their guard against substituting progressive methods for enlightened values. It is all too easy to feel engaged at a technologically detached and alienated distance. Theory and technology—if disembodied—can work against the idea of an enlightened community.

I did not understand some of these human issues until I went to Turkey as a Fulbright lecturer in American literature during 1983 to 1984. I was, in some sense, reluctant to use "human" as a critical term until that year. My students in Turkey, especially the son of a hazelnut farmer from the Black Sea region, helped to reeducate me. I needed to go overseas to understand better this side of the Atlantic.

Overseas and a Quest for America

I'm not quite sure when I first became aware of the Fulbright program. It seemed always to have been part of the educational and intellectual atmosphere for those in my generation who entered college in the 1950s and chose a career in higher education. But I do remember when it first affected my life directly: A young woman with whom I was in love—or certainly with whom I wanted to be in love (she embodied so many positive cultural and aesthetic values)—won a Fulbright, just out of a small, progressive, Eastern college, to study art history in Paris with one of the world's leading experts in what we now would call Mediterranean civilization.

I was dumbfounded. Here was someone, apparently like me, a contemporary, whose life would suddenly become different from mine (as it did) because she had won a Fulbright. I was proud and resentful at the same time: proud, of course, because someone so bright and resourceful, who had given her heart and songs (along with guitar playing) to me for a while, now had the added lustre of being a Fulbright grantee; resentful because we would be separated and because I was not the recipient.

This essay is reprinted with permission from the *Journal of the Association of International Education Administrators,* Spring 1986.

I was less worldly and sophisticated than my friend at that time, and I hadn't even applied. But that didn't stop me from resenting her a little, and I made up my mind that one day I too would "go somewhere on a Fulbright," as I put it to myself, especially when I saw over the years what transformations had become possible for my friend—becoming fluent in French, singing and even recording songs of Piaf and others. In time, when she became a writer, she even lived part of each year in Brittany.

These memories and associations haunted me through graduate school and my early years of teaching, and they became more compelling when as the years passed I became aware of colleagues, sometimes worthy and serious, sometimes gifted and brilliant, setting out for other parts of the world to accept Fulbright lectureships. Romance, achievement, and expansion were now conjoined in my mind as the meaning of the Fulbright.

But I didn't think of applying for many years for different reasons. Life's and history's "cunning passages," as Eliot calls them, kept me toiling in the domestic vineyards of academe instead of teaching abroad, and, at a certain point, I became a single parent and had immense responsibilities to shoulder. Suddenly, I was a baby-sitter, chauffeur, tennis coach, and "laundress." I didn't have time to think about, no less apply for, a Fulbright.

But the time came when my daughter would leave home to go away to college. I had raised her, as my mother would have said, "to fly the coop," even though I knew I would deeply suffer the "empty nest" syndrome; I decided then that the right time had come. I would leave home too for a while. I would apply for a Fulbright and leave Buffalo, if I could, at the same time as my daughter. I knew that she might be able to come along with me if I were chosen, but I thought it best for us to make a clean break at first, if that would be possible.

I thought, at first, of applying for England and Israel. I had a love of English culture and literature, nurtured in the library of my somewhat British-style high school, Horace Mann in New York;

moreover, as someone who mainly taught American literature, I was aware of the deep and complex literary and social relationships between the two countries over the centuries. I also had written a graduate thesis on the American novelist, turned British citizen (some would say "British *writer*"), Henry James.

But as I thought about the possibility of teaching under the auspices of Fulbright, it seemed to me that cultural and literary *difference* was what the experience might offer to me and what I needed. I needed to put myself in a context where I could see my personal history and my country's in a somewhat different light. I wanted to see new modes of family relationships. I wanted to see how young people, different from my daughter and her friends, viewed the world, including the world of their parents. I wanted to replace the loss experience of letting go of a child with a more global perspective in which to view this loss and, finally, to redefine it.

At the same time, I was intrigued by the possibility of going to an ancient homeland. It seemed to me that Israel would provide key terms of difference, even as it would allow me the opportunity to share my miniature experience of recent dispossession with people who also knew loss, many of whom had lost everything. But because of the needs of Fulbright for that year, I was given the opportunity instead to go to Turkey. I was stunned at first. I knew so little about Turkey: remnants of elementary and high school learning, fragments of media images, Hollywood movies set in harems with translucent robes. My appointment seemed remote from the associations that clung to the young woman who had set off for Paris a quarter of a century before.

But I sensed, even in the midst of my apprehension, that my state of cultural innocence might turn out for the best. I would be tested and I might discover—as I did—that initially remote and apparently inhospitable places could become warm and homelike. I sensed that my loss might become or lead me toward and make me ready for a global gain. Still I was unprepared when I accepted an appointment as a Fulbright lecturer in American literature for 1983 to 1984 at Ankara University.

I didn't even know that Ankara had become the capital after the revolution of 1923. I had assumed that Istanbul was the seat of government. I may even have thought that there were two cities— Istanbul and Constantinople—on the Bosphorus. I didn't know that the Bosphorus, connecting the Black and Marmara Seas, divided Turkey into two land masses: one small, lying to the west: Thrace; the other, larger, to the east: Anatolia. I didn't know that this meeting place of West and East at the confluence of the Golden Horn, Bosphorus, and Marmara Sea represented one of the crucibles and crossroads of global history.

I didn't know that Turkey was a Moslem country that looked, by and large, to the West, rather than to Islam, for its cultural identity; that Atatürk ("father of the Turks") was a figure as revered among schoolchildren as George Washington; or that the hands on the ornate clocks in Dolmabahce Palace (the last palace of the Ottoman sultans and Atatürk's residence in Istanbul) would stay fixed at the moment of his death in 1938. I didn't know that Atatürk, virtually single-handedly, had banned the fez, torn off the veil, substituted the Latin alphabet for Arabic, and catapulted Turkey into the modern world after driving the Greeks into the sea at Smyrna (now Izmir).

I had trace memories about the Young Turks, and I had heard of "Turkish delight," but probably assumed it was a close encounter of a perverse sexual nature. So I was ignorant and in some sense open to new arrangements of time and space, history and geography. With a received faith in the "broadening values" of travel and beneficial effects of "difference," with few preconceptions, many apprehensions, too much luggage and less "cool," I left Buffalo in September 1983.

I discovered in Paris, racing to make the connection for Istanbul, that the Turkish Airlines counter had been blown up by Armenian terrorists a month before and that it was now moved every day. "Where is it today?" I asked. "Who knows? You'll have to look," was the Gallic agent's logical response. I mention this part of the antic journey only to hint at a parable about travel, self-discovery, and education: You don't always find what you're looking for directly, and you sometimes find what you're not looking for with simplicity, vividness, and sudden, heartbreaking tenderness. You never know where and when you will see life and yourself somewhat differently.

I soon discovered that Turkey was part of the same ancient Aegean world that had nurtured the now better known "classical" Greeks (a sore point for contemporary Turks). Troy and Ephesus, to name two of a hundred major sites, lay on Turkish soil; Herodotus was born in Bodrum (then Halicarnassus), an Aegean coastal resort now called "Bed-room" by the Turkish jet-setters and disco set.

Turkey was so old that its Byzantine capital, Constantinople, had been sacked by Turkish invaders in 1453, half a century before the discovery of America by European voyagers. This was old, older than my Russian grandfather, so I prepared myself imaginatively for teaching in a hoary university like Oxford or Coimbra in Portugal.

I wondered if I would teach in a robe, perhaps one with feathers or fur, and stroll across tiled courtyards with young scholars who would, glancing at gilt-edge illuminated books, ask wise questions. I was looking, after all, for tradition, civilization, the Jamesian sense of accrued time, memorable place. I learned on my first day in the Faculty of Language, History, and Geography, *Dil Tarih Cografya* (our Arts and Letters, more or less), that my Faculty had been organized and built in the 1930s. I was as old as the Faculty. When I told a colleague that my undergraduate *alma mater* had been founded in 1821 and that I had earned another degree from a university established in 1754, he asked, "What is it like to go to venerable institutions?" I was speechless; I had come after all as a representative of the New World, looking for antique ways, Byzantine design, and glimpses of Attic Aegean architecture.

I felt this doubleness throughout my teaching experience in Turkey. I represented an older society, with respect to the organization of higher education, the checks and balances of liberal democracy, and the application of science and technology to everyday living. Colleagues would often say, if I were critical of static bureaucracy, imperious treatment of students, obsolete caliphatic patterns of hierarchy separating junior from senior faculty: "Give us time; you've been doing this kind of thing longer than we have."

Everyone assumed, nonetheless, that I expected to have the latest state-of-the-art technologies as an aid to teaching: video and audio tapes, electric typewriter, xerox machine, personal computer, etc. Students, always self-effacing in Turkey, apologized for the lack of heat in the building, poor lighting, scored blackboard, soot-filled air that wafted in from the railroad tracks outside our classroom window. "Soon we'll have your means of pollution control," they would say, knowing that the military government wanted F-14s, not a higher quality of expensive fuel for its people.

America was somehow old *and* new. America was far away, farther than ninety-nine percent of my students would ever be able to afford to visit, but it was there as an image, an omnipresent visual fact of life through the export of television and movies (even if they were grade-B reruns), cars (even if they were 1958 Chevrolets), and song (even if it was Nat King Cole). Sometimes I felt as if I were reliving America in the fifties. American "entertainment" gave Turkey a second environment. Russia, though it shares a border, is invisible to all except the USAF logistical analysts.

I represented older traditions of secular learning to my students, even as they subscribed to the sacred laws of Islam; they wanted to know about the Empire State Building (the World Trade Center has not captured the near Third World's imagination yet, perhaps because it lacks a spire), space shuttle launches and moon landings—the most dazzling proof to the Turks of American technological supremacy. Nothing pleased my students more than when I arranged for them to see a film in the temperature-controlled and comfortable screening rooms of the United States Information Service (USIS) building.

They couldn't believe that the cultural officers welcomed us!

I was then in the paradoxical and somewhat topsy-turvy position of teaching them a literature, ours, that pre-dated their own modern state (1923)—the puritans, Poe, Hawthorne, Whitman, Emerson— although I represented a window to modernity. I had come to teach the new and discover the old, but I was beginning to discover the old in my own culture and the problem of the new, so to speak, for my students.

I also was beginning to see more clearly the price my culture had paid for modernity as I travelled through their time-worn villages, and I had mixed feelings about what it would mean for my students and their country to try to catch up with us. The act of talking about books was not so simple. I approached American books from a point of view fixed in a time and place different from theirs. How would we meet?

Literary interpretation and discussion became something more than identifying myself with one academic school or another as I taught in Ankara second, third, and fourth year classes in one room, alongside the railroad track, watching cheap, sulfurous coal being freighted in from the provinces. I struggled all year to find ways in which we could understand how and why Turks looked at the world in terms somewhat different from me, their *American* teacher, and I could never forget that I was a representative of my country, for better and worse.

My gestures, my dress, to say nothing of my language and what I said were, to dress up the issue a little, a *semiotic system*. If I wore an overcoat in class, as I did once or twice, to protest quietly the lack of heat (all that coal was rolling somewhere other than to our university), I was making a statement as important as anything I might say about our books, for their professors would not—in those still politically anxious times, in the aftermath of near civil war—have acted so brazenly. Books were important, yes, and so was what I wore when I talked about those books.

And these books were precious. They were dearly bought new and equally valuable in a useable secondhand state. Many of my students came from rural families with incomes less than two thousand dollars a year. One student, "Zecki," gave me a kilo of hazelnuts as a lavish expression of his father's appreciation for my role as teacher ("hodja"). My students were concerned, in talking about books as they were concerned in buying them, with what was basic, essential, necessary, useful.

They could understand Steinbeck more easily than Poe because the labor of farming was a more obvious feature of their national lives than nightmare; Twain made more sense than Irving because illiteracy was a more common condition than playing nine-pins with leprechauns; they preferred "The Scarlet Letter" to Emerson's "Self-Reliance" because Turkish family and social life are still scrupulously traditional and conservative: young women do not date until marriage is virtually arranged, and premarital sex can lead to a woman's banishment from her family, can drive her to the Buñuel-like Alley of the Lonely in Istanbul.

They preferred Hemingway to Faulkner because he was easier to read, and they needed to learn functional English if they wanted careers in the government, military, tourism, or business. Money talks in Turkey for a struggling generation, and it speaks English.

They preferred Thornton Wilder's "Our Town" to his "The Skin of Our Teeth" because one affirmed social cohesion, continuity between generations, stability of village life, the need for companionship and friendship, while the other inverted time and space, showed a world absurdly out of joint. Turks do not understand aloneness, loneliness, or social pathology. They gather ritualistically in groups—in homes, barber shops, tailor shops, offices—to drink tea (çay, pronounced chĭ) the elixir of social life.

My students were, in a word, essentially premodern. Hawthorne was, in a sense, their contemporary. I had come bearing news of the new, and my students had unearthed the puritan tradition in our literature. I had come looking for civilization, expecting Byzantine ornateness, exotic architecture, and exquisite figures in the carpet and found, instead, a culture largely made up of 40,000 villages, with a dignity based on "poor" values: the lean, bare, and economical. The modern temper, to say nothing of the abstruseness of postmodernism, made little sense to them.

There is, of course, a Turkish avant-garde, but its influence doesn't go much beyond Istanbul, and even there doesn't spring from or touch the life of the people. Postmodernist attitudes are the privilege, or affectation, of a small class of Turks who have been educated in America, Germany, Britain, France, and Italy (in about that order). Nearly two million Turks live in Germany as industrial workers ("Gastarbeiter"), not students of advanced aesthetic culture.

Literary study in English of American literature meant something more practical and, potentially, more dangerous for my students in Turkey than it did at home. Knowing and speaking English opened doors for students in banking, tourism, and the foreign ministry, to say nothing of teaching and study abroad. At the same time, embracing certain American ideas of individualism, set deeply in our literature from the Quaker John Woolman through Emerson to Frost and the Beats, might inaugurate a path of inquiry that would lead to difficult and risky choices.

An editor of one journal told me she did not know one literary person possessing honor and courage, who had not been arrested at one time or other under the alternate regimes of Right and Left that have shaped Turkey's domestic political history since the death of Atatürk. I submittted an essay to this editor and referred in it—historically, not from a partisan point of view—to the Paris communes of the early 1870s. The editor encouraged me to delete the reference for both our sakes.

I was, in this sense, sometimes wary of teaching certain texts, such as Thoreau's "Civil Disobedience," as if I might encourage too facile a sense of opposition to established authority. Many of my students would return to provincial communities, not to the salons of Istanbul. I could not encourage easy assumptions about the dismantling of authority. I had to know where I was. I was teaching the young in Ankara, not Berkeley.

I began to see contrastively into the displacement of tradition in America, the substitution of media families for real families, the replication of experience through symbols, slogans, and "soaps." I wondered how my students could bring about necessary social and political change while maintaining a dignified stability rooted in the rhythms of agrarian and sacred life, and I didn't know how they were going to become new (and I, old) without a painful rearrangement of the self in relation to place and history.

I didn't know the answers and took some comfort in riding the archaic Wagon Lits (1920s) night-train—the Istanbul Express—on the first step of the return to the U.S.; I rocked and swayed in a middle region of time between cultures and wondered how much the leaders of my country paid attention to the subtle ratios of difference in time and geography between countries in making decisions that shape the future of the world.

It seemed to me, as I was about to leave Turkey (and that awareness has grown since then), that foreign policy often misses the actual life of the people about whom we, as a government, are making policy. I hoped, as I was about to leave Turkey, that some of the U.S. graduate students whom I met in Turkey as Fulbrighters in the program's fortieth year would enter the Foreign Service eventually as diplomats or cultural officers. Those American students who had rubbed shoulders with Turkish students would have a clearer sense of the needs and style of the country than people trained strictly within theoretical frameworks and the terms of power. And who knows what difference these people would make in the next forty years?

I thought of these corridors of time and, crossing the "Bos" at dawn, with the sun slanting across the missile-like minarets on the European side, wondered what sense I would make in the future of the drum-beats and flutes I had heard at a village wedding on the edge of the Aegean, while hillside fields burned, preparing the stubble for harvest.

What would I make of the child who had kissed my hand and touched it reverentially to her forehead? How would I relate these gestures of old time to the new world? I wasn't sure, but for a moment, as Europe and Asia were joined in the morning flood of light across the Bosphorus Bridge, I felt suspended in time. Turkey is like that, sometimes, especially on a spring night in the Passage of Flowers.

I have been back almost two years now. I don't think of Turkey every day, or even every week, and I can't say that an outsider would think that I had changed very much. I probably haven't, but there are moments, in the classroom, especially when I look at a foreign student (Remla, Unal, Jaehwan), or when I talk with a visiting Fulbright scholar (Biyot, Adi, Mihali), when I am painfully aware of the adventure and excitement, the displacement and even fear, of being a cultural outsider.

I think of myself in Turkey, of my friend in Paris all those years ago. I try to imagine my Turkish students in the U.S.; I think of my daughter making a long and strange trip to visit me in Turkey (leaving the U.S. for the first time, coming through Germany, losing a day for the first time). I imagine us all as strangers on the globe and try, imperceptibly I suppose, to make patient efforts toward understanding.

And when spring comes to Buffalo, as it usually does, my heart goes back to the "Bos."

I spent ten months in Turkey in 1983 and 1984 as a Fulbright lecturer in American literature in the Faculty of Language, History, and Geography (*Dil Tarih Cografya*) in Ankara University. During this time, I made a number of trips to Istanbul, Izmir, Gordion, Konya, Cappadocia, and Alanya, and when my daughter came to visit me during her winter holiday, we drove from Ankara to Antalya.

From Antalya, we followed the Mediterranean coast around to Faselis, Kas (pronounced Kahsh), Fethiye, Bodrum, Milas, Priene, Ephesus, Pamukkale, and back to Ankara. During this trip, we visited many ancient archeological sites and learned that much of what we had thought of as the ancient Greek world was really part of a larger Mediterranean and Aegean civilization.

During this trip, we stayed one night in a *pension* in Kas for one dollar. Kas has the distinction, therefore, for me of being the most beautiful village I have ever stayed in for so little money, and it reminds me that it is still possible to live inexpensively in certain parts of the world; that it is still possible to imagine that there are places to which one might escape if one gets too world-weary. It must also be said that these inexpensive havens of romantic and artistic

This essay is reprinted with permission from *Spree*, Fall 1986.

retreat are made possible because of the lack of economic development and easy transportation.

We had to drive carefully and painstakingly through the Bey Mountains to get to Kas; it is not a place to which tourists flock. It is likely for this reason to remain a fairly chic resort for the affluent for some time to come—a place to which mainly the *cognoscenti* are likely to come on a "blue sail."

If and when Turkey steps fully into the mainstream of the twentieth century, or perhaps I should now say twenty-first century, places like Kas will cease to exist as havens for the Western traveller, exile, and artist; just as comparable places in France and Italy disappeared after the twenties and thirties, just as comparable places in Spain and Portugal are disappearing now.

As early as 1935, Ernest Hemingway was lamenting, in the *Green Hills of Africa,* that more and more places were becoming spoiled for the Western traveller, for a privileged and, in some cases, adventurous class of people who had sufficient time and money to live off the economies and low-cost labor of less developed countries.

By 1931, Karen Blixen (Isak Dinesen) had already returned to Denmark to write her memoir, *Out of Africa* (1937), in which she would record her seventeen-year experience of living on a six thousand acre farm in Kenya. By 1931, the pristine Kenya which Isak Dinesen knew was already fading.

We might even say that the success of *Out of Africa*—along with a number of recent movies (*The Shooting Party,* E. M. Forster's *A Room With a View*) and many PBS programs (*All Creatures Great and Small, Treasure Houses of Britain*)—depends on the fact that the innocent beauty of its landscape has vanished or is fading; that its quality of being a natural paradise is now only a matter of nostalgic retrospection. We might say, in fact, that the number of programs celebrating nature on public television itself signifies the degree to which we think that all of nature is threatened.

As my daughter and I walked along the harbor in Kas, watching fishermen repair their nets, as we watched the alabaster ledges of sunken ancient Lycian tombs appear above the rise and fall of the gentle waves, as we walked out beyond the village to a modest amphitheatre, I knew that I would one day look back to this moment as a kind of sunken treasure.

I knew all too self-consciously that my daughter and I were academic Romans, budget-priced jet-setters living on the cheap off the poverty of many people who, in their innocence and hospitality, smiled at us as we enjoyed the beauty of their simple culture, or should I say the simplicity of their beautiful culture? I knew that we—my daughter and I, people like us—were living under a penalty of time, and I wasn't sure if it was a good or bad thing that the end of the American empire was in sight. I knew that a day would come when I would spread my maps before me and try to re-create the coordinates of lost simplicity.

So as I said at the outset, I taught in Turkey for ten months and made a number of trips, the ones I have mentioned, and a glorious sail at the end with the other Fulbrighters in our group that year in the Mediterranean waters, the Turquoise Coast, in and around the peninsulas of Marmaris.

If I claim any knowledge about Turkey, its brush with the modern world, such incidental revelations are based on what I saw during these trips. Much of what the traveller knows, especially the traveller who lacks the native language, is based on seeing; and perhaps there is something to be said for the distance between oneself and the world that an absence of language creates. One can develop an objective love in that distance; one can understand the clearest outlines of existence in that silence. But still it is not a defensible silence in face of the world's urgent need for understanding.

Our sail was uneventful. The most exciting moment came when the bowsprit snapped, carrying my bathing suit (hung out to dry) to the four winds and with it almost, but for a bit of good luck, one of the Fulbrighters. Yet there were many moments which I recognized then as lovely and precious, which have become even more precious in memory and which seem to contain more meaning now.

The name of the boat was the *Acıklı* (pronounced Ajakluh). I did not know until a few weeks ago that *acıklı* means both "sorrowful" and "touching," "tragic" and "sentimental." This word now seems appropriate to me as a description of many of the Turkish people whom I met during my stay in Turkey. The Turks live with a sense of loss, the sense that they once dominated the world; it is not a loss they view with a complete sense of homage and elegy, however, for modern Turkey is built upon the rejection of the Ottoman Empire.

There is, indeed, something touching about this relation to the past. Many Turks I met had relatives who had played some important and cosmopolitan role under the reign of the sultans. These friends had parents and grandparents who had played, therefore, some central role in world history, but they themselves felt that they and their language were now, in a fundamental sense, marginal.

Still, they do not look back with complete pride. One man told me that his grandmother had been one of the only women ever to be set free from the harem and then to get a secular education. This man became a writer, and though he wishes that his native language were one which could give him a greater world audience in his mother tongue, he does not wish for the return of the empire that had subjugated women. He prefers Turkey in its modern phase, its republican form, with its sorrow for the writer.

Our captain, who had lived in the village of Selimiye all his life, called himself Captain Acıklı. It didn't sound strange to me then—because all Turkish words are equally exotic to me—but I suppose it would be like calling someone Captain Sentimental. What seems revealing to me in retrospect is that the captain identified with his boat so much.

It was a simple craft, a typical fishing boat of that region, but the captain owned it, and he proudly bore its name because that fact of ownership gave him a real as well as symbolic position in the village.

He not only stood for pride, but he had the spars—at least all but one—and the beams to prove it.

Our captain slept on deck, as much for the fresh air as the extra bunk it gave him to rent, and he awoke with the first light, noiselessly. He could well have been one of Ernest Hemingway's heroes, but he doubtless would have turned out to be too gentle in the end for Papa, who liked his violence neat, as the English say about their Scotch.

Captain Acıklı was not a man who looked for show-downs to set anything straight; he was no village primitive looking to have an international affair. Captain Acıklı knew his village and the villages near it well, and he used his familiarity with skill to make the sail pleasant for his passengers and profitable for himself and his friends.

He lived in a small corner of the world, but he worked that corner well. I used to say in Turkey, somewhat jokingly, that if the Turks could weave an empire, they would once more dominate the world. I meant a number of things by that: the wonderful facility the Turks possessed in the woven and decorative arts and their ability to work in small spaces—both pictorially and economically. It occurred to me that the average Turk survived by marking out one corner of the market, or marketplace, and making it exclusively his own, and, of course, this was true for individual villages as well.

Turks specialized in showing one kind of ware at a marketplace —say, copper pots; or a village was known for the particular kind of carpet that it turned out—say, Malatya.

In the first thing I ever wrote about Turkey, I said:

> It dawned on me then that one might do better here to live, in some sense, as a *villager in the city*—to stop looking for contemporary American solutions to problems and to turn back the clock imaginatively to an earlier, frontier era in America. I realized that I would do better to look for the design in the Turkish carpet and to let go of high-tech consciousness. I was beginning to learn something about the Turkish structure of social and aesthetic miniaturization.[1]

It now seems to me that I can apply this notion of miniaturization to Captain Acıkli and the way he wove us in and out of the Marmaris peninsulas.

It is hard to imagine who would be Captain Acıklı's equivalent in America. It is hard to imagine someone as competent as the captain, as worldly (because of his contact with international tourists), who also would be so cut off from global information.

So far as I could tell, the captain was not someone who read newspapers (I'm not even sure if he was literate), listened to the radio, or watched television (if, indeed, he owned a set). The captain lived mainly in the context and medium of village gossip, of words spoken between men at cafés and tea-houses.

He knew a great deal about a small world firsthand, and he could imagine quite a lot by extrapolating from the lives and styles of his passengers. It might be possible to compare the captain with a logger in eastern Oregon, an endangered farmer in Nebraska, a poor black fisherman on one of the Carolina sea-islands, but all these comparisons would break down along one line or another.

The captain was special, from my point of view, because he only knew an inlet of the world quite well, while at the same time having a cosmopolitan reach and worldliness. Something very much like this might be said of all of Turkey with variations and modifications, depending upon locale. The captain was also special, from my point of view, because his life seemed so unalienated—so untouched by all the forms of communication, bureaucracy, and technological baggage that have made human life both possible and difficult in the twentieth century.

And yet it must be said that the captain himself may wish to have this baggage, and it is doubtless true that the same conditions that make personal humanness possible for the captain and many other Turks also constitute a problem. One need only think of the number of Turks who must leave Turkey in order to work in other countries (especially Germany, as *Gastarbeiten,* because the economy remains preindustrial in so many aspects) to see that there is a price paid for the integrity of lives like the one lived by the captain.

I suppose that everything that I have said so far and can think of saying relates to this essential doubleness: the dignity, harmony, and wholeness of village life that exist alongside the hardships and difficulties that come with a meagre economy and limited technology. Some scene, in each of the villages which we visited and anchored in during our sail, makes this doubleness clear to me.

In Bozurun, I saw peasant families bringing cut wheat across the water in decorated skiffs to be threshed at a central mill. My heart went out to these people, and I envied their "togetherness," as we might say in America, for lack of a better word. Then I saw the usually small women carry bundled staves on their backs. I saw them, after the wheat had been threshed, lie on the ground, with their burlap sacks spread out behind them, so they could be loaded in order to roll forward and lift the load with their momentum. These women had great dignity in their acceptance of work, but I wondered if it was right for women to work so hard when there was equipment somewhere, elsewhere, to make their lives easier.

Even as I saw these beautiful hardships, I walked the ramparts of an ancient ruin with a young scholar from our group. He explained the plan of the Aegean coastal fortress and port to me, and we snorkled for shards in the transparent water. I knew that the beautiful calm of these "shard-infested" waters would fade when the machines came to make life easier for the women I had seen laboring under such difficulty.

While others on the sail played card games and listened to rock music on their cassettes, the young scholar and I kept diving and snorkling, walking the ramparts, engraving in memory the shield-bright light as it pierced the fragmentary arches.

We knew that we were living under a sentence of time, as were the people in the village. The day would soon come when their lives would improve significantly, and a certain beauty would go with it.

With the conveniences of new culture and civilization—much of it only thirty kilometres away in disco-noisy Marmaris—would go the haunting echoes of antiquity and the classical harmonies that have given Western civilization a model and icon of balance.

In Loryma, at the western tip of the southern arm of the Marmaris peninsula, we dropped anchor for a night in a hill-enclosed harbor on one of those clear, moonlit evenings when you think, even if you're approaching middle age, that you don't want to sleep, when you want to welcome the dawn.

As we sat on the deck, listening to the gentle lap-tide against the side of the *Acıklı,* we heard a solitary drum beat in the distance. We asked the captain about it, and he told us that it was a village wedding and that, if we wished, we could go as *honored* guests, for he knew the village. If anything, we might have thought that the terms of meeting should be reversed, but we did want to see the wedding—to go to the source of the drumbeat and fifes that accompanied it.

We went ashore in our small boat and followed the captain through the wheat fields that grew to the edge of the path. The path twisted through the fields with small rocks underfoot. We came out of the fields into the village. Women and children sat at one end of the village square, an informal amphitheatre carved out of the coastal rocks; young men and their male elders sat at wooden tables and on the ledges of rocks at the other end.

The women, huddled together (as they so often do in Turkey, even in the large cities), held their children close. All the women wore their finery: embroidered calico and tassled shawls; all displayed their jewelry, but none so much as the young bride whose golden earrings and bracelets were, as we understood it, emblems of her trousseau. We asked the captain why all the young girls wore jewelry, and he told us that this gave the families a chance to see how much each was worth.

The young men and their male elders danced in the center of the square: traditional Turkish dancing to the words of traditional songs that were chanted as much as sung with the *saz*. Turkish women of the old school were not supposed to dance with men in public, so the men danced with one another. Between dances they drank *rakı* (pronounced rahkuh). They danced until they fell down and others took their place.

Our group was given a special table in the center of the square, and we were brought food. Even though we had eaten, we had to eat again. And we were asked to dance. Even though we were unable to master the special movements of Turkish shoulder-shaking, we tried our best to move our stiff American limbs; even though we were unaccustomed, as puritanical Americans, to dance with other men, we tried our best not to be too self-conscious. The villagers were kind and applauded our awkward gestures.

After we withdrew from the stage, only a group of young men danced. We were told that this gave them a chance to flirt with the nearly veiled young women, and it gave the mothers a chance to choose husbands for their daughters. Eventually, only one young man, the groom, was left. Then there was a good deal of clapping and laughing, and the young bride—no more than sixteen—was sent forward by the crowd of women. They danced toward and around one another without touching.

The young couple—who would eventually repair to their new home and enact the consummation of the marriage ceremony—looked at one another fleetingly and then avoided sharing glances (a visual ballet of interest and modest avoidance). They danced to the beat of the drum, as the sounds of the clapping and laughter echoed off the ledges of the rocks under the dome of heaven (with the soft aroma of grain-scented air taking the scent out of the *rakı*). I watched and responded to all of this; I knew that I might never witness such a perfect moment again.[2]

At the same time, I wondered about the fate of the young couple: The girl, for she was hardly a woman, would probably have few rights and privileges and would doubtless grow up to bear the burden of wheat on her back; the young man would be proud for a while, but if he could not find work as meaningful as the captain's (if he couldn't, in time, buy his own boat and see its keel raised along the harbor front), he might well find himself without hope.

I often said in Turkey—observing the rhythms and manners of country life, the rhythms and manners of country people in the city (*gecekondu*)—that women in Turkey live on adoration and approval while the men survive on hope, and there is a scarcity of the latter. I wondered, as we sat in the village square as honored guests, how it might be possible, if it would be possible, for Turkey in the coming years to preserve the beauty of the pageant to which we had been witness while stepping into the twenty-first century.

These thoughts were on my mind as we wended our way back through the fields. "Embosomed" for a moment, if not a "season," in nature, I wondered about the doubleness of life in Turkey, or I should say, the doubleness of my consciousness about life in Turkey, as we made our way back to the *Acıklı* for the last part of our sail.[3]

We set sail at first light for Dalyan, across the Bay of Marmaris, leaving the emerald traces of the Aegean for the seemingly darker waters of the Mediterranean (though, for the Turks, it is the "white-sea," (*Ak-deniz*). Making five or ten knots in the open sea, with a cool wind taking the heat out of the strong sun overhead, we reached the marsh-surrounded estuary leading to the sleepy river port of Dalyan and the adjacent ruin of Kaunos, a Lycian settlement dis-covered in the nineteenth century, west of the Toros Mountains and the Pampylian sites of Side, Aspendos, and Perge, west of the Xan-thus Hills.

The Lycians, "a kindred people" of the Greeks mentioned in the *Iliad,* built their tombs on the side of hills, with columned façades, carved to imitate timber-built houses and barns; though we could see these tombs during the day, it was at night, illumined by moonlight that these testaments to domesticity and eternity came into clearer view.[4] Rocking slightly in the slip, we looked from the tombs to the café near us on the quay, where the villagers watched video under a vine covered arbor (*çardak*).

I looked at the tombs on the hill and then at the men in the teahouse, turned now into an outdoor video parlor (a common sight in contemporary rural Turkey). I remembered that the first object I had asked about in Turkey, the first word I had learned, was *çardak*. The opposition of the *çardak* and the video, the opposition between the video and the tombs seemed to me at the end of our sail, soon before my departure from Turkey, to be a symbol of Turkey's problematic destiny.

If my thoughts seem typical of Western "primitivism," of a longing for a simpler life, these thoughts are not inconsistent with some of Atatürk's analysis of Turkish culture, and in the end one's thoughts must go to Atatürk, the founder and creator, in many ways, of modern Turkey, who had the wisdom to see that the new must be built out of the old without preserving the outdated elements of the old.

Atatürk said, "The true master of this country and the basic element of our social structure is the peasant. But the peasant has been deprived of the light of education until now."[5] He also said: "As long as the peasant is not master of the country, there can be no real progress in Turkey."[6]

As the young scholar and I talked late into the night on the foredeck of the *Acıklı*, we agreed that we hoped to return one day to a Turkey that would preserve the beauty and antiquity of its classics-haunted village culture while overcoming many of the hardships of its essentially agrarian economy and displaced geopolitical position. We did not know if this would be possible; we did not know if we would risk this return in years to come.

When I think of going back to Turkey, my heart sinks. I am not quite sure why. I sometimes think it is because my daughter and I were last there as a unified child-parent team—undivided by space and the inevitable pressures of life in America. I sometimes think it is because I got a glimpse of family, village, and cultural unity in

Turkey—a unity rooted in the land and in the past, a unity I can never really be a part of, but one which I imagined as a possibility for a brief period of my life.[7]

Despite what I had heard about Turkey (so many people had asked me about *Midnight Express* that I felt as if I knew its oppressive horrors firsthand), my preparations to leave America for a year to go to Turkey had gone well for six months. Documents circulated efficiently from Buffalo to Washington to Ankara and back to Buffalo again. Sometimes the loop worked differently, but in one direction or other the flow of information between this trio of cities seemed to suggest that the McLuhanesque vision of the global village was an operative fact of our time.

All my plans for an orchestrated departure from North America and harmonious arrival at the western edge of Asia had fallen in place as smoothly as a sequence of carefully arranged dominos, but when the moment came to set the sequence in motion—to fly from Buffalo to New York to catch the plane for Frankfurt and from there to get the only non-stop flight to Ankara—it turned out that I had, for the first time in my life, missed a flight.

I had wanted to go through Germany, not Paris—as my new rerouted itinerary dictated—because a group of alleged Armenian

This essay was presented as the keynote address at *Reading and Writing*: The 3rd Annual Colloquium on Language Learning of the Centre for English Language Programs, Brock University, St. Catharines, Ontario, 21-22 March 1986.

terrorists had blown up the Turkish Airlines counter in Paris a few months before, and I was not eager to fly Turkish Airlines in any case. But Paris it would be, and Turkish Airlines it would be from there to Istanbul, and Turkish Airlines it would be again from Istanbul to Ankara, if I wished to arrive anywhere near the time when someone from Fulbright or the USIS was expecting to meet me. All of this took place, of course, on a weekend, when I assumed it would be impossible to let anyone know just what skewed events were taking place.

Although I did not see myself as a world-traveller (neither Richard Halliburton nor Lowell Thomas), I did pride myself on having more than a modicum of planning abilities and on being able to foresee problems and to build solutions to them into my planning. This was, after all, the age of backup and redundancy.

Now I was suddenly disarmed, and I arrived at Orly from which I would have to make my way to Charles DeGaulle (or the other way around) on a sweltering, mid-September day with too much luggage and not enough French to find out even how someone as discomfited as I was, with an aching, psychosomatic lower back pain, could make his way to the other airport without leaving half his luggage behind. I had to rely on linguistic begging: "Do you speak English?" accompanied with importunate grimaces, in the hope of finding someone strong and compassionate enough to lend a traveller a helping hand.

And, of course, there was someone, even in Paris. The young man turned out to be from the Mideast. I made up my mind then and there that I would always temper my pro-Israel sentiment with a regard for the other people in the region. There's nothing quite like losing your ability to speak and to be understood to gain an appreciation for what it means to be misunderstood. You learn quickly that myths of personal and national self-sufficiency are tenuous and can be dismantled very easily; you learn that it is risky to be alone without speech.

At the airport in Paris, I used my primitive French to try to find the location of the Turkish Airlines counter. If I had felt somewhat ill at ease a few months before because I couldn't keep up with the latest turn of French "theoretical" criticism, I felt more uncomfortable at not being able to communicate the most simple needs. I wished deeply, in this moment, that my college French instructors had stressed the values of survival and tourism instead of civilization. It was becoming clear that one depended on the other, that one built on the other. I wasn't convinced then, nor have I been in my reflections since then that it makes much sense to talk about civilization as a concept separate from the material facts of daily life. I wasn't sure that it made sense to talk about civilization separate from language.

I did find someone who spoke English, of course, and who knew something about the airport; I asked where I might find the Turkish Airlines counter.

"I'm not sure where it is today," she said with a look of bemusement.

"*Today?*" I asked.

"Well, they move it every day now," she said, "since the explosion."

"How will I find it?" I asked.

"You'll have to ask; there's no other way."

"But who?"

"I don't know," she said; "they're keeping a low profile. Ask someone with a submachine gun; they might be guarding it."

Her suggestion sounded sensible, but it wasn't what I wanted to hear. I wasn't eager to try out my "Tarzan" French on guards who might well be suspicious of someone asking them incoherent questions about the very place they were trying to defend, and it seemed absurd, in any case, for them to tell me even if they knew.

Sweating and anxious, the steady state of travelers, I decided to rely on intuition, hope, and gesture (body language)—the universal semiotics of the lost tourist. I decided that, in my soul and stored-up visual archive, I would somehow recognize a Turk.

As I scanned the faces in the airport, I looked for some sign of Turkish identity, though, as I have said, I didn't really know what I was looking for; still I had a writer's faith that the fund of shareable symbolism was more complex than I might have assumed. Where diplomats and power-statesmen often look for points of difference to dramatize national self-interest, to reveal contrastively the virtue of nation against nation (*pro* versus *contra*), the traveler-teacher looks for points of rapproachement.

As if looking for me (with a faith in North American know-how, with a hope that proximity to a U.S. passport might steer him through some of the indignities of search and interrogation), a tall man, with a waxed scimitar-shaped mustache appeared next to me. We examined the contents of each other's carts—as one might decode a stack of wash in a laundromat, or scan a wagon full of canned goods in a supermarket to read the secret and social life of the other—in order to find out if we were the national person each was looking for.

"Ankara? Turkey?" I asked, if such utterances can be called questions as much as pleas for rescue and protection.

"Istanbul. Türkiye," he answered with a smile.

Never had an umlaut, a diacritical element meant so much; never had the phonemic differentiation of speech suggested salvation. It became clear then, if it hadn't been before, that these mysterious sounds were the constituents of meaningful reality; that one needed to pay attention, at home as well as abroad, to the slightest variations of speech as indices of the living drama.

"U.S. Okay?" he asked.

"Okay," I said, hoping, more than knowing, that he wanted me to be a U.S. citizen, though it passed through my mind that he might not want to be identified with a U.S. citizen, given the worldwide terrorism directed against America. As apprehensive as he might be as a Turk about Armenian terrorism, it occurred to me that he might be even more apprehensive about Armenian terrorism as a Turk seen with an American. I did not want to believe this, though ten months later, as I was about to leave Ankara, the U.S. Embassy was fortifying *after* Beirut, and I remembered in retrospect that my new friend —and he had, instantly, become my friend—might well have been apprehensive.

But I refused to believe that he wanted anything other than some help in his way as I wanted help in mine. He wanted me to help him get past the guards, and I wanted him to show me where to go. I sensed, rather than knew, this. If friendship comes easily in this situation—when one has been unhomed—so does intuition. International travel, especially when one crosses the border of language, like psychoanalysis and sex, takes one beyond or below the barriers of rational communication. One is forced to go deeper into the sensorium to discover who and what one fears and wants, what one does and doesn't know about others and the environment.

With only a few words to bind us together, we set off towards a small elevator. It seemed clear to me that we should go separately, but "Hasan," as I came to know him, insisted that we go in together. It was a gesture at once, I think now, of Turkish hospitality and some fear that he would get separated from someone who might help him—in those still anxious times in Turkey, only a few years after a near Civil War—get through security. So: he needed help with security and I, typically American, with insecurity.

Huddled in the elevator, the wheels of our carts became entangled. When the door opened, we couldn't move for a moment. Locked together in the elevator, we shrugged, threw up our arms, and burst into laughter. Magically, the laughter got us disentangled, and we were relieved, partially, to find ourselves in front of two gendarmes with submachine guns who were guarding the entrance to the unmarked Turkish Airlines counter.

"Turkish friend," I said, looking at the guard, patting my new friend on the shoulder.

"American friend," said my Turkish companion, patting me, a

little awkwardly on the shoulder.

The guards looked at us as though we were a vaudeville act and let us through with only a cursory glance at our passports. The red Turkish crescent and star which had seemed so forbidding in Buffalo now looked like an emblem of familiarity—my passport to a new world.

Somewhere I have written that "even terror can be domesticated in time," and I think I came close in that phrase to describing something important about the passage from one culture to another: one must go through a period of disorientation before deeper levels of familiarity become possible. And it may be true that one comes closest to understanding another country at precisely those places where one was initially most uncomfortable.

It seems to be true that we remember most fondly and profoundly just what upset us most at first. It may be just that our experience, like language, is distinguished by difference, so that the heart, like memory, recalls contrasts.

Now Hasan and I were separated—set at opposite corners of a room—while the French and Turkish officials took their time to determine if we were safe cargo. As we looked at one another somewhat forlornly, sharing half-smiles, shrugged shoulders, opened palms, and raised eyebrows, it didn't seem possible that we were new companions who would have to struggle to find out the most basic facts of our lives.

It didn't seem possible that I could feel such empathy and sympathy for someone who under different circumstances, for all I knew, might have seen me as another "ambassador of cultural imperialism" or its mirror image, a righteous defender of the military interventionist regime whose mission it was to suppress dangerous and disruptive socialist tendencies. (These were, as it turned out, two standard ways in which Turks, of some standing, were likely to view Americans.)

In this instant, though, we were bound by common needs and fear, and we seemed to understand and accept one another at a basic level. It occurred to me, waiting there, that the transit from culture to culture, language to language, might just serve as an antidote to the penchant for abstraction and intellectual mystification that has characterized so much of academic life in the past few decades.

My premonition turned out to be true for me. My students forced me, through their interest, to see and rediscover what was essential in American literature, to embrace writers (like Twain and London) whom the newer criticism couldn't yet accommodate; they led me, through their situation (often poor, neglected, and deferential to authority), to meet and confront them, against Turkish custom, the way I would not have related to my students at home. I sometimes gave them gifts of books, erasers, modest sums of money, and even loaves of bread (if it seemed to me that they needed these items to go on, if I could give these items discreetly without impoverishing myself, and if I could find the right moment).

I am not saying that I always acted wisely in these acts of giving; I may only have reinvented certain forms of American lendlease, but I want to stress that I felt impelled to meet my students at a more essential level than tends to be the case at home. I want to stress that the encounter in the waiting room—the need and effort to communicate at a level where language begins—may serve as a guide, to some extent, to those who will teach in other lands. It may well be that those who teach language at basic levels are present at the creation of the most important messages between peoples; that the most enduring bonds may be formed through this instruction.

We managed to pass muster with the authorities after a few hours, by which time I had lost hope for reaching Ankara that day, and we were then led into a room where a larger group was waiting for the flight to Istanbul. Finally, we were given a signal by a pleasant-looking stewardess—stewardesses remain, somehow, above international politics—to go onto the tarmac that led to the plane.

Where I had hoped for a 747, I found a DC-10 and a rather weather-beaten-looking one at that. If this big-bellied monster meant high-tech to my Turkish friends, it meant faults and defects to me; but when Hasan pointed to the plane and said, grinning broadly, "Modern," I knew that I had to conceal my dismay. I was learning here, as later, that it is all too easy for North Americans to convey a more-technological-than-thou righteousness even as they pride themselves on having understanding of the world's needy and oppressed.

"Great!" I said, scrambling aboard.

Seated next to Hasan in the half-empty plane—only the rich, and the poor who are going to work in Germany, leave Turkey, more or less—I wondered how Hasan and I would communicate for three hours. It seemed to me that we owed it to one another to impart some essential truths before we parted.

As we flew east Hasan and I began to exchange documents and photos from our wallets and passport folders. We struggled to find out who we were at an official and external level. I showed him letters with SUNY-Buffalo letterhead—an acronym that must mystify him to this day, calling up, as it probably does, bright and solar images in a region where there are only seventy hours of sunlight in the month of February.

I showed him documents from Fulbright with some paragraphs in Turkish, so that he understood more than I did about the terms of my teaching mission. I showed him photographs of my parents, brother, and daughter and despaired that I couldn't make clear to him the difficulties of keeping the family together in America; though I think he would have been dismayed if I had been able to describe our particular constellation to him. Turks really don't understand, as I learned later, alienation within the family. Or if they understand, they don't accept it, and they have meaningful rituals and customs to bring family members and friends back into the fold.

Hasan did not understand the complex relationships that I might have been able to describe to him if I had spoken Turkish or he English, but perhaps it was for the best—for we had had a long day. As it was, he smiled and showed me pictures of his brood. So many

people of different ages were crowded around so many tables under
so many arbors and vine-laden trellises—somewhere along the Bosphorus, I surmised later—that I thought he might be showing me his
village; and perhaps he was. Individual identity, family identity, and
village identity are all bound up for many Turks.

I wanted to know where all these people were from and where
the photos were taken, so I took out a map of Turkey and pointed
back and forth from the photos to the map. Hasan was bewildered.
He couldn't quite make out what information I wanted—in part, I
think because he couldn't break this family group into separate components, as we may take it for granted that an aunt lives in Ottawa,
an uncle in Pembroke (where, in fact, my mother went to high
school), a great-uncle lives in Detroit, while everyone else goes back
and forth from New York to Florida, or something like that.

After struggling with the maps and photos for a while, we were
only successful, I think, in establishing that he would be in Istanbul
and that I would be in Ankara, wherever it was. Hasan gave me his
card, and I wondered if he really meant for me to visit him, for as it
turned out, most adult Turks give their cards to every other adult
they meet. I wanted to think that he really meant for me to visit,
though I'm sure it would have been a social disaster, for he would
have been impelled, like all Turks, to extend ample hospitality, and
we would have had to sit in silence again.

It occurred to me that I understood for the first time something
of what my grandfather must have felt in coming from Russia to
New York in 1909, bereft of language, uncertain about geography,
unclear about the alpha and omega of America's strange mores. It
seemed strange that I should be heading for Islam after seventy-five
years of our family's effort to be comfortable in the U.S. But that
was part of the North American destiny in the twentieth century. We
were the new Romans: our jets, our chariots.

As the fading light played on the minarets and domes of Istanbul, as we descended to land, I felt exhilarated and deeply lonely. I felt some strange measure of pride in going through what my grandfather might have experienced; I felt and was homeless. Only language could have been a bridge to join and explain these paradoxical feelings, but it wasn't there.

Before Hasan and I parted, I tried foolishly to find out the name of a hotel in Ankara where I might stay if I were unable to get in touch with anyone from the embassy or Fulbright.

"Hotel, HOTEL," I said. "Hotel, ANKARA," I said emphatically.

"BUICK," he seemed to say.

I was at once gratified and alarmed that the long arm of the U.S. auto industry reached Ankara: gratified that the environment I had just left would be present in some form; alarmed, for almost the same reason, that I would step into a world of "ugly" Americans. As it turned out, there was no Buick Ankara (it was the Büyük Grand), though there were more used and vintage U.S. autos in Ankara than I've ever seen anywhere.

Dream-shaped 1950 Chevrolets and Hudsons floated along the avenues and boulevards of Ankara, just as the early songs of Frank Sinatra and Nat "King" Cole wafted over the airwaves of the TRT (Turkish Radio and Television) and the Voice Of America: "Red sails . . . open fire. . . ." There was no "Buick" Ankara, but I had flown in some ways into the immediate postwar period in America.

Hasan and I exchanged small gifts, and we went our separate ways: strangers in the twilight, the meeting and parting of East and West, just as the guidebooks always describe Asia Minor.

I did not think I would be going on to Ankara, but it turned out that ticket reservations meant nothing. It seemed to be first come, first served, so long as the planes were leaving and there was room. So on I went.

I was exhausted, edgy, and dislocated in time and space, but why not go on? I wouldn't be able to sleep anyway. We hurtled above the

Anatolian darkness. Never had a landscape seemed so black. The village lights, clustered in valleys, seemed yellowish—more like gaslights than electric bulbs. I wanted, in that instant, to turn back, to go home, but I knew that I would always feel this way en route to anywhere and that I had to stick to one of my few life principles: always spend one night in a strange place before you run away.

I wanted to go home, but I found myself after several more confusing and disruptive episodes in the home of two charming young American Foreign Service career officers. They seemed to know immediately what I would want. They had welcomed more than a few weary night-travellers; they were expert at reading the signs and gestures of dislocation. A beautiful double-scotch, with seemingly sculpted ice, appeared in an elegant Steuben tumbler. Diplomats obviously know how to live.

They talked patiently with me, answering my questions, allaying my fears, and replenishing my scotch. The more I drank, the less I feared, though I knew I would be anxious in the morning and for some time afterward. I also knew, as I spun off into sleep, that I had to be careful about casting my lot with the diplomats and official American presence in Ankara—including the military—if I really wanted to learn anything about Turkey and its people. I would do better, I knew, to try to get to know my students and colleagues, my neighbors. I would do better to get out into the country.

It sometimes seems to me that I lived years in those first few weeks in Ankara, and it is especially clear to me now, after two years, that I spent much of those first few weeks trying, in one way or other, either to re-create the terms of home or to identify myself with others who were, in one form or other, displaced; who were, in one way or other, outsiders. I was not ready immediately to meet Turkey on its own terms.

And in needing to identify myself with other outsiders (who were, at the same time, ready to extend hospitality to me), I ran a few risks, I disappointed a few people, and I embarrassed myself. I think especially of a kindly and intelligent bookseller who had served five years of a sixty-year sentence for publishing a journal that the government, before the 1981 intervention, had condemned as being dangerously leftist.

I met him in his bookstore, and though we did not share much language, I was able to communicate my love of books. I suppose he inferred, from some of the English titles at which I looked, my tastes and preferences.

I managed somehow to let him know that I had a birthday coming up, and he quickly invited me to his home for a celebration. I learned at the party through his wife (who had studied in the U.S. for a year under the auspices of the American Field Service) that he had carried a pistol for years before his arrest and just afterward, for fear that someone from the Right or Left, but probably the Right, might try to kill him for nothing more than reading a liberal magazine at a café. I learned further that the guest next to me was the widow of an honorable judge who had been murdered by ultrarightwing henchmen.

As the champagne flowed and the stories became more desperate, I wondered if it was wise for me to cast my lot so early with a group whose deepest political motivations I could hardly guess at. I wondered if it was wise for me to identify myself so early with a group if such an association might mean a cancellation of my Fulbright or a knife in the back. I was pretty sure that these were melodramatic speculations, but I was a newcomer and virtually speechless.

As the champagne continued to flow and the party began to sing some songs of the Spanish Civil War, I felt at once a sense of rising up with the tide of history and a fear of being washed out in the usually muddy Ankara streets. The more we sang, the happier my new friend became, and he invited me, his wife explained, to join them, when the warm weather came, for a trip to his native Malatya where he would introduce me to a poet-shepherd whom he had always admired.

I did not know how to tell him that I was immensely flattered to be trusted so quickly, that I wanted very much to go to those distant hills to hear the poet's stories, but that I was, in Prufrock's word, "afraid" to jeopardize my new position when I knew so little and couldn't begin to estimate costs and risks.

I could have asked his wife to translate these thoughts, but I was embarrassed, I think, to speak them so publicly, and I hoped that somehow my feelings would shift soon, my understanding would grow, and I would be able to join him. I never did get it all sorted out, and I never saw him again. This is, I suppose, my apology *in absentia* to him.

I had a few other experiences like this, but I learned soon that I had to pass through a period of disorientation without making too strong an affiliation with either official or alienated groups if I were going to face the country alone on my own two feet and discover some kind of meaningful reorientation: some kind of meeting between my self and the western Orient.

Because I lacked Turkish, I was able most deeply to gain this sense of meeting through my eyes: I was haunted, in time, with images of rubble burning up the sides of hills in the Aegean, of a train switchman playing a lonely flute at a remote crossing, of the fishing villages near Marmaris where women carry threshed wheat like mules.

I am haunted by these images and others—a peasant woman pushing her amputee husband up through the streets of Istanbul in a wheel-barrow, a steamy camel-fight festival at Ephesus.

If I could, I would like to learn Turkish and go back to that historically displaced country and speak to its soul and learn from it, to go into its remote mountain regions and learn something about cohesive community life, but this is unlikely to happen for some time. I have classes to teach.

Notes

A collection of essays does not seem to demand an index, but the reader who wishes to locate the significant references in *The Education of a Teacher: Essays on American Culture* can, with relative ease, use these notes to find page references within individual chapters. The reader can also, as it were, scan the notes at the outset to see, through citation, if some chapters might be of special interest, though I hope that section headings and titles will serve this purpose.

Chapter 1

1. See John C. Louis, *English 1-2 at Amherst College: Composition and the Unity of Knowledge,* U.M.I. Dissertation Information Service.

Chapter 3

1. *New York Times,* 8 January 1968, 22.

Chapter 4

1. There are, of course, good teachers in all of these institutions,

and the State University of New York at Buffalo, as a whole, is beginning to make radical changes in education. This is especially true of the English Department, one of the most progressive in the country.

2. I take the phrase from Paul Velde, a contributor to *Commonweal.*

3. *College English,* December 1971.

4. A. H. Maslow, "Some Education Implications of the Humanistic Psychologies," *Harvard Educational Review* 38 (Fall 1968): 4.

5. Harold Taylor, *Art and Intellect* (New York, 1960), 12-13.

Chapter 6

1. See R. D. Laing, *Self and Others* (New York, 1969); *The Politics of the Family* (New York, 1971).

2. I have noticed a disparity between activism in the political sphere and passivity in the classroom. Experiments such as ours might serve to reconcile this dichotomy. Passivity might move towards a truer inwardness and aggression towards active self-expression.

3. There are many reasons why psychoanalysis is in disfavor among undergraduates. For one, Freud's vision is infused with stoicism and tragedy; the sense of the moment is utopian and futuristic.

4. Philip E. Slater, "Teaching as an Erotic Irritant," *Microcosm* (New York: John Wiley & Sons, Inc., 1966).

5. For elaborations of this point, see Sigmund Freud, "Mourning and Melancholia," in *Collected Papers,* vol. 4, trans. Joan Riviere (New York: Basic Books, Inc., 1959).

Chapter 7

1. *Freud: Dictionary of Psychoanalysis,* ed. N. Fodor and F.

Gaynor (New York, 1966), 158-59. I realize that questions of *resistance* must be faced if one is going to try to deal with transference in the classroom, but an atmosphere of trust, a less judgmental ambience, will contribute greatly to meeting this difficulty. I realize, at the same time, that there are some conflict-free areas between student and teacher, many creative and successfully sublimated attitudes towards learning, which should be recognized as egosyntonic. A friend and colleague, Professor Robert Rogers, justly raises these issues.

2. Ibid., 103.

3. S. Freud, *General Introduction to Psychoanalysis,* tran. Joan Riviere (New York, 1968), 345.

4. Ibid., 451.

5. Ibid., 461.

6. S. Freud, "Mourning and Melancholia (1917)," vol. 4 of *Collected Papers,* ed. Joan Riviere (New York, 1959), 152-70.

7. Freud, *Psychoanalysis,* 467.

8. Ibid., 364.

9. Herbert Marcuse, *Eros and Civilization* (New York, 1961), 139-40.

10. David Holbrook, "R. D. Laing and the Death-Circuit," *Encounter* XXXI, 2 (August 1968): 34-46.

11. Marcuse, *Eros and Civilization,* 101.

12. John Weightman, "The Concept of the Avant-Garde," *Encounter* XXXIII, 1 (July 1969): 5-17; Robert Brustein, "Revolution as Theatre," *New Republic,* 14 March 1970, 13-17; Virgil Thomson, "Cage and the Collage of Noises," *New York Review of Books,* 23 April 1970, 9-15; Hilton Kramer, "The Seamless Web," *The New York Times Book Review,* 22 February 1970, 4.

13. Ernst Kris, *Psychoanalytic Explorations in Art* (New York, 1964).

Chapter 8

1. R. D. Laing, *Self and Others* (New York, 1969), 154.
2. William James, *Varieties of Religious Experience* (New York, 1964), 124-25.
3. John Bowlby, "Childhood Mourning and Psychiatric Illness," in the *Predicament of the Family,* ed. Peter Lomas (New York, 1967), 140-68. See also: Sigmund Freud, "Mourning and Melancholia," in *Collected Papers,* vol. 4, trans. Joan Riviere (New York, 1959), 152-70.
4. D. W. Winnicott, "Mirror-role of Mother and Family in Child Development," in *The Predicament of the Family,* 27:

> What does the baby see when he or she looks at the mother's face? I am suggesting that, ordinarily, what the baby sees is himself or herself. In other words, the mother is looking at the baby and *what she looks like is related to what she sees there.* All this is too easily taken for granted. I am asking that this which is naturally done well by mothers who are caring for their infants shall not be taken for granted. I can make my point by going straight over to the case of the baby whose mother reflects her own mood, or worse still, the rigidity of her own defenses.

5. Ibid., 32.

Chapter 9

1. H. R. Wolf, "Classroom as Microcosm," *College English,* December 1971; "Composition and Group Dynamics," *College English,* March 1969; "Teaching and Human Development: Truth's Body," *New Directions in Teaching,* Summer-Fall 1969.
2. See R. D. Laing, "Mystification, Confusion, and Conflict," in *Intensive Family Therapy,* ed. Ivan Boszormenyl-Nagy and James L. Framo (New York, 1969).
3. David Bakan, *Towards a Psychology of Suffering* (Toronto, 1968).

4. Cf. R. D. Laing, *The Divided Self* (Baltimore, 1966).

5. T. S. Eliot, "Ash Wednesday," *Collected Poems, 1909-1935* (New York, 1936), 110.

6. Cf. Theodore Roszak, "The Myth of Objective Consciousness," *The Making of a Counter Culture* (New York, 1969).

7. Cf. Aldous Huxley, *The Doors of Perception* (New York, 1963).

Chapter 10

1. Richard Schechner, *Public Domain: Essays on the Theatre* (New York, 1969).

2. George Orwell, *A Collection of Essays* (New York, 1954), 52-53.

3. Harvey Swados, "The Joys and Terrors of Sending the Kids to College," *New York Times Magazine,* 14 February 1971, 13.

4. Ibid., 13.

5. See my "British Fathers and Sons, 1773-1913: from Filial Submissiveness to Creativity," *The Psychoanalytic Review,* Summer 1965, 53-70.

6. Mark Gerzon, *The Whole World is Watching* (New York, 1969), 235-36.

7. Carl Rogers, *On Encounter Groups* (New York, 1970), 108.

8. Ibid., 108-109.

9. Ibid., 113.

10. Eugene O'Neill, *Long Day's Journey Into Night* (New Haven, 1965), 151.

11. Arthur Miller, *Death of a Salesman* (New York, 1969), 133.

12. *The New Group Therapies,* ed. H. Ruitenbeck (New York, 1970), 224.

13. L. L. Whyte, "Towards a Science of Form," *Hudson Review* (Winter 1970-71): 623.

14. Ibid., 621.

15. Alvin B. Kernan, "A New Context for Literature," *Ventures: Magazines of the Yale Graduate School* IX (1969): 43.

16. The human, mythic, and subjective content of much contemporary art is to be found in open form, not in "objective ratiocination." See Hilton Kramer, "From 'Open-Form' to the Monolithic Cube," *New York Times,* 4 April 1971. Harold Rosenberg makes a similar point by opposing the "human energy" of the Action Painters to the limited "grammar of dimensions" in the work of the contemporary formalists. See "The Art World," *New Yorker,* 27 March 1971, 117-120. Lionel Trilling points to the profound connection between rational and primitive thought processes when he says, "The ultimate questions of conscious and rational thought about the nature of man and his destiny match easily in the literary mind with the dark *un*conscious and with the most primitive human relationships." See "The Meaning of a Literary Idea," *The Liberal Imagination* (New York, 1950), 284.

Chapter 12

1. Harold Rosenberg, "The Art World: What's New," *The New Yorker,* 24 February 1973, 90-95.

2. George Steiner, *In Bluebeard's Castle* (New Haven, 1971), 92.

3. Stuart N. Hampshire, *Modern Writers and Other Essays* (New York, 1970), 197-98.

4. Eugene Mallove, "The Universe Has A Sense of Rhythm," Viewpoints section, *Buffalo News,* 13 July 1986, F-11, F-12. We need a new "Harmonia Mundi" (Harmony of the World).

Chapter 13

1. Thomas S. Kuhn, *The Structure of Scientific Revolutions*

(Chicago, 1962).

2. Theodore Roszak, "The Myth of Objective Consciousness," in *The Making of a Counter Culture* (New York, 1969).

3. L. L. Whyte, "Towards a Science of Form," *Hudson Review* 4 (Winter 1970-71): 613-32; Karen Horney, "A Morality of Evolution," in *Neurosis and Human Growth: The Struggle Toward Self-Realization* (New York, 1950), 15; Alvin R. Kernan, "A New Context for Literature," *Ventures* (1969): 43.

4. See my "Composition and Group Dynamics," *College English* (March 1969); "Teaching and Human Development: Truth's Body," *New Directions in Teaching* (Summer-Fall 1969); "Freud and Marcuse: Transference and the Demystification of Authority in the Classroom," *New Directions in Teaching* (Winter 1971); "Education and Social Discontinuity," *Soundings* (Spring 1971); "Classroom as Microcosm," *College English* (December 1971).

5. Philip Slater, *The Pursuit of Loneliness* (Boston, 1970). The relationship between loneliness in the culture and passivity in the classroom needs to be pursued further.

6. Carl Rogers, "The Lonely Person—and his Experiences in an Encounter Group," in *On Encounter Groups* (New York, 1970), 106-16.

7. Katherine Anne Porter, "Holiday," in *American Literature*, vol. 2, eds. Poirier and Vance (Boston, 1970), 719.

8. Ibid., 705.

9. For psychological implications of mutuality, see D. W. Winnicott, "Mirror-role of Mother and Family in Child Development," in *The Predicament of the Family*, ed. Peter Lomas (New York, 1967) and D. W. Winnicott, "The Mother-Infant Experience of Mutuality," in *Parenthood*, eds. E. James Anthony and Therese Benedek (Boston, 1970).

10. Karen Horney, "Morality of Evolution," 105.

Chapter 14

1. Lionel Trilling, "The Meaning of a Literary Idea," in *The Liberal Imagination* (New York, 1950).

2. Robert M. Adams, "The Sense of Verification: Pragmatic Commonplaces about Literary Criticism," *Daedalus* (Winter 1972): 203-14.

3. Robert Jay Lifton, "Self," in *Boundaries* (New York, 1970).

4. The liberal-humanist and liberal-left critics were, in the main, either outside the university and writing for journals devoted to literature and politics (e.g., *Dissent, Partisan Review, Commentary, Encounter, The Nation,* and *The New Leader*), or they were teaching in the New York area. I am thinking of Irving Howe, Alfred Kazin, Lionel Trilling, Clement Greenberg, Harold Rosenberg, Philip Rahv, Robert Warshow, and Leslie Fiedler, among others.

5. D. W. Winnicott, *Playing and Reality* (New York, 1971).

6. Ibid.

7. Heinz Lichtenstein, M.D., "Identity and Sexuality," *Journal American Psychoanalytic Association* 9 (1961): 208.

8. John Bowlby, "Childhood Mourning and Psychiatric Illness," in *The Predicament of the Family,* ed. Peter Lomas (New York, 1967).

9. C. L. Barber, *Shakespeare's Festive Comedies* (Princeton, 1959).

10. Winnicott, *Playing and Reality.*

Chapter 15

1. F. Scott Fitzgerald, *The Great Gatsby* (New York, 1953), 36.

2. Ernst Cassirer, *An Essay On Man* (New Haven, 1967), 52.

3. George Steiner, *In Bluebeard's Castle* (New Haven, 1971), 133.

4. George Holton, "On Trying To Understand Scientific Genius," *American Scholar* (Winter 1971-72): 95-110. See also, John C. Eccles, "The Discipline of Science with Special Reference to the Neurosciences," *Daedalus* (Spring 1973): 85-99.

5. Holton, "Scientific Genius," 97.

6. Ibid., 102.

7. Ibid., 106.

8. Ibid., 108.

9. Roger Shattuck, "Project for a Revolution in New York," *The New York Times Book Review,* 28 May 1972, 5, 24. See also John Weightman, "Refrigerated Dreams," 1 June 1972, *The New York Review of Books,* 6, 8-10; Michael Holquist, "Whodunit and Other Questions: Metaphysical Detective Stories in Post-War Fiction," *New Literary History* (Autumn 1971): 113-56.

10. Virginia Woolf, "The Modern Essay," *Common Reader, First Series* (New York, 1953), 222.

Chapter 17

1. *The Drama Review* (March 1979): 79-86.

2. "Gaping at Studio 54," *New York Times,* 2 February 1979, C16.

3. Orde Coombs, "Le Freak C'est Chic on 45th Street," *New York,* 8 January 1979, 47-50.

4. Mel Gussow, "The Time of the Wounded Hero," *New York Times,* 15 April 1979, Arts and Leisure section, 1, 30.

5. Jerry Buck, "'Galactica' to Travel in High Circles," *Buffalo Courier Express,* 16 September 1979.

6. Joy Horowitz, "What's a Surf Nazi?" *Buffalo Evening News,* 5 March 1979.

7. Val Hennessy, *In the Gutter* (London, 1978).

8. Norman Podhoretz, "How the North Was Won," *The New York Times Magazine,* 30 September 1979, 20, 50-64.

Chapter 19

1. Howard Wolf, "From Frisco to Disco (1960-1980): The Cultural Legacy of Protest," *Journal of Thought* (Winter 1980): 37-51.

2. Lionel Trilling discusses some of this ambivalence with customary brilliance and suppleness in his "F. Scott Fitzgerald," *The Liberal Imagination* (New York, 1950).

3. Ernest Hemingway, "The Snows of Kilimanjaro," in *The Short Stories of Ernest Hemingway* (New York, 1966), 72.

4. Matthew J. Bruccoli, *Scott and Earnest* (New York, 1978), 4.

5. There's usually a subtle and unacknowledged correspondence between "high" and "low" culture, between the academy and popular culture, even as the academy rails against popular culture and sees itself engaged in self-defense against that culture: e.g., the connection between metafiction and "fabulous" literature on the "high" side and sci-fi escape movies on the "low."

6. Harold Bloom, *The Anxiety of Influence* (New York, 1973), 11.

7. Roland Barthes, *Camera Lucida* (New York, 1981), 76.

8. Ibid., 77.

9. Trilling, *The Liberal Imagination,* 245.

Chapter 24

1. Amitai Etzioni, "Blue-Collar Work Is Wave of Future," *Buffalo Evening News,* Viewpoints, 21 September 1980.

2. George Orwell, "Why I Write," *A Collection of Essays* (New York, 1953), 309.

3. William Hazlitt, "Of Familiar Style," in *Eight Modern Essayists,* ed. W. Smart (New York, 1980), 353.

4. Frederick Douglass, *Narrative* (New York, 1968), 90.

5. Stephen Spender, "Stephen Spender," *The God That Failed* (New York, 1964), 248.

6. Czeslaw Milosz, "Writers and Utopias," *Partisan Review/2,* vol. LIII, no. 2, 177-79.

Chapter 26

1. Howard Wolf, "An American in Ankara," *Reporter,* 26 January 1984, 4.

2. Mahmut Makal, *A Village in Anatolia* (London, 1965), 121-132.

3. Ralph Waldo Emerson, "Nature," *The Selected Writings of Ralph Waldo Emerson,* ed. Brooks Atkinson (New York, 1950), 3.

4. Freya Stark, *Turkey: A Sketch of Turkish History* (London, 1971), 82-83.

5. Office of the Ambassador of Cultural Affairs, *Atatürk's Republic of Culture* (New York, 1981), 8.

6. Robert Paul Jordan, "Turkey: Cross Fire at an Ancient Crossroads," *National Geographic,* vol. 152, no. 1 (July 1977): 88-123.

7. (Map) *Türkei/Turkey,* Kummerly and Frey, Bern Edition, 1982.